Vice Versa

Or, A Lesson to Fathers

F. Anstey

Alpha Editions

This edition published in 2024

ISBN : 9789362923264

Design and Setting By
Alpha Editions
www.alphaedis.com
Email - info@alphaedis.com

As per information held with us this book is in Public Domain.
This book is a reproduction of an important historical work. Alpha Editions uses the best technology to reproduce historical work in the same manner it was first published to preserve its original nature. Any marks or number seen are left intentionally to preserve its true form.

Contents

PREFACE .... - 1 -
1. Black Monday .... - 2 -
2. A Grand Transformation Scene .... - 12 -
3. In the Toils .... - 25 -
4. A Minnow amongst Tritons .... - 38 -
5. Disgrace .... - 55 -
6. Learning and Accomplishments .... - 69 -
7. Cutting the Knot .... - 82 -
8. Unbending the Bow .... - 94 -
9. A Letter from Home .... - 105 -
10. The Complete Letter-Writer .... - 116 -
11. A Day of Rest .... - 123 -
12. Against Time .... - 134 -
13. A Respite .... - 147 -
14. An Error of Judgment .... - 155 -
15. The Rubicon .... - 164 -
16. Hard Pressed .... - 175 -
17. A Perfidious Ally .... - 191 -
18. Run to Earth .... - 205 -
19. The Reckoning .... - 215 -

PREFACE

There is an old story of a punctiliously polite Greek, who, while performing the funeral of an infant daughter, felt bound to make his excuses to the spectators for "bringing out such a ridiculously small corpse to so large a crowd."

The Author, although he trusts that the present production has more vitality than the Greek gentleman's child, still feels that in these days of philosophical fiction, metaphysical romance, and novels with a purpose, some apology may perhaps be needed for a tale which has the unambitious and frivolous aim of mere amusement.

However, he ventures to leave the tale to be its own apology, merely contenting himself with the entreaty that his little fish may be spared the rebuke that it is not a whale.

In submitting it with all possible respect to the Public, he conceives that no form of words he could devise would appeal so simply and powerfully to their feelings as that which he has ventured to adopt from a certain Anglo-Portuguese Phrase-Book of deserved popularity.

Like the compilers of that work, he—"expects then who the little book, for the care what he wrote him and her typographical corrections, will commend itself to the—*British Paterfamilias*—at which he dedicates him particularly."

1.
Black Monday

> "In England, where boys go to boarding schools, if the holidays were not long there would be no opportunity for cultivating the domestic affections."—*Letter of Lord Campbell's, 1835.*

On a certain Monday evening late in January, 1881, Paul Bultitude, Esq. (of Mincing Lane, Colonial Produce Merchant), was sitting alone in his dining-room at Westbourne Terrace after dinner.

The room was a long and lofty one, furnished in the stern uncompromising style of the Mahogany Age, now supplanted by the later fashions of decoration which, in their outset original and artistic, seem fairly on the way to become as meaningless and conventional.

Here were no skilfully contrasted shades of grey or green, no dado, no distemper on the walls; the woodwork was grained and varnished after the manner of the Philistines, the walls papered in dark crimson, with heavy curtains of the same colour, and the sideboard, dinner-waggon, and row of stiff chairs were all carved in the same massive and expensive style of ugliness. The pictures were those familiar presentments of dirty rabbits, fat white horses, bloated goddesses, and misshapen boors, by masters who, if younger than they assume to be, must have been quite old enough to know better.

Mr. Bultitude was a tall and portly person, of a somewhat pompous and overbearing demeanour; not much over fifty, but looking considerably older. He had a high shining head, from which the hair had mostly departed, what little still remained being of a grizzled auburn, prominent pale blue eyes with heavy eyelids and fierce, bushy whitey-brown eyebrows. His general expression suggested a conviction of his own extreme importance, but, in spite of this, his big underlip drooped rather weakly and his double chin slightly receded, giving a judge of character reason for suspecting that a certain obstinate positiveness observable in Mr. Bultitude's manner might possibly be due less to the possession of an unusually strong will than to the circumstance that, by some fortunate chance, that will had hitherto never met with serious opposition.

The room, with all its æsthetic shortcomings, was comfortable enough, and Mr. Bultitude's attitude—he was lying back in a well-wadded leather arm-chair, with a glass of claret at his elbow and his feet stretched out towards the ruddy blaze of the fire—seemed at first sight to imply that happy after-dinner condition of perfect satisfaction with oneself and things in general, which is the natural outcome of a good cook, a good conscience, and a good digestion.

At first sight; because his face did not confirm the impression—there was a latent uneasiness in it, an air of suppressed irritation, as if he expected and even dreaded to be disturbed at any moment, and yet was powerless to resent the intrusion as he would like to do.

At the slightest sound in the hall outside he would half rise in his chair and glance at the door with a mixture of alarm and resignation, and as often as the steps died away and the door remained closed, he would sink back and resettle himself with a shrug of evident relief.

Habitual novel readers on reading thus far will, I am afraid, prepare themselves for the arrival of a faithful cashier with news of irretrievable ruin, or a mysterious and cynical stranger threatening disclosures of a disgraceful nature.

But all such anticipations must at once be ruthlessly dispelled. Mr. Bultitude, although he was certainly a merchant, was a fairly successful one—in direct defiance of the laws of fiction, where any connection with commerce seems to lead naturally to failure in one of the three volumes.

He was an elderly gentleman, too, of irreproachable character and antecedents; no Damocles' sword of exposure was swinging over his bald but blameless head; he had no disasters to fear and no indiscretions to conceal. He had not been intended for melodrama, with which, indeed, he would not have considered it a respectable thing to be connected.

In fact, the secret of his uneasiness was so absurdly simple and commonplace that I am rather ashamed to have made even a temporary mystery of it.

His son Dick was about to return to school that evening, and Mr. Bultitude was expecting every moment to be called upon to go through a parting scene with him; that was really all that was troubling him.

This sounds very creditable to the tenderness of his feelings as a father—for there are some parents who bear such a bereavement at the close of the holidays with extraordinary fortitude, if they do not actually betray an unnatural satisfaction at the event.

But it was not exactly from softness of heart that he was restless and impatient, nor did he dread any severe strain upon his emotions. He was not much given to sentiment, and was the author of more than one of those pathetically indignant letters to the papers, in which the British parent denounces the expenses of education and the unconscionable length and frequency of vacations.

He was one of those nervous and fidgety persons who cannot understand their own children, looking on them as objectionable monsters whose next movements are uncertain—much as Frankenstein must have felt towards *his* monster.

He hated to have a boy about the house, and positively writhed under the irrelevant and irrepressible questions, the unnecessary noises and boisterous high spirits which nothing would subdue; his son's society was to him simply an abominable nuisance, and he pined for a release from it from the day the holidays began.

He had been a widower for nearly three years, and no doubt the loss of a mother's loving tact, which can check the heedless merriment before it becomes intolerable, and interpret and soften the most peevish and unreasonable of rebukes, had done much to make the relations between parent and children more strained than they might otherwise have been.

As it was, Dick's fear of his father was just great enough to prevent any cordiality between them, and not sufficient to make him careful to avoid offence, and it is not surprising if, when the time came for him to return to his house of bondage at Dr. Grimstone's, Crichton House, Market Rodwell, he left his father anything but inconsolable.

Just now, although Mr. Bultitude was so near the hour of his deliverance, he still had a bad quarter of an hour before him, in which the last farewells must be said, and he found it impossible under these circumstances to compose himself for a quiet half-hour's nap, or retire to the billiard-room for a cup of coffee and a mild cigar, as he would otherwise have done—since he was certain to be disturbed.

And there was another thing which harassed him, and that was a haunting dread lest at the last moment some unforeseen accident should prevent the boy's departure after all. He had some grounds for this, for only a week before, a sudden and unprecedented snowstorm had dashed his hopes, on the eve of their fulfilment, by forcing the Doctor to postpone the day on which his school was to re-assemble, and now Mr. Bultitude sat on brambles until he had seen the house definitely rid of his son's presence.

All this time, while the father was fretting and fuming in his arm-chair, the son, the unlucky cause of all this discomfort, had been standing on the mat outside the door, trying to screw up enough courage to go in as if nothing was the matter with him.

He was not looking particularly boisterous just then. On the contrary, his face was pale, and his eyelids rather redder than he would quite care for them to be seen by any of the "fellows" at Crichton House. All the life and spirit had gone out of him for the time; he had a troublesome dryness in his throat, and a general sensation of chill heaviness, which he himself would have described—expressively enough, if not with academical elegance—as "feeling beastly."

The stoutest hearted boy, returning to the most perfect of schools, cannot always escape something of this at that dark hour when the sands of the holidays have run out to their last golden grain, when the boxes are standing corded and labelled in the hall, and some one is going to fetch the fatal cab.

Dick had just gone the round of the house, bidding dreary farewells to all the servants; an unpleasant ordeal which he would gladly have dispensed with, if possible, and which did not serve to raise his spirits.

Upstairs, in the bright nursery, he had found his old nurse sitting sewing by the high wire fender. She was a stern, hard-featured old lady, who had systematically slapped him through infancy into boyhood, and he had had some stormy passages with her during the past few weeks; but she softened now in the most unexpected manner as she said good-bye, and told him he was a "pleasant, good-hearted young gentleman, after all, though that aggravating and contrairy sometimes." And then she predicted, with some of the rashness attaching to irresponsibility, that he would be "the best boy this next term as ever was, and work hard at all his lessons, and bring home a prize"—but all this unusual gentleness only made the interview more difficult to come out of with any credit for self-control.

Then downstairs, the cook had come up in her evening brown print and clean collar, from her warm spice-scented kitchen, to remark cheerily that "Lor bless his heart, what with all these telegrafts and things, time flew so fast nowadays that they'd be having him back again before they all knew where they were!" which had a certain spurious consolation about it, until one saw that, after all, it put the case entirely from her own standpoint.

After this Dick had parted from his elder sister Barbara and his young brother Roly, and had arrived where we found him first, at the mat outside the dining-room door, where he still lingered shivering in the cold foggy hall.

Somehow, he could not bring himself to take the next step at once; he knew pretty well what his father's feelings would be, and a parting is a very unpleasant ceremony to one who feels that the regret is all on his own side.

But it was no use putting it off any longer; he resolved at last to go in and get it over, and opened the door accordingly. How warm and comfortable the room looked—more comfortable than it had ever seemed to him before, even on the first day of the holidays!

And his father would be sitting there in a quarter of an hour's time, just as he was now, while he himself would be lumbering along to the station through the dismal raw fog!

How unspeakably delightful it must be, thought Dick enviously, to be grown up and never worried by the thoughts of school and lesson-books; to be able to look forward to returning to the same comfortable house, and living the same easy life, day after day, week after week, with no fear of a swiftly advancing Black Monday.

Gloomy moralists might have informed him that we cannot escape school by simply growing up, and that, even for those who contrive this and make a long holiday of their lives, there comes a time when the days are grudgingly counted to a blacker Monday than ever made a school-boy's heart quake within him.

But then Dick would never have believed them, and the moralists would only have wasted much excellent common sense upon him.

Paul Bultitude's face cleared as he saw his son come in. "There you are, eh?" he said, with evident satisfaction, as he turned in his chair, intending to cut the scene as short as possible. "So you're off at last? Well, holidays can't last for ever—by a merciful decree of Providence, they don't last quite for ever! There, good-bye, good-bye, be a good boy this term, no more scrapes, mind. And now you'd better run away, and put on your coat—you're keeping the cab waiting all this time."

"No, I'm not," said Dick, "Boaler hasn't gone to fetch one yet."

"Not gone to fetch a cab yet!" cried Paul, with evident alarm, "why, God bless my soul, what's the man thinking about? You'll lose your train! I know you'll lose the train, and there will be another day lost, after the extra week gone already through that snow! I must see to this myself. Ring the bell, tell Boaler to start this instant—I insist on his fetching a cab this instant!"

"Well, it's not my fault, you know," grumbled Dick, not considering so much anxiety at all flattering, "but Boaler has gone now. I just heard the gate shut."

"Ah!" said his father, with more composure, "and now," he suggested, "you'd better shake hands, and then go up and say good-bye to your sister—you've no time to spare."

"I've said good-bye to them," said Dick. "Mayn't I stay here till—till Boaler comes?"

This request was due, less to filial affection than a faint desire for dessert, which even his feelings could not altogether stifle. Mr. Bultitude granted it with a very bad grace.

"I suppose you can if you want to," he said impatiently, "only do one thing or the other—stay outside, or shut the door and come in and sit down quietly. I cannot sit in a thorough draught!"

Dick obeyed, and applied himself to the dessert with rather an injured expression.

His father felt a greater sense of constraint and worry than ever; the interview, as he had feared, seemed likely to last some time, and he felt that he ought to improve the occasion in some way, or, at all events, make some observation. But, for all that, he had not the remotest idea what to say to this red-haired, solemn boy, who sat staring gloomily at him in the intervals of filling his mouth. The situation grew more embarrassing every moment.

At last, as he felt himself likely to have more to say in reproof than on any other subject, he began with that.

"There's one thing I want to talk to you about before you go," he began, "and that's this. I had a most unsatisfactory report of you this last term; don't let me have that again. Dr. Grimstone tells me—ah, I have his letter here—yes, he says (and just attend, instead of making yourself ill with preserved ginger)—he says, 'Your son has great natural capacity, and excellent abilities; but I regret to say that, instead of applying himself as he might do, he misuses his advantages, and succeeds in setting a mischievous example to—if not actually misleading—his companions.' That's a pleasant account for a father to read! Here am I, sending you to an expensive school, furnishing you with great natural capacity and excellent abilities, and—and—every other school requisite, and all you do is to misuse them! It's disgraceful! And misleading your companions, too! Why, at your age, they ought to mislead *you*—No, I don't mean that—but what I may tell you is that I've written a very strong letter to Dr. Grimstone, saying what pain it gave me to hear you misbehaved yourself, and telling him, if he ever caught you setting an example of any sort, mind that, *any* sort, in the future—he was to, ah, to remember some of Solomon's very sensible remarks on the subject. So I should strongly advise you to take care what you're about in future, for your own sake!"

This was not a very encouraging address, perhaps, but it did not seem to distress Dick to any extent; he had heard very much the same sort of thing several times before, and had been fully prepared for it then.

He had been seeking distraction in almonds and raisins, but now they only choked instead of consoling him, and he gave them up and sat brooding silently over his hard lot instead, with a dull, blank dejection which those only who have gone through the same thing in their boyhood will understand. To others, whose school life has been one unchequered course of excitement and success, it will be incomprehensible enough—and so much the better for them.

He sat listening to the grim sphinx clock on the black marble chimneypiece, as it remorselessly ticked away his last few moments of home-life, and he ingeniously set himself to crown his sorrow by reviving recollections of happier days.

In one of the corners of the overmantel there was still a sprig of withered laurel left forgotten, and his eye fell on it now with grim satisfaction. He made his thoughts travel back to that delightful afternoon on Christmas Eve, when they had all come home riotous through the brilliant streets, laden with purchases from the Baker Street Bazaar, and then had decorated the rooms with such free and careless gaiety.

And the Christmas dinner too! He had sat just where he was sitting now, with, ah, such a difference in every other respect—the time had not come then when the thought of "only so many more weeks and days left" had begun to intrude its grisly shape, like the skull at an ancient feast.

And yet he could distinctly recollect now, and with bitter remorse, that he had not enjoyed himself then as much as he ought to have done; he even remembered an impious opinion of his that the proceedings were "slow." Slow! with plenty to eat, and three (four, if he had only known it) more weeks of holiday before him; with Boxing Day and the brisk exhilarating drive to the Crystal Palace immediately following, with all the rest of a season of licence and varied joys to come, which he could hardly trust himself to look back upon now! He must have been mad to think such a thing.

Overhead his sister Barbara was playing softly one of the airs from "The Pirates" (it was Frederic's appeal to the Major-General's daughters), and the music, freed from the serio-comic situation which it illustrates, had a tenderness and pathos of its own which went to Dick's heart and intensified his melancholy.

He had gone (in secret, for Mr. Bultitude disapproved of such dissipations) to hear the Opera in the holidays, and now the piano conjured the whole scene up for him again—there would be no more theatre-going for him for a very long time!

By this time Mr. Bultitude began to feel the silence becoming once more oppressive, and roused himself with a yawn. "Heigho!" he said, "Boaler's an uncommonly long time fetching that cab!"

Dick felt more injured than ever, and showed it by drawing what he intended for a moving sigh.

Unfortunately it was misunderstood.

"I do wish, sir," said his parent testily, "you would try to break yourself of that habit of breathing hard. The society of a grampus (for it's no less) delights no one and offends many—including me—and for Heaven's sake, Dick, don't kick the leg of the table in that way; you know it simply maddens me. What do you do it for? Why can't you learn to sit at table like a gentleman?"

Dick mumbled some apology, and then, having found his tongue and remembered his necessities, said, with a nervous catch in his voice, "Oh, I say, father, will you—can you let me have some pocket-money, please, to go back with?"

Mr. Bultitude looked as if his son had petitioned for a latch-key.

"Pocket-money!" he repeated, "why, you can't want money. Didn't your grandmother give you a sovereign as a Christmas-box? And I gave you ten shillings myself!"

"I do want it, though," said Dick; "that's all spent. And you know you always *have* given me money to take back."

"If I do give you some, you'll only go and spend it," grumbled Mr. Bultitude, as if he considered money an object of art.

"I shan't spend it all at once, and I shall want some to put in the plate on Sundays. We always have to put in the plate when it's a collection. And there's the cab to pay."

"Boaler has orders to pay your cab—as you know well enough," said his father, "but I suppose you must have some, though you cost me enough, Heaven knows, without this additional expense."

And at this he brought up a fistful of loose silver and gold from one of his trouser-pockets, and spread it deliberately out on the table in front of him in shining rows.

Dick's eyes sparkled at the sight of so much wealth; for a moment or two he almost forgot the pangs of approaching exile in the thought of the dignity and credit which a single one of those bright new sovereigns would procure for him.

It would ensure him surreptitious luxuries and open friendships as long as it lasted. Even Tipping, the head boy of the school, who had gone into tails, brought back no more, and besides, the money would bring him handsomely out of certain pecuniary difficulties to which an unexpected act of parental authority had exposed him; he could easily dispose of all claims with such a sum at command, and then his father could so easily spare it out of so much!

Meanwhile Mr. Bultitude, with great care and precision, selected from the coins before him a florin, two shillings, and two sixpences, which he pushed across to his son, who looked at them with a disappointment he did not care to conceal.

"An uncommonly liberal allowance for a young fellow like you," he observed. "Don't buy any foolishness with it, and if, towards the end of the term you want a little more, and write an intelligible letter asking for it, and I think proper to let you have it—why, you'll get it, you know."

Dick had not the courage to ask for more, much as he longed to do so, so he put the money in his purse with very qualified expressions of gratitude.

In his purse he seemed to find something which had escaped his memory, for he took out a small parcel and unfolded it with some hesitation.

"I nearly forgot," he said, speaking with more animation than he had yet done, "I didn't like to take it without asking you, but is this any use? May I have it?"

"Eh?" said Mr. Bultitude, sharply, "what's that? Something else—what is it you want now?"

"It's only that stone Uncle Duke brought mamma from India; the thing, he said, they called a 'Pagoda stone,' or something, out there."

"Pagoda stone? The boy means Garudâ Stone. I should like to know how you got hold of that; you've been meddling in my drawers, now, a thing I will not put up with, as I've told you over and over again."

"No, I haven't, then," said Dick, "I found it in a tray in the drawing-room, and Barbara said, perhaps, if I asked you, you might let me have it, as she didn't think it was any use to you."

"Then Barbara had no right to say anything of the sort."

"But may I have it? I may, mayn't I?" persisted Dick.

"Have it? certainly not. What could you possibly want with a thing like that? It's ridiculous. Give it to me."

Dick handed it over reluctantly enough. It was not much to look at, quite an insignificant-looking little square tablet of greyish green stone, pierced at one angle, and having on two of its faces faint traces of mysterious letters or symbols, which time had made very difficult to distinguish.

It looked harmless enough as Mr. Bultitude took it in his hand; there was no kindly hand to hold him back, no warning voice to hint that there might possibly be sleeping within that small marble block the pent-up energy of long-forgotten Eastern necromancy, just as ready as ever to awake into action at the first words which had power to evoke it.

There was no one; but even if there had been such a person, Paul Bultitude was a sober prosaic individual, who would probably have treated the warning as a piece of ridiculous superstition.

As it was, no man could have put himself in a position of extreme peril with a more perfect unconsciousness of his danger.

2.
A Grand Transformation Scene

"Magnaque numinibus vota exaudita malignis."

Paul Bultitude put on his glasses to examine the stone more carefully, for it was some time since he had last seen or thought about it. Then he looked up and said once more, "What use would a thing like this be to you?"

Dick would have considered it a very valuable prize indeed; he could have exhibited it to admiring friends—during lessons, of course, when it would prove a most agreeable distraction; he could have played with and fingered it incessantly, invented astonishing legends of its powers and virtues; and, at last, when he had grown tired of it, have bartered it for any more desirable article that might take his fancy. All these advantages were present to his mind in a vague shifting form, but he could not find either courage or words to explain them.

Consequently he only said awkwardly, "Oh, I don't know, I should like it."

"Well, any way," said Paul, "you certainly won't have it. It's worth keeping, whatever it is, as the only thing your uncle Marmaduke was ever known to give to anybody."

Marmaduke Paradine, his brother-in-law, was not a connection of whom he had much reason to feel particularly proud. One of those persons endowed with what are known as "insinuating manners and address," he had, after some futile attempts to enter the army, been sent out to Bombay as agent for a Manchester firm, and in that capacity had contrived to be mixed up in some more than shady transactions with rival exporters and native dealers up the country, which led to an unceremonious dismissal by his employers.

He had brought home the stone from India as a propitiatory token of remembrance, more portable and less expensive than the lacquered cabinets, brasses, stuffs and carved work which are expected from friends at such a distance, and he had been received with pardon and started once more, until certain other proceedings of his, shadier still, had obliged Paul to forbid him the house at Westbourne Terrace.

Since then little had been heard of him, and the reports which reached Mr. Bultitude of his disreputable relative's connection with the promotion of a series of companies of the kind affected by the widow and curate, and exposed in money articles and law courts, gave him no desire to renew his acquaintance.

"Isn't it a talisman, though?" said Dick, rather unfortunately for any hopes he might have of persuading his father to entrust him with the coveted treasure.

"I'm sure I can't tell you," yawned Paul, "how do you mean?"

"I don't know, only Uncle Duke once said something about it. Barbara heard him tell mamma. I say, perhaps it's like the one in Scott, and cures people of things, though I don't think it's that sort of talisman either, because I tried it once on my chilblains, and it wasn't a bit of good. If you would only let me have it, perhaps I might find out, you know."

"You might," said his father drily, apparently not much influenced by this inducement, "but you won't have the chance. If it has a secret, I will find it out for myself" (he little knew how literally he was to be taken at his word), "and, by the way, there's your cab—at last."

There was a sound of wheels outside, and, as Dick heard them, he grew desperate in his extremity; a wish he had long secretly cherished unspoken, without ever hoping for courage to give it words, rose to his lips now; he got up and moved timidly towards his father.

"Father," he said, "there's something I want to say to you so much before I go. Do let me ask you now."

"Well, what is it?" said Paul. "Make haste, you haven't much time."

"It's this. I want you to—to let me leave Grimstone's at the end of the term."

Paul stared at him, angry and incredulous, "Let you leave Dr. Grimstone's (oblige me by giving him his full title when you speak of him)," he said slowly. "Why, what do you mean? It's an excellent school—never saw a better expressed prospectus in my life. And my old friend Bangle, Sir Benjamin Bangle, who's a member of the School Board, and ought to know something about schools, strongly recommended it—would have sent his own son there, if he hadn't entered him at Eton. And when I pay for most of the extras for you too. Dancing, by Gad, and meat for breakfast. I'm sure I don't know what you would have."

"I'd like to go to Marlborough, or Harrow, or somewhere," whimpered Dick. "Jolland's going to Harrow at Easter. (Jolland's one of the fellows at Grimstone's—Dr. Grimstone's I mean.) And what does old Bangle know about it? He hasn't got to go there himself! And—and Grimstone's jolly enough to fellows he likes, but he doesn't like *me*—he's always sitting on me for something—and I hate some of the fellows there, and altogether it's beastly. Do let me leave! If you don't want me to go to a public school, I—I could stop at home and have a private tutor—like Joe Twitterley!"

"It's all ridiculous nonsense, I tell you," said Paul angrily, "ridiculous nonsense! And, once for all, I'll put a stop to it. I don't approve of public schools for boys like you, and, what's more, I can't afford it. As for private tutors, that's absurd! So you will just make up your mind to stay at Crichton House as long as I think proper to keep you there, and there's an end of that!"

At this final blow to all his hopes, Dick began to sob in a subdued hopeless kind of way, which was more than his father could bear. To do Paul justice, he had not meant to be quite so harsh when the boy was about to set out for school, and, a little ashamed of his irritation, he sought to justify his decision.

He chose to do this by delivering a short homily on the advantages of school, by which he might lead Dick to look on the matter in the calm light of reason and common sense, and commonplaces on the subject began to rise to the surface of his mind, from the rather muddy depths to which they had long since sunk.

He began to give Dick the benefit of all this stagnant wisdom, with a feeling of surprise as he went on, at his own powerful and original way of putting things.

"Now, you know, it's no use to cry like that," he began. "It's—ah—the usual thing for boys at school, I'm quite aware, to go about fancying they're very ill-used, and miserable, and all the rest of it, just as if people in my position had their sons educated out of spite! It's one of those petty troubles all boys have to go through. And you mark my words, my boy, when they go out into the world and have real trials to put up with, and grow middle-aged men, like me, why, they see what fools they've been, Dick; they see what fools they've been. All the—hum, the innocent games and delights of boyhood, and that sort of thing, you know—come back to them—and then they look back to those hours passed at school as the happiest, aye, the very happiest time of their life!"

"Well," said Dick, "then I hope it won't be the happiest time in mine, that's all! And you may have been happy at the school you went to, perhaps, but I don't believe you would very much care about being a boy again like me, and going back to Grimstone's, you know you wouldn't!"

This put Paul on his mettle; he had warmed well to his subject, and could not let this open challenge pass unnoticed—it gave him such an opening for a cheap and easy effect.

He still had the stone in his hand as he sank back into his chair, smiling with a tolerant superiority.

"Perhaps you will believe me," he said, impressively, "when I tell you, old as I am and much as you envy me, I only wish, at this very moment, I could be a boy again, like you. Going back to school wouldn't make me unhappy, I can tell you."

It is so fatally easy to say more than we mean in the desire to make as strong an impression as possible. Well for most of us that—more fortunate than Mr. Bultitude—we can generally do so without fear of being taken too strictly at our word.

As he spoke these unlucky words, he felt a slight shiver, followed by a curious shrinking sensation all over him. It was odd, too, but the arm-chair in which he sat seemed to have grown so much bigger all at once. He felt a passing surprise, but concluded it must be fancy, and went on as comfortably as before.

"I should like it, my boy, but what's the good of wishing? I only mention it to prove that I was not speaking at random. I'm an old man and you're a young boy, and, that being so, why, of course—What the dooce are you giggling about?"

For Dick, after some seconds of half-frightened open-mouthed staring, had suddenly burst into a violent fit of almost hysterical giggling, which he seemed trying vainly to suppress.

This naturally annoyed Mr. Bultitude, and he went on with immense dignity, "I—ah—I'm not aware that I've been saying anything particularly ridiculous. You seem to be amused?"

"Don't!" gasped Dick. "It, it isn't anything you're saying—it's, it's—oh, can't you feel any difference?"

"The sooner you go back to school the better!" said Paul angrily. "I wash my hands of you. When I do take the trouble to give you any advice, it's received with ridicule. You always were an ill-mannered little cub. I've had quite enough of this. Leave the room, sir!"

The wheels must have belonged to some other cab, for none had stopped at the pavement as yet; but Mr. Bultitude was justly indignant, and could stand the interview no longer. Dick, however, made no attempt to move; he remained there, choking and shaking with laughter, while his father sat stiffly on his chair, trying to ignore his son's unmannerly conduct, but only partially succeeding.

No one can calmly endure watching other people laughing at him like idiots, while he is left perfectly incapable of guessing what he has said or done to amuse them. Even when this is known, it requires a peculiarly keen sense of humour to see the point of a joke against oneself.

At last his patience gave out, and he said coldly, "Now, perhaps, if you are quite yourself again, you will be good enough to let me know what the joke is?"

Dick, looking flushed and half-ashamed, tried again and again to speak, but each time the attempt was too much for him. After a time he did succeed, but his voice was hoarse and shaken with laughter as he spoke. "Haven't you found it out yet? Go and look at yourself in the glass—it will make you roar!"

There was the usual narrow sheet of plate glass at the back of the sideboard, and to this Mr. Bultitude walked, almost under protest, and with a cold dignity. It occurred to him that he might have a smudge on his face or something wrong with his collar and tie—something to account to some extent for his son's frivolous and insulting behaviour. No suspicion of the terrible truth crossed his mind as yet.

Meanwhile Dick was looking on eagerly with a chuckle of anticipation, as one who watches the dawning appreciation of an excellent joke.

But no sooner had Paul met the reflection in the glass than he started back in incredulous horror—then returned and stared again and again.

Surely, surely, this could not be he!

He had expected to see his own familiar portly bow-windowed presence there—but somehow, look as he would, the mirror insisted upon reflecting the figure of his son Dick. Could he possibly have become invisible and have lost the power of casting a reflection—or how was it that Dick, and only Dick, was to be seen there?

How was it, too, when he looked round, there was the boy still sitting there? It could not be Dick, evidently, that he saw in the glass. Besides, the reflection opposite him moved when he moved, returned when he returned, copied his every gesture!

He turned round upon his son with angry and yet hopeful suspicion. "You, you've been playing some of your infernal tricks with this mirror, sir," he cried fiercely. "What have you done to it?"

"Done! how could I do anything to it? As if you didn't know that!"

"Then," stammered Paul, determined to know the worst, "then do you, do you mean to tell me you can see any—alteration in me? Tell me the truth now!"

"I should just think I could!" said Dick emphatically. "It's very queer, but just look here," and he came up to the sideboard and placed himself by the side of his horrified father. "Why," he said, with another giggle, "we're—he-he—as like as two peas!"

They were indeed; the glass reflected now two small boys, each with chubby cheeks and auburn hair, both dressed, too, exactly alike, in Eton jackets and broad white collars; the only difference to be seen between them was that, while one face wore an expression of intense glee and satisfaction, the other—the one which Mr. Bultitude was beginning to fear must belong to him—was lengthened and drawn with dismay and bewilderment.

"Dick," said Paul faintly, "what is all this? Who has been, been taking these liberties with me?"

"I'm sure I don't know," protested Dick. "It wasn't me. I believe you did it all yourself."

"Did it all myself!" repeated Paul indignantly. "Is it likely I should? It's some trickery, I tell you, some villainous plot. The worst of it is," he added plaintively, "I don't understand who I'm supposed to be now. Dick, who am I?"

"You can't be me," said Dick, "because here I am, you know. And you're not yourself, that's very plain. You must be *somebody*, I suppose," he added dubiously.

"Of course I am. What do you mean?" said Paul angrily. "Never mind who I am. I feel just the same as I always did. Tell me when you first began to notice any change. Could you see it coming on at all, eh?"

"It was all at once, just as you were talking about school and all that. You said you only wished—— Why of course; look here, it must be the stone that did it!"

"Stone! what stone?" said Paul. "I don't know what you're talking about."

"Yes, you do—the Garudâ Stone! You've got it in your hand still. Don't you see? It's a real talisman after all! How jolly!"

"I didn't do anything to set it off; and besides, oh, it's perfectly absurd! How can there be such things as talismans nowadays, eh? Tell me that."

"Well, something's happened to you, hasn't it? And it must have been done somehow," argued Dick.

"I was holding the confounded thing, certainly," said Paul, "here it is. But what could I have said to start it? What has it done this to me for?"

"I know!" cried Dick. "Don't you remember? You said you wished you were a boy again, like me. So you are, you see, exactly like me! What a lark it is, isn't it? But, I say, you can't go up to business like that, you know, can you? I tell you what, you'd better come to Grimstone's with me now, and see how you like it. I shouldn't mind so much if you came too. Grimstone's face would be splendid when he saw two of us. Do come!"

"That's ridiculous nonsense you're talking," said Paul, "and you know it. What should I do at school at my age? I tell you I'm the same as ever inside, though I may have shrunk into a little rascally boy to look at. And it's simply an abominable nuisance, Dick, that's what it is! Why on earth couldn't you let the stone alone? Just see what mischief you've done by meddling now—put me to all this inconvenience!"

"You shouldn't have wished," said Dick.

"Wished!" echoed Mr. Bultitude. "Why, to be sure," he said, with a gleam of returning hopefulness, "of course—I never thought of that. The thing's a wishing stone; it must be! You have to hold it, I suppose, and then say what you wish aloud, and there you are. If that's the case, I can soon put it all right by simply wishing myself back again. I—I shall have a good laugh at all this by and by—I know I shall!"

He took the stone, and got into a corner by himself where he began repeating the words, "I wish I was back again," "I wish I was the man I was five minutes ago," "I wish all this had not happened," and so on, until he was very exhausted and red in the face. He tried with the stone held in his left hand, as well as his right, sitting and standing, under all the various conditions he could think of, but absolutely nothing came of it; he was just as exasperatingly boyish and youthful as ever at the end of it.

"I don't like this," he said at last, giving it up with a rather crestfallen air. "It seems to me that this diabolical invention has got out of order somehow; I can't make it work any more!"

"Perhaps," suggested Dick, who had shown throughout the most unsympathetic cheerfulness, "perhaps it's one of those talismans that only give you one wish, and you've had it, you know?"

"Then it's all over!" groaned Paul. "What the dooce am I to do? What shall I do? Suggest something, for Heaven's sake; don't stand cackling there in that unfeeling manner. Can't you see what a terrible, mess I've got into? Suppose—only suppose your sister or one of the servants were to come in, and see me like this!"

This suggestion simply enchanted Dick. "Let's have 'em all up," he laughed; "it would be such fun! How they will laugh when we tell them!" And he rushed to the bell.

"Touch that bell if you dare!" screamed Paul. "I won't be seen in this condition by anybody! What on earth could have induced that scoundrelly uncle of yours to bring such a horrible thing as this over I can't imagine! I never heard of such a situation as this in my life. I can't stay like this, you know—it's not to be thought of! I—I wonder whether it would be any use to send over to Dr. Bustard and ask him to step in; he might give me something to bring me round. But then the whole neighbourhood would hear about it! If I don't see my way out of this soon, I shall go raving mad!"

And he paced restlessly up and down the room with his brain on fire.

All at once, as he became able to think more coherently, there occurred to him a chance, slender and desperate enough, but still a chance, of escaping even yet the consequences of his folly.

He was forced to conclude that, however improbable and fantastic it might appear in this rationalistic age, there must be some hidden power in this Garudâ Stone which had put him in his present very unpleasant position. It was plain too that the virtues of the talisman refused to exert themselves any more at his bidding.

But it did not follow that in another's hands the spell would remain as powerless. At all events, it was an experiment well worth the trial, and he lost no time in explaining the notion to Dick, who, by the sparkle in his eyes and suppressed excitement in his manner, seemed to think there might be something in it.

"I may as well try," he said, "give it to me."

"Take it, my dear boy," said Paul, with a paternal air that sorely tried Dick's recovered gravity, it contrasted so absurdly with his altered appearance. "Take it, and wish your poor old father himself again!"

Dick took it, and held it thoughtfully for some moments, while Paul waited in nervous impatience. "Isn't it any use?" he said dolefully at last, as nothing happened.

"I don't know," said Dick calmly, "I haven't wished yet."

"Then do so at once," said Paul fussily, "do so at once. There's no time to waste, every moment is of importance—your cab will be here directly. Although, although I'm altered in this ridiculous way, I hope I still retain my authority as a father, and as a father, by Gad, I expect you to obey me, sir!"

"Oh, all right," said Dick indifferently, "you may keep the authority if you like."

"Then do what I tell you. Can't you see how urgent it is that a scandal like this shouldn't get about? I should be the laughing-stock of the city. Not a soul must ever guess that such a thing has happened. You must see that yourself."

"Yes," said Dick, who all this time was sitting on a corner of the table, swinging his legs, "I see that. It will be all right. I'm going to wish in a minute, and no one will guess there has been anything the matter."

"That's a good boy!" said Paul, much relieved, "I know your heart is in the right place—only do make haste."

"I suppose," Dick asked, "when you are yourself again, things would go on just as usual?"

"I—I hope so."

"I mean you will go on sitting here, and I shall go off to Grimstone's?"

"Of course, of course," said Paul; "don't ask so many questions. I'm sure you quite understand what has to be done, so get on. We might be found like this any minute."

"That settles it," said Dick, "any fellow would do it after that."

"Yes, yes, but you're so slow about it!"

"Don't be in a hurry," said Dick, "you mayn't like it after all when I've done it."

"Done what?" asked Mr. Bultitude sharply, struck by something sinister and peculiar in the boy's manner.

"Well, I don't mind telling you," said Dick, "it's fairer. You see, you wished to be a boy just like me, didn't you?"

"I didn't mean it," protested Paul.

"Ah, you couldn't expect a stone to know that; at any rate, it made you into a boy like me directly. Now, if I wish myself a man just like you were ten minutes ago, before you took the stone, that will put things all right again, won't it?"

"Is the boy mad?" cried Paul, horrified at this proposal. "Why, why, that would be worse than ever!"

"I don't see that," objected Dick, stubbornly. "No one would know anything about it then."

"But, you little blockhead, can't I make you understand? It wouldn't do at all. We should both of us be wrong then—each with the other's personal appearance."

"Well," said Dick blandly, "I shouldn't mind that."

"But I should—I mind very much. I object strongly to such a—such a preposterous arrangement. And what's more, I won't have it. Do you hear, I forbid you to think of any such thing. Give me back that stone. I can't trust you with it after this."

"I can't help it," said Dick doggedly. "You've had your wish, and I don't see why I shouldn't have mine. I mean to have it, too."

"Why, you unnatural little rascal!" cried the justly-enraged father, "do you mean to defy me? I tell you I will have that stone! Give it up this instant!" and he made a movement towards his son, as if he meant to recover the talisman by main force.

But Dick was too quick for him. Slipping off the table with great agility, he planted himself firmly on the hearth-rug, with the hand that held the stone clenched behind his back, and the other raised in self-defence.

"I'd much rather you wouldn't make me hit you, you know," he said, "because, in spite of what's happened, you're still my father, I suppose. But if you interfere with me before I've done with this stone, I'm afraid I shall have to punch your head."

Mr. Bultitude retreated a few steps apprehensively, feeling himself no match for his son, except in size and general appearance; and for some moments of really frightful intensity they stood panting on the hearth-rug, each cautiously watching the other, on his guard against stratagem and surprise.

It was one of those painful domestic scenes which are fortunately rare between father and son.

Overhead, the latest rollicking French polka was being rattled out, with a savage irony of which pianos, even by the best makers, can at times be capable.

Suddenly Dick drew himself up. "Stand out of my way!" he cried excitedly, "I am going to do it. I wish I was a man like you were just now!"

And as he spoke, Mr. Bultitude had the bitterness of seeing his unscrupulous son swell out like the frog in the fable, till he stood there before him the exact duplicate of what Paul had so lately been!

The transformed Dick began to skip and dance round the room in high glee, with as much agility as his increased bulk would allow. "It's all right, you see," he said. "The old stone's as good as ever. You can't say anyone would ever know, to look at us."

And then he threw himself panting into a chair, and began to laugh excitedly at the success of his unprincipled manœuvres.

As for Paul, he was perfectly furious at having been so outwitted and overreached. It was a long time before he could command his voice sufficiently to say, savagely: "Well, you've had your way, and a pretty mess you've made of it. We're both of us in false positions now. I hope you're satisfied, I'm sure. Do you think you'll care about going back to Crichton House in that state?"

"No," said Dick, very decidedly: "I'm quite sure I shouldn't."

"Well, I can't help it. You've brought it on yourself; and, provided the Doctor sees no objection to take you back as you are and receive you as one of his pupils, I shall most certainly send you there."

Paul did not really mean this, he only meant to frighten him; for he still trusted that, by letting Boaler into the secret, the charm might be set in motion once more, and the difficulty comfortably overcome. But his threat had a most unfortunate effect upon Dick; it hardened him to take a course he might otherwise have shrunk from.

"Oh," he said, "you're going to do that? But doesn't it strike you that things are rather altered with us now?"

"They are, to a certain extent, of course," said Paul, "through my folly and your wicked cunning; but a word or two of explanation from me——"

"You'll find it will take more explanation than you think," said Dick; "but, of course, you can try, if you think it worth while—when you get to Grimstone's."

"When I,—I don't understand. When I,—what did you say?" gasped Paul.

"Why, you see," exclaimed Dick, "it would never have done for us both to go back; the chaps would have humbugged us so, and as I hate the place and you seem so fond of being a boy and going back to school and that, I thought perhaps it would be best for you to go and see how you liked it!"

"I never will! I'll not stir from this room! I dare you to try to move me!" cried Paul. And just then there was the sound of wheels outside once more. They stopped before the house, the bell rang sharply—the long-expected cab had come at last.

"You've no time to lose," said Dick, "get your coat on."

Mr. Bultitude tried to treat the affair as a joke. He laughed a ghastly little laugh.

"Ha! ha! you've fairly caught your poor father this time; you've proved him in the wrong. I admit I said more than I exactly meant. But that's enough. Don't drive a good joke too far; shake hands, and let us see if we can't find a way out of this!"

But Dick only warmed his coat tails at the fire as he said, with a very ungenerous reminiscence of his father's manner: "You are going back to an excellent establishment, where you will enjoy all the comforts of home—I can specially recommend the stickjaw; look out for it on Tuesdays and Fridays. You will once more take part in the games and lessons of happy boyhood. (Did you ever play 'chevy' when you were a boy before? You'll enjoy chevy.) And you will find your companions easy enough to get on with, if you don't go giving yourself airs; they won't stand airs. Now good-bye, my boy, and bless you!"

Paul stood staring stupidly at this outrageous assumption; he could scarcely believe yet that it was meant in cruel earnest. Before he could answer, the door opened and Boaler appeared.

"Had a deal of trouble to find a keb, sir, on a night like this," he said to the false Dick, "but the luggage is all on top, and the man says there's plenty of time still."

"Good-bye then, my boy," said Dick, with well-assumed tenderness, but a rather dangerous light in his eye. "My compliments to the Doctor, remember."

Paul turned indignantly from him to the butler; he, at least, would stand by him. Boaler would not see a master who had always been fair, if not indulgent, to him driven from his home in this cold-blooded manner!

He made two or three attempts to speak, for his brain whirled so with scathing, burning things to say. He would expose the fraud then and there, and defy the impudent usurper; he would warn every one against this spurious pinchbeck imitation of himself. The whole household should be summoned and called upon to judge between the two!

No doubt, if he had had enough self-command to do all this effectually, while Dick had as yet not had the time thoroughly to adapt himself to his altered circumstances, he might have turned the situation at the outset, and spared himself some very painful experiences.

But it is very often precisely those words which are the most vitally important to be said that refuse to pass our lips on a sudden emergency. We feel all the necessity of saying something at once, but the necessary words unaccountably desert us at the critical moment.

Mr. Bultitude felt himself in this unfortunate position. He made more wild efforts to explain, but the sense of his danger only petrified his mind instead of stimulating it. Then he was spared further conflict. A dark mist rose before his eyes; the walls of the room receded into infinite space; and, with a loud singing in his ears, he fell, and seemed to himself to be sinking down, down, through the earth to the very crust of the antipodes. Then the blackness closed over him—and he knew no more.

3.
In the Toils

> "I beseech you let his lack of years be no impediment to let
> him lack a reverend estimation, for I never knew so young
> a body with so old a head."—*Merchant of Venice*, Act iv.

When Mr. Bultitude recovered his senses, which was not for a considerable time, he found that he was being jolted along through a broad well-lit thoroughfare, in a musty four-wheeler.

His head was by no means clear yet, and for some minutes he could hardly be said to think at all; he merely lay back dreamily listening to the hard grinding jar of the cab windows vibrating in their grooves.

His first distinct sensation was a vague wonder what Barbara might be intending to give him for dinner, for, oddly enough, he felt far from hungry, and was conscious that his palate would require the adroitest witching.

With the thought of dinner his dining-room was almost inseparably associated, and then, with an instant rush of recollection, the whole scene there with the Garudâ Stone surged into his brain. He shuddered as he did so; it had all been so real, so hideously vivid and coherent throughout. But all unpleasant impressions soon yielded to the delicious luxury of his present security.

As his last conscious moment had been passed in his own dining-room, the fact that he opened his eyes in a cab, instead of confirming his worst fears, actually helped to restore the unfortunate gentleman's serenity; for he frequently drove home from the city in this manner, and believed himself now, instead of being, as was actually the case, in that marvellous region of cheap photography, rocking-horses, mild stone lions, and wheels and ladders—the Euston Road—to be bowling along Holborn.

Now that he was thoroughly awake he found positive amusement in going over each successive incident of his nightmare experience with the talisman, and smiling at the tricks his imagination had played him.

"I wonder now how the dickens I came to dream such outrageous nonsense!" he said to himself, for even his dreams were, as a rule, within the bounds of probability. But he was not long in tracing it to the devilled kidneys he had had at the club for lunch, and some curious old brown sherry Robinson had given him afterwards at his office.

"Gad, what a shock the thing has given me!" he thought. "I can hardly shake off the feeling even now."

As a rule, after waking up on the verge of a fearful crisis, the effect of the horror fades swiftly away, as one detail after another evades a memory which is never too anxious to retain them, and each moment brings a deeper sense of relief and self-congratulation.

But in Paul's case, curiously enough, as he could not help thinking, the more completely roused he became, the greater grew his uneasiness.

Perhaps the first indication of the truth was suggested to him by a lurking suspicion—which he tried to dismiss as mere fancy—that he filled rather less of the cab than he had always been accustomed to do.

To reassure himself he set his thoughts to review all the proceedings of that day, feeling that if he could satisfactorily account for the time up to his taking the cab, that would be conclusive as to the unreality of any thing that appeared to have happened later in his own house. He got on well enough till he came to the hour at which he had left the office, and then, search his memory as he would, he could not remember hailing any cab!

Could it be another delusion, too, or was it the fact that he had found himself much pressed for time and had come home by the Underground to Praed Street? It must have been the day before, but that was Sunday. Saturday, then? But the recollection seemed too recent and fresh; and besides, on Saturday, he had left at two, and had taken Barbara to see Messrs. Maskelyne and Cooke's performance.

Slowly, insidiously, but with irresistible force, the conviction crept upon him that he had dined, and dined well.

"If I have dined already," he told himself, "I can't be going home to dinner; and if I am not going home to dinner, what—what am I doing in this cab?"

The bare idea that something might be wrong with him after all made him impatient to put an end to all suspense. He must knock this scotched nightmare once for all on the head by a deliberate appeal to his senses.

The cab had passed the lighted shops now, and was driving between squares and private houses, so that Mr. Bultitude had to wait until the sickly rays of a street lamp glanced into the cab for a moment, and, as they did so, he put his feet up on the opposite seat and examined his boots and trousers with breathless eagerness.

It was not to be denied; they were not his ordinary boots, nor did he ever wear such trousers as he saw above them! Always a careful and punctiliously neat person, he was more than commonly exacting concerning the make and polish of his boots and the set of his trousers.

These boots were clumsy, square-toed, and thick-soled; one was even patched on the side. The trousers were heavy and rough, of the kind advertised as "wear-resisting fabrics, suitable for youths at school," frayed at the ends, and shiny—shamefully shiny—about the knees!

In hot despair he rapidly passed his hands over his body. It felt unusually small and slim, Mr. Bultitude being endowed with what is euphemistically termed a "presence," and it was with an agony rarely felt at such a discovery that he realised that, for the first time for more than twenty years, he actually had a waist.

Then, as a last resource, he took off his hat and felt for the broad, smooth, egg-like surface, garnished by scanty side patches of thin hair, which he knew he ought to find.

It was gone—hidden under a crop of thick close curling locks!

This last disappointment completely overcame him; he had a kind of short fit in the cab as the bitter truth was brought home to him unmistakably.

Yes, this was no dream of a distempered digestion, but sober reality. The whole of that horrible scene in the dining-room had really taken place; and now he, Paul Bultitude, the widely-respected merchant of Mincing Lane, a man of means and position, was being ignominiously packed off to school as if he were actually the schoolboy some hideous juggle had made him appear!

It was only with a violent effort that he could succeed in commanding his thoughts sufficiently to decide on some immediate action. "I must be cool," he kept muttering to himself, with shaking lips, "quite cool and collected. Everything will depend on that now!"

It was some comfort to him in this extremity to recognise on the box the well-known broad back of Clegg, a cabman who stabled his two horses in some mews near Praed Street, and whom he had been accustomed to patronise in bad weather for several years.

Clegg would know him, in spite of his ridiculous transformation.

His idea was to stop the cab, and turn round and drive home again, when they would find that he was not to be got rid of again quite so easily. If Dick imagined he meant to put up tamely with this kind of treatment, he was vastly mistaken; he would return home boldly and claim his rights!

No reasonable person could be perverse enough to doubt his identity when once matters came to the proof; though at first, of course, he might find a difficulty in establishing it. His children, his clerks, and his servants would soon get used to his appearance, and would learn to look below the mere surface, and then there was always the possibility of putting everything right by means of the magic stone.

"I won't lose a minute!" he said aloud; and letting down the window, leaned out and shouted "Stop!" till he was hoarse.

But Clegg either could not or would not hear; he drove on at full speed, a faster rate of progress than that adopted by most drivers of four-wheeled cabs being one of his chief recommendations.

They were now passing Euston. It was a muggy, slushy night, with a thin brown fog wreathing the houses and fading away above their tops into a dull, slate-blue sky. The wet street looked like a black canal; the blurred forms, less like vehicles than nondescript boats, moving over its inky surface, were indistinctly reflected therein; the gas-lights flared redly through the murky haze. It was not a pleasant evening in which to be out-of-doors.

Paul would have opened the cab-door and jumped out had he dared, but his nerve failed him, and, indeed, considering the speed of the cab, the leap would have been dangerous to a far more active person. So he was forced to wait resignedly until the station should be reached, when he determined to make Clegg understand his purpose with as little loss of time as possible.

"I must pay him something extra," he thought; "I'll give him a sovereign to take me back." And he searched his pockets for the loose coin he usually carried about with him in such abundance; there was no gold in any of them.

He found, however, a variety of minor and less negotiable articles, which he fished out one by one from unknown depths—a curious collection. There was a stumpy German-silver pencil case, a broken prism from a crystal chandelier, a gilded Jew's harp, a little book in which the leaves on being turned briskly, gave a semblance of motion to the sails of a black windmill drawn therein, a broken tin soldier, some Hong-Kong coppers with holes in them, and a quantity of little cogged wheels from the inside of a watch; while a further search was rewarded by an irregular lump of toffee imperfectly enfolded in sticky brown paper.

He threw the whole of these treasures out of the window with indescribable disgust, and, feeling something like a purse in a side pocket, opened it eagerly.

It held five shillings exactly, the coins corresponding to those he had pushed across to his son such a little while ago! It did not seem to him quite such a magnificent sum now as it had done then; he had shifted his point of view.

It was too clear that the stone must have carried out his thoughtless wish with scrupulous and conscientious exactness in every detail. He had wanted, or said he wanted, to be a boy again like Dick, and accordingly he had become a perfect duplicate, even to the contents of the pockets. Evidently nothing on the face of things showed the slightest difference. Yet—and here lay the sting of the metamorphosis—he was conscious under it all of being his old original self, in utter discordance with the youthful form in which he was an unwilling prisoner.

By this time the cab had driven up the sharp incline, and under the high pointed archway of St. Pancras terminus, and now drew up with a jerk against the steps leading to the booking office.

Paul sprang out at once in a violent passion. "Here, you, Clegg!" he said, "why the devil didn't you pull up when I told you? eh?"

Clegg was a burly, red-faced man, with a husky voice and a general manner which conveyed the impression that he regarded teetotalism, as a principle, with something more than disapproval.

"Why didn't I pull up?" he said, bending stiffly down from his box. "'Cause I didn't want to lose a good customer, that's why I didn't pull up!"

"Do you mean to say you don't know me?"

"Know yer?" said Clegg, with an approach to sentiment: "I've knowed yer when you was a babby in frocks. I've knowed yer fust nuss (and a fine young woman she were till she took to drinking, as has been the ruin of many). I've knowed yer in Infancy's hour and in yer byhood's bloom! I've druv yer to this 'ere werry station twice afore. Know yer!"

Paul saw the uselessness of arguing with him. "Then, ah—drive me back at once. Let those boxes alone. I—I've important business at home which I'd forgotten."

Clegg gave a vinous wink. "Lor, yer at it agin," he said with admiration. "What a artful young limb it is! But it ain't what yer may call good enough, so to speak, it ain't. Clegg don't do that no more!"

"Don't do what?" asked Paul.

"Don't drive no young gents as is a-bein' sent to school back agin into their family's bosims," said Clegg sententiously. "You was took ill sudden in my cab the larst time. Offal bad you was, to be sure—to hear ye, and I druv' yer back; and I never got no return fare, I didn't, and yer par he made hisself downright nasty over it, said as if it occurred agin he shouldn't employ me no more. I durstn't go and offend yer par; he's a good customer to me, he is."

"I'll give you a sovereign to do it," said Paul.

"If yer wouldn't tell no tales, I might put yer down at the corner p'raps," said Clegg, hesitating, to Paul's joy; "not as it ain't cheap at that, but let's see yer suffering fust. Why," he cried with lofty contempt as he saw from Paul's face that the coin was not producible, "y'ain't got no suffering! Garn away, and don't try to tempt a pore cabby as has his livin' to make. What d'ye think of this, porter, now? 'Ere's a young gent a tryin' to back out o' going to school when he ought to be glad and thankful as he's receivin' the blessin's of a good eddication. Look at me. I'm a 'ard-workin' man. I am. I ain't 'ad no eddication. The kids, they're a learnin' French, and free'and drorin, and the bones on a skellington at the Board School, and I pays my coppers down every week cheerful. And why, porter? Why, young master? 'Cause I knows the vally on it! But when I sees a real young gent a despisin' of the oppertoonities as a bountiful Providence and a excellent par has 'eaped on his 'ed, it—it makes me sick, it inspires Clegg with a pity and a contemp' for such ingratitood, which he cares not for to 'ide from public voo!"

Clegg delivered this harangue with much gesture and in a loud tone, which greatly edified the porters and disgusted Mr. Bultitude.

"Go away," said the latter, "that's enough. You're drunk!"

"Drunk!" bellowed the outraged Clegg, rising on the box in his wrath. "'Ear that. 'Ark at this 'ere young cock sparrer as tells a fam'ly man like Clegg as he's drunk! Drunk, after drivin' his par in this 'ere werry cab through frost and fine fifteen year and more! I wonder yer don't say the old 'orse is drunk; you'll be sayin' that next! Drunk! oh, cert'nly, by all means. Never you darken my cab doors no more. I shall take and tell your par, I shall. Drunk, indeed! A ill-conditioned young wiper as ever I see. Drunk! yah!"

And with much cursing and growling, Clegg gathered up his reins and drove off into the fog, Boaler having apparently pre-paid the fare.

"Where for, sir, please?" said a porter, who had been putting the playbox and portmanteau on a truck during the altercation.

"Nowhere," said Mr. Bultitude. "I—I'm not going by this train; find me a cab with a sober driver."

The porter looked round. A moment before there had been several cabs discharging their loads at the steps; now the last had rolled away empty.

"You might find one inside the station by the arrival platform," he suggested; "but there'll be sure to be one comin' up here in another minute, sir, if you like to wait."

Paul thought the other course might be the longer one, and decided to stay where he was. So he walked into the lofty hall in which the booking offices are placed and waited there by the huge fire that blazed in the stove until he should hear the cab arrive which could take him back to Westbourne Terrace.

One or two trains were about to start, and the place was full. There were several Cambridge men "going up" after the Christmas vacation, in every variety of ulster; some tugging at refractory white terriers, one or two entrusting bicycles to dubious porters with many cautions and directions. There were burly old farmers going back to their quiet countryside, flushed with the prestige of a successful stand under cross-examination in some witness-box at the Law Courts; to tell and retell the story over hill and dale, in the market-place and bar-parlour, every week for the rest of their honest lives. There was the usual pantomime "rally" on a mild scale, with real frantic passengers, and porters, and trucks, and trays of lighted lamps.

Presently, out of the crowd and confusion, a small boy in a thick pilot jacket and an immensely tall hat, whom Paul had observed looking at him intently for some time, walked up to the stove and greeted him familiarly.

"Hallo, Bultitude!" he said, "I thought it was you. Here we are again, eh? Ugh!" and he giggled dismally.

He was a pale-faced boy with freckles, very light green eyes, long, rather ragged black hair, a slouching walk, and a smile half-simpering, half-impudent.

Mr. Bultitude was greatly staggered by the presumption of so small a boy venturing to address him in this way. He could only stare haughtily.

"You might find a word to say to a fellow!" said the boy in an aggrieved tone. "Look here; come and get your luggage labelled."

"I don't want it labelled," said Paul stiffly, feeling bound to say something. "I'm waiting for a cab to take me home again."

The other gave a loud whistle. "That'll make it rather a short term, won't it, if you're going home for the holidays already? You're a cool chap, Bultitude! If I were to go back to my governor now, he wouldn't see it. It would put him in no end of a bait. But you're chaffing——"

Paul walked away from him with marked coolness. He was not going to trouble himself to talk to his son's schoolfellows.

"Aren't you well?" said the boy, not at all discouraged by his reception, following him and taking his arm. "Down in the mouth? It is beastly, isn't it, having to go back to old Grimstone's! The snow gave us an extra week, though—we've that much to be thankful for. I wish it was the first day of the holidays again, don't you? What's the matter with you? What have I done to put you in a wax?"

"Nothing at present," said Paul. "I don't speak to you merely because I don't happen to have the—ah—pleasure of your acquaintance."

"Oh, very well, then; I daresay you know best," said the other huffily. "Only I thought—considering we came the same half, and have been chums, and always sat next one another ever since—you might perhaps just recollect having met me before, you know."

"Well, I don't," said Mr. Bultitude. "I tell you I haven't the least idea what your name is. The fact is there has been a slight mistake, which I can't stop to talk about now. There's a cab just driven up outside now. You must excuse me, really, my boy, I want to go."

He tried to work his arm free from the close and affectionate grip of his unwelcome companion, who was regarding him with a sort of admiring leer.

"What a fellow you are, Bultitude!" he said; "always up to something or other. You know me well enough. What is the use of keeping it up any longer? Let's talk, and stop humbugging. How much grub have you brought back this time?"

To be advised to stop humbugging, and be persecuted with such idle questions as these, maddened the poor gentleman. A hansom really had rolled up to the steps outside. He must put an end to this waste of precious time, and escape from this highly inconvenient small boy.

He forced his way to the door, the boy still keeping fast hold of his arm. Fortunately the cab was still there, and its late occupant, a tall, broad man, was standing with his back to them paying the driver. Paul was only just in time.

"Porter!" he cried. "Where's that porter? I want my box put on that cab. No, I don't care about the luggage; engage the cab. Now, you little ruffian, are you going to let me go? Can't you see I'm anxious to get away?"

Jolland giggled more impishly than ever. "Well, you *have* got cheek!" he said. "Go on, I wish you may get that cab, I'm sure!"

Paul, thus released, was just hurrying towards the cab, when the stranger who had got out of it settled the fare with satisfaction to himself and turned sharply round.

The gas-light fell full on his face, and Mr. Bultitude recognised that the form and features were those of no stranger—he had stumbled upon the very last person he had expected or desired to meet just then—his flight was intercepted by his son's schoolmaster, Dr. Grimstone himself!

The suddenness of the shock threw him completely off his balance. In an ordinary way the encounter would not of course have discomposed him, but now he would have given worlds for presence of mind enough either to rush past to the cab and secure his only chance of freedom before the Doctor had fully realised his intention, or else greet him affably and calmly, and, taking him quietly aside, explain his awkward position with an easy man-of-the-world air, which would ensure instant conviction.

But both courses were equally impossible. He stood there, right in Dr. Grimstone's path, with terrified starting eyes and quivering limbs, more like an unhappy guinea-pig expecting the advances of a boa, than a British merchant in the presence of his son's schoolmaster! He was sick and faint with alarm, and the consciousness that appearances were all against him.

There was nothing in the least extraordinary in the fact of the Doctor's presence at the station. Mr. Bultitude might easily have taken this into account as a very likely contingency and have provided accordingly, had he troubled to think, for it was Dr. Grimstone's custom, upon the first day of the term, to come up to town and meet as many of his pupils upon the platform as intended to return by a train previously specified at the foot of the school-bills; and Paul had even expressly insisted upon Dick's travelling under surveillance in this manner, thinking it necessary to keep him out of premature mischief.

It makes a calamity doubly hard to bear when one looks back and sees by what a trivial chance it has come upon us, and how slight an effort would have averted it altogether; and Mr. Bultitude cursed his own stupidity as he stood there, rooted to the ground, and saw the hansom (a "patent safety" to him in sober earnest) drive off and abandon him to his fate.

Dr. Grimstone bore down heavily upon him and Jolland, who had by this time come up. He was a tall and imposing personage, with a strong black beard and small angry grey eyes, slightly blood-tinged; he wore garments of a semi-clerical cut and colour, though he was not in orders. He held out a hand to each with elaborate geniality.

"Ha, Bultitude, my boy, how are you? How are you, Jolland? Come back braced in body and mind by your vacation, eh? That's as it should be. Have you tickets? No? follow me then. You're both over age, I believe. There you are; take care of them."

And before Paul could protest, he had purchased tickets for all three, after which he laid an authoritative hand upon Mr. Bultitude's shoulder and walked him out through the booking hall upon the platform.

"This is awful," thought Paul, shrinking involuntarily; "simply awful. He evidently has no idea who I really am. Unless I'm very careful I shall be dragged off to Crichton House before I can put him right. If I could only get him away alone somewhere."

As if in answer to the wish, the Doctor guided him by a slight pressure straight along by the end of the station, saying to Jolland as he did so, "I wish to have a little serious conversation with Richard in private. Suppose you go to the bookstall and see if you can find out any of our young friends. Tell them to wait for me there."

When they were alone the Doctor paced solemnly along in silence for some moments, while Paul, who had always been used to consider himself a fairly prominent object, whatever might be his surroundings, began to feel an altogether novel sensation of utter insignificance upon that immense brown plain of platform and under the huge span of the arches whose girders were lost in wreaths of mingled fog and smoke.

Still he had some hope. Was it not possible, after all, that the Doctor had divined his secret and was searching for words delicate enough to convey his condolences?

"I wished to tell you, Bultitude," said the Doctor presently, and his first words dashed all Paul's rising hopes, "that I hope you are returning this term with the resolve to do better things. You have caused your excellent father much pain in the past. You little know the grief a wilful boy can inflict on his parent."

"I think I have a very fair idea of it," thought Paul, but he said nothing.

"I hope you left him in good health? Such a devoted parent, Richard—such a noble heart!"

At any other time Mr. Bultitude might have felt gratified by these eulogies, but just then he was conscious that he could lay no claim to them. It was Dick who had the noble heart now, and he himself felt even less of a devoted parent than he looked.

"I had a letter from him during the vacation," continued Dr. Grimstone, "a sweet letter, Richard, breathing in every line a father's anxiety and concern for your welfare."

Paul was a little staggered. He remembered having written, but he would scarcely perhaps have described his letter as "sweet," as he had not done much more than enclose a cheque for his son's account and object to the items for pew-rent and scientific lectures with the diorama as excessive.

"But—and this is what I wanted to say to you, Bultitude—his is no blind doting affection. He has implored me, for your own sake, if I see you diverging ever so slightly from the path of duty, not to stay my hand. And I shall not forget his injunctions."

A few minutes ago, and it would have seemed to Paul so simple and easy a matter to point out to the Doctor the very excusable error into which he had fallen. It was no more than he would have to do repeatedly upon his return, and here was an excellent opportunity for an explanation.

But, somehow the words would not come. The schoolmaster's form seemed so tremendous and towering, and he so feeble and powerless before him, that he soon persuaded himself that a public place, like a station platform, was no scene for domestic revelations of so painful a character.

He gave up all idea of resistance at present. "Perhaps I had better leave him in his error till we get into the train," he thought; "then we will get rid of that other boy, and I can break it to him gradually in the railway carriage as I get more accustomed to him."

But in spite of his determination to unbosom himself without further delay, he knew that a kind of fascinated resignation was growing upon him and gaining firmer hold each minute.

Something must be done to break the spell and burst the toils which were being woven round him before all effort became impossible.

"And now," said the Doctor, glancing up at the great clock-face on which a reflector cast a patch of dim yellow light, "we must be thinking of starting. But don't forget what I have said."

And they walked back towards the book-stalls with their cheery warmth of colour, past the glittering buffet, and on up the platform, to a part where six boys of various sizes were standing huddled forlornly together under a gaslight.

"Aha!" said Dr. Grimstone, with a slight touch of the ogre in his tone, "more of my fellows, eh? We shall be quite a party. How do you do, boys? Welcome back to your studies."

And the six boys came forward, all evidently in the lowest spirits, and raised their tall hats with a studied politeness.

"Some old friends here, Bultitude," said the Doctor, impelling the unwilling Paul towards the group. "You know Tipping, of course; Coker, too, you've met before—and Coggs. How are you, Siggers? You're looking well. Ah, by the way, I see a new face—Kiffin, I think? Kiffin, this is Bultitude, who will make himself your mentor, I hope, and initiate you into our various manners and customs."

And, with a horrible dream-like sense of unreality, Mr. Bultitude found himself being greeted by several entire strangers with a degree of warmth embarrassing in the extreme.

He would have liked to protest and declare himself there and then in his true colours, but if this had been difficult alone with the Doctor under the clock, it was impossible now, and he submitted ruefully enough to their unwelcome advances.

Tipping, a tall, red-haired, raw-boned boy, with sleeves and trousers he had outgrown, and immense boots, wrung Paul's hand with misdirected energy, saying "how-de-do?" with a gruff superiority, mercifully tempered by a touch of sheepishness.

Coggs and Coker welcomed him with open arms as an equal, while Siggers, a short, slight, sharp-featured boy, with a very fashionable hat and shirt-collars, and a horse-shoe pin, drawled, "How are you, old boy?" with the languor of a confirmed man about town.

The other two were Biddlecomb, a boy with a blooming complexion and a singularly sweet voice, and the new-comer, Kiffin, who did not seem much more at home in the society of other boys than Mr. Bultitude himself, for he kept nervously away from them, shivering with the piteous self-abandonment of an Italian greyhound.

Paul was now convinced that unless he exerted himself considerably, his identity with his son would never even be questioned, and the danger roused him to a sudden determination.

However his face and figure might belie him, nothing in his speech or conduct should encourage the mistake. Whatever it might cost him to overcome his fear of the Doctor, he would force himself to act and talk ostentatiously, as much like his own ordinary self as possible, during the journey down to Market Rodwell, so as to prepare the Doctor's mind for the disclosures he meant to make at the earliest opportunity. He was beginning to see that the railway carriage, with all those boys sitting by and staring, would be an inconvenient place for so delicate and difficult a confession.

The guard having warned intending passengers to take their seats, and Jolland, who had been unaccountably missing all this time, having appeared from the direction of the refreshment buffet, furtively brushing away some suspicious-looking flakes and crumbs from his coat, and contrived to join the party unperceived, they all got into a first-class compartment—Paul with the rest.

He longed for moral courage to stand out boldly and refuse to leave town, but, as we have seen, it was beyond his powers, and he temporised. Very soon the whistle had sounded and the train had begun to glide slowly out beyond the platform and arch, past the signal boxes and long low sheds and offices which are the suburbs of a large terminus—and then it was too late.

4.
A Minnow amongst Tritons

> "Boys are capital fellows in their own way among their mates; but they are unwholesome companions for grown people."—*Essays of Elia*.

For some time after they were fairly started the Doctor read his evening paper with an air of impartial but severe criticism, and Mr. Bultitude as he sat opposite him next to the window, found himself overwhelmed with a new and very unpleasant timidity.

He knew that, if he would free himself, this utterly unreasonable feeling must be wrestled with and overcome; that now, if ever, was the time to assert himself, and prove that he was anything but the raw youth he was conscious of appearing. He had merely to speak and act, too, in his ordinary everyday manner; to forget as far as possible the change that had affected his outer man, which was not so very difficult to do after all—and yet his heart sank lower and lower as each fresh telegraph post flitted past.

"I will let him speak first," he thought; "then I shall be able to feel my way." But there was more fear than caution in the resolve.

At last, however, the Doctor laid down his paper, and, looking round with the glance of proprietorship on his pupils, who had relapsed into a decorous and gloomy silence, observed: "Well, boys, you have had an unusually protracted vacation this time—owing to the unprecedented severity of the weather. We must try to make up for it by the zest and ardour with which we pursue our studies during the term. I intend to reduce the Easter holidays by a week by way of compensation."

This announcement (which by no means relieved the general depression—the boys receiving it with a sickly interest) was good news to Paul, and even had the effect of making him forget his position for the time.

"I'm uncommonly glad to hear it, Dr. Grimstone," he said heartily, "an excellent arrangement. Boys have too many holidays as it is. There's no reason, to my mind, why parents should be the sufferers by every snowstorm. It's no joke, I can assure you, to have a great idle boy hanging about the place eating his empty head off!"

A burglar enlarging upon the sanctity of the law of property, or a sheep exposing the fallacies of vegetarianism, could hardly have produced a greater sensation.

Every boy was roused from his languor to stare and wonder at these traitorous sentiments, which, from the mouth of any but a known and tried companion, would have roused bitter hostility and contempt. As it was, their wonder became a rapturous admiration, and they waited for the situation to develop with a fearful and secret joy.

It was some time before the Doctor quite recovered himself; then he said with a grim smile, "This is indeed finding Saul amongst the prophets; your sentiments, if sincere, Bultitude—I repeat, if sincere—are very creditable. But I am obliged to look upon them with suspicion!" Then, as if to dismiss a doubtful subject, he inquired generally, "And how have you all been spending your holidays, eh!"

There was no attempt to answer this question, it being felt probably that it was, like the conventional "How do you do?" one to which an answer is neither desired nor expected, especially as he continued almost immediately, "I took my boy Tom up to town the week before Christmas to see the representation of the 'Agamemnon' at St. George's Hall. The 'Agamemnon,' as most of you are doubtless aware, is a drama by Æschylus, a Greek poet of established reputation. I was much pleased by the intelligent appreciation Tom showed during the performance. He distinctly recognised several words from his Greek Grammar in the course of the dialogue."

No one seemed capable of responding except Mr. Bultitude, who dashed into the breach with an almost pathetic effort to maintain his accustomed stiffness.

"I may be old-fashioned," he said, "very likely I am; but I—ah—decidedly disapprove of taking children to dramatic exhibitions of any kind. It unsettles them, sir—unsettles them!"

Dr. Grimstone made no answer, but he put a hand on each knee, and glared with pursed lips and a leonine bristle of the beard at his youthful critic for some moments, after which he returned to his *Globe* with a short ominous cough.

"I've offended him now," thought Paul. "I must be more careful what I say. But I'll get him into conversation again presently."

So he began at the first opportunity: "You have this evening's paper, I see. No telegrams of importance, I suppose?"

"No, sir," said the Doctor shortly.

"I saw a report in to-day's *Times*," said poor Mr. Bultitude, with a desperate attempt at his most conversational and instructive manner, "I saw a report that the camphor crop was likely to be a failure this season. Now, it's a very singular thing about camphor, that the Japanese——" (he hoped to lead the conversation round to colonial produce, and thus open the Doctor's eyes by the extent of his acquaintance with the subject).

"I am already acquainted with the method of obtaining camphor, thank you, Bultitude," said the Doctor, with dangerous politeness.

"I was about to observe, when you interrupted me," said Paul, "(and this is really a fact that I doubt if you are aware of), that the Japanese never——"

"Well, well," said the Doctor, with some impatience, "probably they never do, sir, but I shall have other opportunities of finding out what you have read about the Japanese."

But he glanced over the top of the paper at the indignant Paul, who was not accustomed to have his information received in this manner, with less suspicion and a growing conviction that some influence during the holidays had changed the boy from a graceless young scapegrace into a prig of the first water.

"He's most uncivil"—Mr. Bultitude told himself—"almost insulting, but I'll go on. I'm rousing his curiosity. I'm making way with him; he sees a difference already." And so he applied himself once more.

"You're a smoker, of course, Dr. Grimstone?" he began. "We don't stop anywhere, I think, on the way, and I must confess myself, after dinner, a whiff or two—I think I can give you a cigar you'll appreciate."

And he felt for his cigar-case, really forgetting that it was gone, like all other incidents of his old self; while Jolland giggled with unrestrained delight at such charming effrontery.

"If I did not know, sir," said the Doctor, now effectually roused, "that this was ill-timed buffoonery, and not an intentional insult, I should be seriously angry. As it is, I can overlook any exuberance of mirth which is, perhaps, pardonable when the mind is elated by the return to the cheerful bustle and activity of school-life. But be very careful."

"He needn't be so angry," thought Paul, "how could I know he doesn't smoke? But I'm afraid he doesn't quite know me, even now."

So he began again: "Did I hear you mention the name of Kiffin amongst those of your pupils here, Doctor? I thought so. Not the son of Jordan Kiffin, of College Hill, surely? Yes? Why, bless my soul, your father and I, my little fellow, were old friends in days before you were born or thought of—born or thought of. He was in a very small way then, a very small—— Eh, Dr. Grimstone, don't you feel well?"

"I see what you're aiming at, sir. You wish to prove to me that I'm making a mistake in my treatment of you."

"That was my idea, certainly," said Paul, much pleased. "I'm very glad you take me, Doctor."

"I shall take you in a way you won't appreciate soon, if this goes on," said the Doctor under his breath.

"When the time comes I shall know how to deal with you. Till then you'll have the goodness to hold your tongue," he said aloud.

"It's not a very polite way of putting it," Paul said to himself, "but, at any rate, he sees how the case stands now, and after all, perhaps, he only speaks like that to put the boys off the scent. If so, it's uncommonly considerate and thoughtful of him, by Gad. I won't say any more."

But by-and-by, the open window made him break his resolution. "I'm sorry to inconvenience you, Dr. Grimstone," he said, with the air of one used to having his way in these matters, "but I positively must ask you either to allow me to have this window up or to change places with you. The night air, sir, at this time of the year is fatal, my doctor tells me, simply fatal to a man of my constitution."

The Doctor pulled up the window with a frown, and yet a somewhat puzzled expression. "I warn you, Bultitude," he said, "you are acting very imprudently."

"So I am," thought Paul, "so I am. Good of him to remind me. I must keep it up before all these boys. This unpleasant business mustn't get about. I'll hold my tongue till we get in. Then, I daresay, Grimstone will see me off by the next train up, if there is one, and lend me enough for a bed at an hotel for the night. I couldn't get to St. Pancras till very late, of course. Or he might offer to put me up at the school. If he does, I think I shall very possibly accept. It might be better."

And he leant back in his seat in a much easier frame of mind; it was annoying, of course, to have been turned out of his warm dining-room, and sent all the way down to Market Rodwell on a fool's errand like this; but still, if nothing worse came of it, he could put up with the temporary inconvenience, and it was a great relief to be spared the necessity of an explanation.

The other boys watched him furtively with growing admiration, which expressed itself in subdued whispers, varied by little gurgles and "squirks" of laughter; they tried to catch his eye and stimulate him to further feats of audacity, but Mr. Bultitude, of course, repulsed all such overtures with a coldness and severity which at once baffled and piqued them.

At last his eccentricity took a shape which considerably lessened their enthusiasm. Kiffin, the new boy, occupied the seat next to Paul; he was a nervous-looking little fellow, with a pale face and big pathetic brown eyes like a seal's, and his dress bore plain evidence of a mother's careful supervision, having all the uncreased trimness and specklessness rarely to be observed except in the toilettes of the waxen prodigies in a shop-window.

It happened that, as he lay back in the padded seat between the sheltering partitions, watching the sickly yellow dregs of oil surging dismally to and fro with the motion in the lamp overhead, or the black indistinct forms flitting past through the misty blue outside, the pathos of his situation became all at once too much for him.

He was a home-bred boy, without any of that taste for the companionship and pursuits of his fellows, or capacity for adapting himself to their prejudices and requirements, which give some home-bred boys a ready passport into the roughest communities.

His heart throbbed with no excited curiosity, no conscious pride, at this his first important step in life; he was a forlorn little stranger, in an unsympathetic strange land, and was only too well aware of his position.

So that it is not surprising that as he thought of the home he had left an hour or two ago which now seemed so shadowy, so inaccessible and remote, his eyes began to smart and sting, and his chest to heave ominously, until he felt it necessary to do something to give a partial vent to his emotions and prevent a public and disgraceful exhibition of grief.

Unhappily for him he found this safety-valve in a series of suppressed but distinctly audible sniffs.

Mr. Bultitude bore this for some time with no other protest than an occasional indignant bounce or a lowering frown in the offender's direction, but at last his nerves, strung already to a high pitch by all he had undergone, could stand it no longer.

"Dr. Grimstone," he said with polite determination, "I'm not a man to complain without good reason, but really I must ask you to interfere. Will you tell this boy here, on my right, either to control his feelings or to cry into his pocket-handkerchief, like an ordinary human being? A good honest bellow I can understand, but this infernal whiffling and sniffing, sir, I will not put up with. It's nothing less than unnatural in a boy of that size."

"Kiffin," said the Doctor, "are you crying?"

"N—no, sir," faltered Kiffin; "I—I think I must have caught cold, sir."

"I hope you are telling me the truth, because I should be sorry to believe you were beginning your new life in a spirit of captiousness and rebellion. I'll have no mutineers in my camp. I'll establish a spirit of trustful happiness and unmurmuring content in this school, if I have to flog every boy in it as long as I can stand over him! As for you, Richard Bultitude, I have no words to express my pain and disgust at the heartless irreverence with which you persist in mimicking and burlesquing a fond and excellent parent. Unless I perceive, sir, in a very short time a due sense of your error and a lively repentance, my disapproval will take a very practical form."

Mr. Bultitude fell back into his seat with a gasp. It was hard to be accused of caricaturing one's own self, particularly when conscious of entire innocence in that respect, but even this was slight in comparison with the discovery that he had been so blindly deceiving himself!

The Doctor evidently had failed to penetrate his disguise, and the dreaded scene of elaborate explanation must be gone through after all.

The boys (with the exception of Kiffin) still found exquisite enjoyment in this extraordinary and original exhibition, and waited eagerly for further experiment on the Doctor's patience.

They were soon gratified. If there was one thing Paul detested more than another, it was the smell of peppermint—no less than three office boys had been discharged by him because, as he alleged, they made the clerks' room reek with it,—and now the subtle searching odour of the hated confection was gradually stealing into the compartment and influencing its atmosphere.

He looked at Coggs, who sat on the seat opposite to him, and saw his cheeks and lips moving in slow and appreciative absorption of something. Coggs was clearly the culprit.

"Do you encourage your boys to make common nuisances of themselves in a public place, may I ask, Dr. Grimstone?" he inquired, fuming.

"Some scarcely seem to require encouragement, Bultitude," said the Doctor pointedly: "what is the matter now?"

"If he takes it medicinally," said Paul, "he should choose some other time and place to treat his complaint. If he has a depraved liking for the abominable stuff, for Heaven's sake make him refrain from it on occasions when it is a serious annoyance to others!"

"Will you explain? Who and what are you talking about?"

"That boy opposite," said Paul, pointing the finger of denunciation at the astonished Coggs; "he's sucking an infernal peppermint lozenge strong enough to throw the train off the rails!"

"Is what Bultitude tells me true, Coggs?" demanded the Doctor in an awful voice.

Coggs, after making several attempts to bolt the offending lozenge, and turning scarlet meanwhile with confusion and coughing, stammered huskily something to the effect that he had "bought the lozenges at a chemist's," which he seemed to consider, for some reason, a mitigating circumstance.

"Have you any more of this pernicious stuff about you?" said the Doctor.

Very slowly and reluctantly Coggs brought out of one pocket after another three or four neat little white packets, made up with that lavish expenditure of time, string, and sealing-wax, by which the struggling chemist seeks to reconcile the public mind to a charge of two hundred and fifty per cent. on cost price, and handed them to Dr. Grimstone, who solemnly unfastened them one by one, glanced at their contents with infinite disgust, and flung them out of window.

Then he turned to Paul with a look of more favour than he had yet shown him. "Bultitude," he said, "I am obliged to you. A severe cold in the head has rendered me incapable of detecting this insidious act of insubordination and self-indulgence, on which I shall have more to say on another occasion. Your moral courage and promptness in denouncing the evil thing are much to your credit."

"Not at all," said Paul, "not at all, my dear sir. I mentioned it because I—ah—happen to be peculiarly sensitive on the subject and——" Here he broke off with a sharp yell, and began to rub his ankle. "One of these young savages has just given me a severe kick; it's that fellow over there, with the blue necktie. I have given him no provocation, and he attacks me in this brutal manner, sir; I appeal to you for protection!"

"So, Coker" (Coker wore a blue necktie), said the Doctor, "you emulate the wild ass in more qualities than those of stupidity and stubbornness, do you? You lash out with your hind legs at an inoffensive school-fellow, with all the viciousness of a kangaroo, eh? Write out all you find in Buffon's Natural History upon those two animals a dozen times, and bring it to me by to-morrow evening. If I am to stable wild asses, sir, they shall be broken in!"

Six pairs of sulky glowering eyes were fixed upon the unconscious Paul for the rest of the journey; indignant protests and dark vows of vengeance were muttered under cover of the friendly roar and rattle of tunnels. But the object of them heard nothing; his composure was returning once more in the sunshine of Dr. Grimstone's approbation, and he almost decided on declaring himself in the station fly.

And now at last the train was grinding along discordantly with the brakes on, and, after a little preliminary jolting and banging over the points, drew up at a long lighted platform, where melancholy porters paced up and down, croaking "Market Rodwell!" like so many Solomon Eagles predicting woe.

Paul got out with the others, and walked forward to the guard's van, where he stood shivering in the raw night air by a small heap of portmanteaux and white clamped boxes.

"I should like to tell him all about it now," he thought, "if he wasn't so busy. I'll get him to go in a cab alone with me, and get it over before we reach the house."

Dr. Grimstone certainly did not seem in a very receptive mood for confidences just then. No flys were to be seen, which he took as a personal outrage, and visited upon the station-master in hot indignation.

"It's scandalous, I tell you," he was saying: "scandalous! No cabs to meet the train. My school reassembles to-day, and here I find no arrangements made for their accommodation! Not even an omnibus! I shall write to the manager and report this. Let some one go for a fly immediately. Boys, go into the waiting room till I come to you. Stay—there are too many for one fly. Coker, Coggs, and, let me see, yes, Bultitude, you all know your way. Walk on and tell Mrs. Grimstone we are coming."

Paul Bultitude was perhaps more relieved than disappointed by this postponement of a disagreeable interview, though, if he had seen Coker dig Coggs in the side with a chuckle of exultant triumph, he might have had misgivings as to the prudence of trusting himself alone with them.

As it was he almost determined to trust the pair with his secret. "They will be valuable witnesses," he said to himself, "that, whoever else I may be, I am not Dick."

So he went on briskly ahead over a covered bridge and down some breakneck wooden steps, and passed through the wicket out upon the railed-in space, where the cabs and omnibuses should have been, but which was now a blank spectral waste with a white ground-fog lurking round its borders.

Here he was joined by his companions, who, after a little whispering, came up one on either side and put an arm through each of his.

"Well," said Paul, thinking to banter them agreeably; "here you are, young men, eh? Holidays all over now! Work while you're young, and then——

Gad, you're walking me off my legs. Stop; I'm not as young as I used to be——"

"Grim can't see us here, can he, Coker?" said Coggs when they had cleared the gates and palings.

"Not he!" said Coker.

"Very well, then. Now then, young Bultitude, you used to be a decent fellow enough last term, though you *were* coxy. So, before we go any further—what do you mean by this sort of thing?"

"Because," put in Coker, "if you aren't quite right in your head, through your old governor acting like a brute all the holidays, as you said he does, just say so, and we won't be hard on you."

"I—he—always an excellent father," stammered Paul. "What am I to explain?"

"Why, what did you go and sneak of *him* for bringing tuck back to school for, eh?" demanded Coker.

"Yes, and sing out when he hacked your shin?" added Coggs; "and tell Grimstone that new fellow was blubbing? Where's the joke in all that, eh? Where's the joke?"

"You don't suppose I was bound to sit calmly down and allow you to suck your villainous peppermints under my very nose, do you?" said Mr. Bultitude. "Why shouldn't I complain if a boy annoys me by sniffing, or kicks me on the ankle? Just tell me that? Suppose my neighbour has a noisy dog or a smoky chimney, am I not to venture to tell him of it? Is he to——"

But his arguments, convincing as they promised to be, were brought to a sudden and premature close by Coker, who slipped behind him and administered a sharp jog below his back, which jarred his spine and caused him infinite agony.

"You little brute!" cried Paul, "I could have you up for assault for that!"

But upon this Coggs did the very same thing only harder. "Last term you'd have shown fight for much less, Bultitude," they both observed severely, as some justification for repeating the process.

"Now, perhaps, you'll drop it for the future," said Coker. "Look here! we'll give you one more chance. This sneaking dodge is all very well for Chawner. Chawner could do that sort of thing without getting sat upon, because he's a big fellow; but we're not going to stand it from you. Will you promise on your sacred word of honour, now, to be a decent sort of chap again, as you were last term?"

But Mr. Bultitude, though he longed for peace and quietness, dreaded doing or saying anything to favour the impression that he was the schoolboy he unluckily appeared to be, and he had not skill and tact enough to dissemble and assume a familiar genial tone of equality with these rough boys.

"You don't understand," he protested feebly. "If I could only tell you——"

"We don't want any fine language, you know," said the relentless Coggs. "Yes or no. Will you promise to be your old self again?"

"I only wish I could," said poor Mr. Bultitude—"but I can't!"

"Very well, then," said Coggs firmly, "we must try the torture. Coker, will you screw the back of his hand, while I show him how they make barley-sugar?"

And he gave Paul an interesting illustration of the latter branch of industry by twisting his right arm round and round till he nearly wrenched it out of the socket, while Coker seized his left hand and pounded it vigorously with the first joint of his forefinger, causing the unfortunate Paul to yell for mercy.

At last he could bear no more, and breaking away from his tormentors with a violent effort, he ran frantically down the silent road towards a house which he knew from former visits to be Dr. Grimstone's.

He was but languidly pursued, and, as the distance was short, he soon gained a gate on the stuccoed posts of which he could read "Crichton House" by the light of a neighbouring gas-lamp.

"This is a nice way," he thought, as he reached it breathless and trembling, "for a father to visit his son's school!"

He had hoped to reach sanctuary before the other two could overtake him; but he soon discovered that the gate was shut fast, and all his efforts would not bring him within reach of the bell-handle—he was too short.

So he sat down on the doorstep in resigned despair, and waited for his enemies. Behind the gate was a large many-windowed house, with steps leading up to a portico. In the playground to his right the school gymnasium, a great gallows-like erection, loomed black and grim through the mist, the night wind favouring the ghastliness of its appearance by swaying the ropes till they creaked and moaned weirdly on the hooks, and the metal stirrups clinked and clashed against one another in irregular cadence.

He had no time to observe more, as Coker and Coggs joined him, and, on finding he had not rung the bell, seized the occasion to pummel him at their leisure before announcing their arrival.

Then the gate was opened, and the three—the revengeful pair assuming an air of lamb-like inoffensiveness—entered the hall and were met by Mrs. Grimstone.

"Why, here you are!" she said, with an air of surprise, and kissing them with real kindness. "How cold you look! So you actually had to walk. No cabs as usual. You poor boys! come in and warm yourselves. You'll find all your old friends in the schoolroom."

Mr. Bultitude submitted to be kissed with some reluctance, inwardly hoping that Dr. Grimstone might never hear of it.

Mrs. Grimstone, it may be said here, was a stout, fair woman, not in the least intellectual or imposing, but with a warm heart, and a way of talking to and about boys that secured her the confidence of mothers more effectually, perhaps, than the most polished conversation and irreproachable deportment could have done.

She did not reserve her motherliness for the reception room either, as some schoolmasters' wives have a tendency to do, and the smallest boy felt less homesick when he saw her.

She opened a green baize outer door, and the door beyond it, and led them into a long high room, with desks and forms placed against the walls, and a writing table, and line of brown-stained tables down the middle. Opposite the windows there was a curious structure of shelves partitioned into lockers, and filled with rows of shabby schoolbooks.

The room had been originally intended for a drawing-room, as was evident from the inevitable white and gold wall-paper and the tarnished gilt beading round the doors and window shutters; the mantelpiece, too, was of white marble, and the gaselier fitted with dingy crystal lustres.

But sad-coloured maps hung on the ink-splashed walls, and a clock with a blank idiotic face (it is not every clock that possesses a decently intelligent expression) ticked over the gilt pier-glass. The boards were uncarpeted, and stained with patches of ink of all sizes and ages; while the atmosphere, in spite of the blazing fire, had a scholastic blending of soap and water, ink and slate-pencil in its composition, which produced a chill and depressing effect.

On the forms opposite the fire some ten or twelve boys were sitting, a few comparing notes as to their holiday experiences with some approach to vivacity. The rest, with hands in pockets and feet stretched towards the blaze, seemed lost in melancholy abstraction.

"There!" said Mrs. Grimstone cheerfully, "you'll have plenty to talk to one another about. I'll send Tom in to see you presently!" And she left them with a reassuring nod, though the prospect of Tom's company did not perhaps elate them as much as it was intended to do.

Mr. Bultitude felt much as if he had suddenly been dropped down a bear-pit, and, avoiding welcome and observation as well as he could, got away into a corner, from which he observed his new companions with uneasy apprehension.

"I say," said one boy, resuming the interrupted conversation, "did you go to Drury Lane? Wasn't it stunning! That goose, you know, and the lion in the forest, and all the wooden animals lumbering in out of the toy Noah's Ark!"

"Why couldn't you come to our party on Twelfth-night?" asked another. "We had great larks. I wish you'd been there!"

"I had to go to young Skidmore's instead," said a pale, spiteful-looking boy, with fair hair carefully parted in the middle. "It was like his cheek to ask me, but I thought I'd go, you know, just to see what it was like."

"What was it like?" asked one or two near him languidly.

"Oh, awfully slow! They've a poky little house in Brompton somewhere, and there was no dancing, only boshy games and a conjurer, without any presents. And, oh! I say, at supper there was a big cake on the table, and no one was allowed to cut it, because it was hired. They're so poor, you know. Skidmore's pater is only a clerk, and you should see his sisters!"

"Why, are they pretty?"

"Pretty! they're just like young Skidmore—only uglier; and just fancy, his mother asked me 'if I was Skidmore's favourite companion, and if he helped me in my studies?'"

The unfortunate Skidmore, when he returned, soon found reason to regret his rash hospitality, for he never heard the last of the cake (which had, as it happened, been paid for in the usual manner) during the rest of the term.

There was a slight laugh at the enormity of Mrs. Skidmore's presumption, and then a long pause, after which some one asked suddenly, "Does any one know whether Chawner really has left this time?"

"I hope so," said a big, heavy boy, and his hope seemed echoed with a general fervour. "He's been going to leave every term for the last year, but I believe he really has done it this time. He wrote and told me he wasn't coming back."

"Thank goodness!" said several, with an evident relief, and some one was just observing that they had had enough of the sneaking business, when a fly was heard to drive up, and the bell rang, whereupon everyone abandoned his easy attitude, and seemed to brace himself up for a trying encounter.

"Look out—here's Grimstone!" they whispered under their breaths, as voices and footsteps were heard in the hall outside.

Presently the door of the schoolroom opened, and another boy entered the room. Dr. Grimstone, it appeared, had not been the occupant of the fly, after all. The new-comer was a tall, narrow-shouldered, stooping fellow, with a sallow, unwholesome complexion, thin lips, and small sunken brown eyes. His cheeks were creased with a dimpling subsmile, half uneasy, half malicious, and his tread was mincing and catlike.

"Well, you fellows?" he said.

All rose at once, and shook hands effusively. "Why, Chawner!" they cried, "how are you, old fellow? We thought you weren't coming back!"

There was a heartiness in their manner somewhat at variance with their recent expressions of opinion; but they had doubtless excellent reasons for any inconsistency.

"Well," said Chawner, in a low, soft voice, which had a suggestion of feminine spitefulness, "I was going to leave, but I thought you'd be getting into mischief here without me to watch over you. Appleton, and Lench, and Coker want looking after badly, I know. So, you see, I've come back after all."

He laughed with a little malevolent cackle as he spoke, and the three boys named laughed too, though with no great heartiness, and shifting the while uneasily on their seats.

After this sally the conversation languished until Tom Grimstone's appearance. He strolled in with a semi-professional air, and shook hands with affability.

Tom was a short, flabby, sandy-haired youth, not particularly beloved of his comrades, and his first remark was, "I say, you chaps, have you done your holiday task? Pa says he shall keep everyone in who hasn't. I've done mine;" which, as a contribution to the general liveliness, was a distinct failure.

Needless to say, the work imposed as a holiday occupation had been first deferred, then forgotten, then remembered too late, and recklessly defied with the confidence begotten in a home atmosphere.

Amidst a general silence Chawner happened to see Mr. Bultitude in his corner, and crossed over to him. "Why, there's Dicky Bultitude there all the time, and he never came to shake hands! Aren't you going to speak to me?"

Paul growled something indistinctly, feeling strangely uncomfortable and confused.

"What's the matter with him?" asked Chawner. "Does anyone know? Has he lost his tongue?"

"He hadn't lost it coming down in the train," said Coker: "I wish he had. I tell you what, you fellows—He—here's Grim at last! I'll tell you all about it up in the bedroom."

And Dr. Grimstone really did arrive at this point, much to Paul's relief, and looked in to give a grip of the hand and a few words to those of the boys he had not seen.

Biddlecomb, Tipping, and the rest, came in with him, and the schoolroom soon filled with others arriving by later trains, amongst the later comers being the two house-masters, Mr. Blinkhorn and Mr. Tinkler; and there followed a season of bustle and conversation, which lasted until the Doctor touched a small hand-bell, and ordered them to sit down round the tables while supper was brought in.

Mr. Bultitude was not sorry to hear the word "supper." He was faint and dispirited, and although he had dined not very long since, thought that perhaps a little cold beef and beer, or some warmed-up trifle, might give him courage to tell his misfortunes before bedtime.

Of one thing he felt certain. Nothing should induce him to trust his person in a bedroom with any of those violent and vindictive boys; whether he succeeded in declaring himself that night or not, he would at least insist on a separate bedroom. Meantime he looked forward to supper as likely to restore geniality and confidence.

But the supper announced so imposingly proved to consist of nothing more than two plates piled with small pieces of thinly-buttered bread, which a page handed round together with tumblers of water; and Paul, in his disappointment, refused this refreshment with more firmness than politeness, as Dr. Grimstone observed.

"You got into trouble last term, Bultitude," he said sternly, "on account of this same fastidious daintiness. Your excellent father has informed me of your waste and gluttony at his own bountifully spread table. Don't let me have occasion to reprove you for this again."

Mr. Bultitude, feeling the necessity of propitiating him, hastened to take the two largest squares of bread and butter on the plate. They were moist and thick, and he had considerable difficulty in disposing of them, besides the gratification of hearing himself described as a "pig" by his neighbours, who reproved him with a refreshing candour.

"I must get away from here," he thought, ruefully. "Dick seems very unpopular. I wish I didn't feel so low-spirited and unwell. Why can't I carry it off easily as—as a kind of joke? How hard these forms are, and how those infernal boys did jog my back!"

Bedtime came at length. The boys filed, one by one, out of the room, and the Doctor stood by the door to shake hands with them as they passed.

Mr. Bultitude lingered until the others had gone, for he had made up his mind to seize this opportunity to open the Doctor's eyes to the mistake he was making. But he felt unaccountably nervous; the diplomatic and well-chosen introduction he had carefully prepared had left him at the critical moment; all power of thought was gone with it, and he went tremblingly up to the schoolmaster, feeling hopelessly at the mercy of anything that chose to come out of his mouth.

"Dr. Grimstone," he began; "before retiring I—I must insist—I mean I must request—— What I wish to say is——"

"I see," said the Doctor, catching him up sharply. "You wish to apologise for your extraordinary behaviour in the railway carriage? Well, though you made some amends afterwards, an apology is very right and proper. Say no more about it."

"It's not that," said Paul hopelessly; "I wanted to explain——"

"Your conduct with regard to the bread and butter? If it was simply want of appetite, of course there is no more to be said. But I have an abhorrence of——"

"Quite right," said Paul, recovering himself; "I hate waste myself, but there is something I must tell you before——"

"If it concerns that disgraceful conduct of Coker's," said the Doctor, "you may speak on. I shall have to consider his case to-morrow. Has any similar case of disobedience come to your knowledge? If so, I expect you to disclose it to me. You have found some other boy with sweetmeats in his possession?"

"Good Heavens, sir!" said Mr. Bultitude, losing his temper; "I haven't been searching the whole school for sweetmeats! I have other things to occupy my mind, sir. And, once for all, I demand to be heard! Dr. Grimstone, there are, ahem, domestic secrets that can only be alluded to in the strictest privacy. I see that one of your assistants is writing at his table there. Cannot we go where there will be less risk of interruption? You have a study, I suppose?"

"Yes, sir," said the Doctor with terrible grimness, "I have a study—and I have a cane. I can convince you of both facts, if you wish it. If you insult me again by this brazen buffoonery, I will! Be off to your dormitory, sir, before you provoke me to punish you. Not another word! Go!"

And, incredible as it may appear to all who have never been in his position, Mr. Bultitude went. It was almost an abdication, it was treachery to his true self; he knew the vital importance of firmness at this crisis. But nevertheless his courage gave way all at once, and he crawled up the bare, uncarpeted stairs without any further protest!

"Good night, Master Bultitude," said a housemaid, meeting him on the staircase: "you know your bedroom. No. 6, with Master Coker, and Master Biddlecomb, and the others."

Paul dragged himself up to the highest landing-stage, and, with a sick foreboding, opened the door on which the figure 6 was painted.

It was a large bare plainly papered room, with several curtainless windows, the blinds of which were drawn, a long deal stand of wash-hand basins, and eight little white beds against the walls.

A fire was lighted in consideration of its being the first night, and several boys were talking excitedly round it. "Here he is! He's stayed behind to tell more tales!" they cried, as Paul entered nervously. "Now then, Bultitude, what have you got to say for yourself?"

Mr. Bultitude felt powerless among all these young wolves. He had no knowledge of boys, nor any notion of acquiring an influence over them, having hitherto regarded them as necessary nuisances, to be rather repressed than studied. He could only stare hopelessly at them in fascinated silence.

"You see he hasn't a word to say for himself!" said Tipping. "Look here, what shall we do to him? Shall we try tossing in a blanket? I've never tried tossing a fellow in one myself, but as long as you don't jerk him too high, or out on the floor, you can't hurt him dangerously."

"No, I say, don't toss him in a blanket," pleaded Biddlecomb, and Paul felt gratefully towards him at the words; "anyone coming up would see what was going on. I vote we flick at him with towels."

"Now just you understand this clearly," said Paul, thinking, not without reason, that this course of treatment was likely to prove painful; "I refuse to allow myself to be flicked at with towels. No one has ever offered me such an indignity in my life! Oh, do you think I've not enough on my mind as it is without the barbarities of a set of young brutes like you!"

As this appeal was not of a very conciliatory nature they at once proceeded to form a circle round him and, judging their distance with great accuracy, jerked towels at his person with such diabolical dexterity that the wet corners cut him at all points like so many fine thongs, and he span round like a top, dancing, and, I regret to add, swearing violently, at the pain.

When he was worked up almost to frenzy pitch Biddlecomb's sweet low voice cried, "*Cave*, you fellows! I hear Grim. Let him undress now, and we can lam it into him afterwards with slippers!"

At this they all cast off such of their clothes as they still wore, and slipped modestly and peacefully into bed, just as Dr. Grimstone's large form appeared at the doorway. Mr. Bultitude made as much haste as he could, but did not escape a reprimand from the Doctor as he turned the gas out; and as soon as he had made the round of the bedrooms and his heavy tread had died away down the staircase, the light-hearted occupants of No. 6 "lammed" it into the unhappy Paul until they were tired of the exercise and left him to creep sore and trembling with rage and fright into his cold hard bed.

Then, after a little desultory conversation, one by one sank from incoherence into silence, and rose from silence to snores, while Paul alone lay sleepless, listening to the creeping tinkle of the dying fire, drearily wondering at the marvellous change that had come over his life and fortunes in the last few hours, and feverishly composing impassioned appeals which were to touch the Doctor's heart and convince his reason.

5.
Disgrace

"Well had the boding tremblers learned to trace

The day's disasters in his morning's face."

Sleep came at last, and brought too brief forgetfulness. It was not till the dull grey light of morning was glimmering through the blinds that Mr. Bultitude awoke to his troubles.

The room was bitterly cold, and he remained shivering in bed for some time, trying to realise and prepare for his altered condition.

He was the only one awake. Now and then from one of the beds around a boy would be heard talking in his sleep, or laughing with holiday glee—at the drolleries possibly of some pantomime performed for his amusement in the Theatre Royal, Dreamland—a theatre mercifully open to all boys free of charge, long after the holidays have come to an end, the only drawbacks being a certain want of definiteness in the plot and scenery, and a liability to premature termination of the vaguely splendid performance.

Once Kiffin, the new boy, awoke with a start and a heavy sigh, but he cried himself to sleep again almost immediately.

Mr. Bultitude could bear being inactive no longer. He thought, if he got up, he might perhaps see his misfortunes shrink to a more bearable, less hopeless scale, and besides, he judged it prudent, for many reasons, to finish his toilet before the sleepers began theirs.

Very stealthily, dreading to rouse anyone and attract attention in the form of slippers, he broke the clinking crust of ice in one of the basins and, shuddering from the shock, bathed face and hands in the biting water. He parted his hair, which from natural causes he had been unable to accomplish for some years, and now found an awkwardness in accomplishing neatly, and then stole down the dark creaking staircase just as the butler in the hall began to swing the big railway bell which was to din stern reality into the sleepy ears above.

In the schoolroom a yawning maid had just lighted the fire, from which turbid yellow clouds of sulphurous smoke were pouring into the room, making it necessary to open the windows and lower a temperature that was far from high originally.

Paul stood shaking by the mantelpiece in a very bad temper for some minutes. If the Doctor had come in then, he might have been spurred by indignation to utter his woes, and even claim and obtain his freedom. But that was not to be.

The door did open presently, however, and a little girl appeared; a very charming little maiden indeed, in a neat dark costume relieved by a fresh white pinafore. She had deep grey eyes and glossy brown hair falling over her forehead and down her back in soft straight masses, her face was oval rather than round, and slightly serious, though her smile was pretty and gay.

She ran towards Mr. Bultitude with a glad little cry, stretching out her hands.

"Dick! dear Dick!" she said, "I am so glad! I thought you'd be down early; as you used to be. I wanted to sit up last night so very much, but mamma wouldn't let me."

Some might have been very glad to be welcomed in this way, even vicariously. As for boys, it must have been a very bad school indeed which Dulcie Grimstone could not have robbed of much of its terrors.

Mr. Bultitude, however, as has been explained, did not appreciate children— being a family man himself. When one sees their petty squabbles and jealousies, hears their cruel din, and pays for their monkeyish mischief, perhaps the daintiest children seem but an earthly order of cherubim. He was only annoyed and embarrassed by the interruption, though he endured it.

"Ah," he said with condescension, "and so you're Dr. Grimstone's little girl, are you? How d'ye do, my dear?"

Dulcie stopped and looked at him, with drawn eyebrows and her soft mouth quivering. "What makes you talk like that?" she asked.

"How ought I to talk?" said Paul.

"You didn't talk like that before," said Dulcie plaintively. "I—I thought perhaps you'd be glad to see me. You were once. And—and—when you went away last you asked me to—to—kiss you, and I did, and I wish I hadn't. And you gave me a ginger lozenge with your name written on it in lead pencil, and I gave you a cough-lozenge with mine; and you said it was to show that you were my sweetheart and I was yours. But I suppose you've eaten the one I gave you?"

"This is dreadful!" thought Mr. Bultitude. "What shall I do now? The child evidently takes me for that little scoundrel Dick." "Tut-tut," he said aloud, "little girls like you are too young for such nonsense. You ought to think about—about your dolls, and—ah, your needlework—not sweethearts!"

"You say that now!" cried Dulcie indignantly. "You know I'm not a little girl, and I've left off playing with dolls—almost. Oh, Dick, don't be unkind! You haven't changed your mind, have you?"

"No," said Paul dismally, "I've changed my body. But there—you wouldn't understand. Run away and play somewhere, like a good little girl!"

"I know what it is!" said Dulcie. "You've been out to parties, or somewhere, and seen some horrid girl ... you like ... better than me!"

"This is absurd, you know," said Mr. Bultitude. "You can't think how absurd it is! Now, you'll be a very foolish little girl if you cry. You're making a mistake. I'm not the Dick you used to know!"

"I know you're not!" sobbed Dulcie. "But oh, Dick, you will be. Promise me you will be!" And, to Paul's horror and alarm, she put her arms round his neck, and cried piteously on his shoulder.

"Good gracious!" he cried, "let me go. Don't do that, for Heaven's sake! I can hear some one coming. If it's your father, it will ruin me!"

But it was too late. Over her head he saw Tipping enter the room, and stand glaring at them menacingly. Dulcie saw him too, and sprang away to the window, where she tried to dry her eyes unperceived, and then ran past him with a hurried good morning, and escaped, leaving Paul alone with the formidable Tipping.

There was an awkward silence at first, which Tipping broke by saying, "What have you been saying to make her cry, eh?"

"What's that to you, sir?" said Paul, trying to keep his voice firm.

"Why, it's just this to me," said Tipping, "that I've been spoons on Dulcie myself ever since I came, and she never would have a word to say to me. I never could think why, and now it turns out to be you! What do you mean by cutting me out like this? I heard her call you 'dear Dick.'"

"Don't be an ass, sir!" said Paul angrily.

"Now, none of your cheek, you know!" said Tipping, edging up against him with a dangerous inclination first to jostle aggressively, and then maul his unconscious rival. "You just mind what I say. I'm not going to have Dulcie bothered by a young beggar in the second form; she deserves something better than that, anyway, and I tell you that if I once catch you talking to her in the way you did just now, or if I hear of her favouring you more than any other fellows, I'll give you the very juiciest licking you ever had in your life. So look out!"

At this point the other boys began to straggle down and cluster round the fire, and Paul withdrew from the aggrieved Tipping, and looked drearily out of the window on the hard road and bare black trees outside.

"I *must* tell the Doctor how I'm situated!" he thought; "and yet directly I open my mouth, he threatens to flog me. If I stay here, that little girl will be always trying to speak to me, and I shall be thrashed by the red-haired boy. If I could only manage to speak out after breakfast!"

It was not without satisfaction that he remembered that he paid extra for "meat for breakfast" in his son's school-bills, for he was beginning to look forward to meal-time with the natural desire of a young and healthy frame for nourishment.

At eight o'clock the Doctor came in and announced breakfast, leading the way himself to what was known in the school as the "Dining Hall." It scarcely deserved so high-sounding a name perhaps, being a long low room on the basement floor, with a big fireplace, fitted with taps, and baking ovens, which provoked the suspicion that it had begun existence as a back kitchen.

The Doctor took his seat alone at a cross table forming the top of one of the two rows of tables, set with white cups and saucers, and plates well heaped with the square pieces of bread and butter, while Mrs. Grimstone with Dulcie and Tom, sat at the foot of the same row, behind two ugly urns of dull block-tin.

But when Mr. Bultitude, more hungry than he had felt for years, found his place at one of the tables, he was disgusted to find upon his plate—not, as he had confidently expected, a couple of plump poached eggs, with their appetising contrast of ruddy gold and silvery white, not a crisp and crackling sausage or a mottled omelette, not even the homely but luscious rasher, but a brace of chill forbidding sardines, lying grim and headless in bilious green oil!

It was a fish he positively loathed, nor could it be reasonably expected that the confidence necessary for a declaration was to be forgotten by so sepulchral a form of nutriment.

He roused himself, however, to swallow them, together with some of the thin and tin-flavoured coffee. But the meal as a whole was so different from the plentiful well-cooked breakfasts he had sat down before for years as a matter of course, that it made him feel extremely unwell.

No talking was allowed during the meal. The Doctor now and then looked up from his dish of kidneys on toast (at which envious glances were occasionally cast) to address a casual remark to his wife across the long row of plates and cups, but, as a rule, the dull champing sound of boys solemnly and steadily munching was all that broke the silence.

Towards the end, when the plates had been generally cleared, and the boys sat staring with the stolidity of repletion at one another across the tables, the junior house-master, Mr. Tinkler, made his appearance. He had lately left a small and little-known college at Cambridge, where he had contrived, contrary to expectation, to evade the uncoveted wooden spoon by just two places, which enabled the Doctor to announce himself as being "assisted by a graduate of the University of Cambridge who has taken honours in the Mathematical Tripos."

For the rest, he was a small insignificant-looking person, who evidently disliked the notice his late appearance drew upon himself.

"Mr. Tinkler," said the Doctor in his most awful voice, "if it were my custom to rebuke my assistants before the school (which it is not), I should feel forced to remind you that this tardiness in rising is a bad beginning of the day's work, and sets a bad example to those under your authority."

Mr. Tinkler made no articulate reply, but sat down with a crushed expression, and set himself to devour bread and butter with an energy which he hoped would divert attention from his blushes; and almost immediately the Doctor looked at his watch and said, "Now, boys, you have half-an-hour for 'chevy'—make the most of it. When you come in I shall have something to say to you all. Don't rise, Mr. Tinkler, unless you have quite finished."

Mr. Tinkler preferred leaving his breakfast to continuing it under the trying ordeal of his principal's inspection. So, hastily murmuring that he had "made an excellent breakfast"—which he had not—he followed the others, who clattered upstairs to put on their boots and go out into the playground.

It was noticeable that they did so without much of the enthusiasm which might be looked for from boys dismissed to their sports. But the fact was that this particular sport, "chevy," commonly known as "prisoners' base," was by no means a popular amusement, being of a somewhat monotonous nature, and calling for no special skill on the part of the performers. Besides this, moreover, it had the additional disadvantage (which would have been fatal to a far more fascinating diversion) of being in a great measure compulsory.

Football and cricket were of course reserved for half-holidays, and played in a neighbouring field rented by the Doctor, and in the playground he restricted them to "chevy," which he considered, rightly enough, both gave them abundant exercise and kept them out of mischief. Accordingly, if any adventurous spirit started a rival game, it was usually abandoned sooner or later in deference to suggestions from headquarters which were not intended to be disregarded.

This, though undoubtedly well meant, did not serve to stimulate their affection for the game, an excellent one in moderation, but one which, if played "by special desire" two or three hours a day for weeks in succession is apt to lose its freshness and pall upon the youthful mind.

It was a bright morning. There had been a hard frost during the night, and the ground was hard, sparkling with rime and ringing to the foot. The air was keen and invigorating, and the bare black branches of the trees were outlined clear and sharp against the pale pure blue of the morning sky.

Just the weather for a long day's skating over the dark green glassy ice, or a bracing tramp on country roads into cheery red-roofed market towns. But now it had lost all power to charm. It was almost depressing by the contrast between the boundless liberty suggested, and the dull reality of a round of uninteresting work which was all it heralded.

So they lounged listlessly about, gravitating finally towards the end of the playground, where a deep furrow marked the line of the base. There was no attempt to play. They stood gossiping in knots, grumbling and stamping their feet to keep warm. By-and-by the day-boarders began to drop in one by one, several of them, from a want of tact in adapting themselves to the general tone, earning decided unpopularity at once by a cheerful briskness and an undisguised satisfaction at having something definite to do once more.

If Mr. Tinkler, who had joined one of the groups, had not particularly distinguished himself at breakfast, he made ample amends now, and by the grandeur and manliness of his conversation succeeded in producing a decided impression upon some of the smaller boys.

"The bore of a place like this, you know," he was saying with magnificent disdain, "is that a fellow can't have his pipe of a morning. I've been used to it, and so, of course, I miss it. If I chose to insist on it Grimstone couldn't say anything; but with a lot of young fellows like you, you see, it wouldn't look well!"

It could hardly have looked worse than little Mr. Tinkler himself would have done, if he had ventured upon more than the mildest of cigarettes, for he was a poor but pertinacious smoker, and his love for the weed was chastened by wholesome fear. There, however, he was in no danger of betraying this, and indeed it would have been injudicious to admit it.

"Talking of smoking," he went on, with a soft chuckle, as at recollections of unspeakable devilry, "did I ever tell you chaps of a tremendous scrape I very nearly got into up at the 'Varsity? Well, you must know there's a foolish rule there against smoking in the streets. Not that that made any difference to some of us! Well, one night about nine, I was strolling down Petty Cury with two other men, smoking (Bosher of "Pothouse," and Peebles of "Cats," both pretty well known up there for general rowdiness, you know—great pals of mine!) and, just as we turned the corner, who should we see coming straight down on us but a Proctor with his bull-dogs (not dogs, you know, but the strongest 'gyps' in college). Bosher said, 'Let's cut it!' and he and Peebles bolted. (They were neither of them funks, of course, but they lost their heads.) I went calmly on, smoking my cigar as if nothing was the matter. That put the Proctor in a bait, I can tell you! He came fuming up to me. 'What do you mean, sir,' says he, quite pale with anger (he was a great bull-headed fellow, one of the strongest dons of his year, that's why they made him a Proctor)—'what do you mean by breaking the University Statutes in this way?' 'It *is* a fine evening,' said I (I was determined to keep cool). 'Do you mean to insult me?' said he. 'No, old boy,' said I, 'I don't; have a cigar?' He couldn't stand that, so he called up his bull-dogs. 'I give him in charge!' he screamed out. 'I'll have him sent down!' 'I'll send you down first,' said I, and I just gave him a push—I never meant to hurt the fellow—and over he went. I rolled over a bull-dog to keep him company, and, as the other fellow didn't want any more and stood aside to let me pass, I finished my stroll and my cigar."

"Was the Proctor hurt, sir?" inquired a small boy with great respect.

"More frightened than hurt, I always said," said Mr. Tinkler lightly, "but somehow he never would proctorise any more—it spoilt his nerve. He was a good deal chaffed about it, but of course no one ever knew I'd had anything to do with it!"

With such tales of Homeric exploit did Mr. Tinkler inculcate a spirit of discipline and respect for authority. But although he had indeed once encountered a Proctor, and at night, he did himself great injustice by this version of the proceedings, which were, as a matter of fact, of a most peaceable and law-abiding character, and though followed by a pecuniary transaction the next day in which six-and-eightpence changed pockets, the Proctors continued their duties much as before, while Mr. Tinkler's feelings towards them, which had ever been reverential in the extreme, were, if anything, intensified by the experience.

Upon this incident, however, he had gradually embroidered the above exciting episode, until he grew to believe at intervals that he really had been a devil of a fellow in his time, which, to do him justice, was far from the case.

He might have gone on still further to calumniate himself, and excite general envy and admiration thereby, if at that moment Dr. Grimstone had not happened to appear at the head of the cast-iron staircase that led down into the playground; whereupon Mr. Tinkler affected to be intensely interested in the game, which, as a kind of involuntary compliment to the principal, about this time was galvanised into a sort of vigour.

But the Doctor, after frowning gloomily down upon them for a minute or so, suddenly called "All in!"

He had several ways of saying this. Sometimes he would do so in a half-regretful tone, as one himself obeying the call of duty; sometimes he would appear for some minutes, a benignant spectator, upon the balcony, and summon them to work at length with a lenient pity—for he was by no means a hard-hearted man; but at other times he would step sharply and suddenly out and shout the word of command with a grim and ominous expression. On these last occasions the school generally prepared itself for a rather formidable quarter of an hour.

This was the case now and, as a further portent, Mr. Blinkhorn was observed to come down and, after a few words with Mr. Tinkler, withdrew with him through the school gate.

"He's sent them out for a walk," said Siggers, who was skilled in omens. "It's a row!"

Rows at Crichton House, although periodical, and therefore things to be forearmed against in some degree, were serious matters. Dr. Grimstone was a quick-tempered man, with a copious flow of words and a taste for indulging it. He was also strongly prejudiced against many breaches of discipline which others might have considered trifling, and whenever he had discovered any such breach he could not rest until by all the means in his power he had ascertained exactly how many were implicated in the offence, and to what extent.

His usual method of doing this was to summon the school formally together and deliver an elaborate harangue, during which he worked himself by degrees into such a state of indignation that his hearers were most of them terrified out of their senses, and very often conscience-stricken offenders would give themselves up as hopelessly detected and reveal transgressions altogether unsuspected by him—much as a net brings up fish of all degrees of merit, or as heavy firing will raise drowned corpses to the surface.

Paul naturally knew nothing of this peculiarity; he had kept himself as usual apart from the others, and was now trying to compel himself to brave the terrors of an avowal at the first opportunity. He followed the others up the steps with an uneasy wonder whether, after all, he would not find himself ignominiously set down to learn lessons.

The boys filed into the schoolroom in solemn silence, and took their seats at the desks and along the brown tables. The Doctor was there before them, standing up with one elbow resting upon a reading-stand, and with a suggestion of coming thunder in his look and attitude that, combined with the oppressive silence, made some of the boys feel positively ill.

Presently he began. He said that, since they had come together again, he had made a discovery concerning one among them which, astounding as it was to him, and painful as he felt it to be compelled to make it known, concerned them all to be aware of.

Mr. Bultitude could scarcely believe his ears. His secret was discovered, then; the injury done him by Dick about to be repaired, and open restitution and apology offered him! It was not perhaps precisely delicate on the Doctor's part to make so public an affair of it, but so long as it ended well, he could afford to overlook that.

So he settled himself comfortably on a form with his back against a desk and his legs crossed, his expression indicating plainly that he knew what was coming and, on the whole, approved of it.

"Ever since I have devoted myself to the cause of tuition," continued the Doctor, "I have made it my object to provide boys under my roof with fare so abundant and so palatable that they should have no excuse for obtaining extraneous luxuries. I have presided myself at their meals, I have superintended their very sports with a fatherly eye———"

Here he paused, and fixed one or two of those nearest him with the fatherly eye in such a manner that they writhed with confusion.

"He's wandering from the point," thought Paul, a little puzzled.

"I have done all this on one understanding—that the robustness of your constitutions, acquired by the plain, simple, but abundant regimen of my table, shall not be tampered with by the indulgence in any of the pampering products of confectionery. They are absolutely and unconditionally prohibited—as every boy who hears me now knows perfectly well!

"And yet" (here he began gradually to relax his self-restraint and lash himself into a frenzy of indignation), "what do I find? There are some natures so essentially base, so incapable of being affected by kindness, so dead to honour and generosity, that they will not scruple to conspire or set themselves individually to escape and baffle the wise precautions undertaken for their benefit. I will not name the dastards at present—they themselves can look into their hearts and see their guilt reflected there———"

At this every boy, beginning to see the tendency of his denunciations, tried hard to assume an air of conscious innocence and grieved interest, the majority achieving conspicuous failure.

"I do not like to think," said Dr. Grimstone, "that the evil has a wider existence than I yet know of. It may be so; nothing will surprise me now. There may be some before me trembling with the consciousness of secret guilt. If so, let those boys make the only reparation in their power, and give themselves up in an honourable and straightforward manner!"

To this invitation, which indeed resembled that of the duck-destroying Mrs. Bond, no one made any response. They had grown too wary, and now preferred to play a waiting game.

"Then let the being—for I will not call him boy—who is known to me, step forth and confess his fault publicly, and sue for pardon!" thundered the Doctor, now warmed to his theme.

But the being declined from a feeling of modesty, and a faint hope that somebody else might, after all, be the person aimed at.

"Then I name him!" stormed Dr. Grimstone; "Cornelius Coggs—stand up!"

Coggs half rose in a limp manner, whimpering feebly, "Me, sir? Oh, please sir—no, not me, sir!"

"Yes, you, sir, and let your companions regard you with the contempt and abhorrence you so richly merit!" Here, needless to say, the whole school glared at poor Coggs with as much virtuous indignation as they could summon up at such short notice; for contempt is very infectious when communicated from high quarters.

"So, Coggs," said the Doctor, with a slow and withering scorn, "so you thought to defy me; to smuggle compressed illness and concentrated unhealthiness into this school with impunity? You flattered yourself that after I had once confiscated your contraband poisons, you would hear no more of it! You deceived yourself, sir! I tell you, once for all, that I will not allow you to contaminate your innocent schoolmates with your gifts of surreptitious sweetmeats; they shall not be perverted with your pernicious peppermints, sir; you shall not deprave them by jujubes, or enervate them with Turkish Delight! I will not expose myself or them to the inroads of disease invited here by a hypocritical inmate of my walls. The traitor shall have his reward!"

All of which simply meant that the Doctor, having once had a small boy taken seriously ill from the effects of overeating himself, was naturally anxious to avoid such an inconvenience for the future. "Thanks to the fearless honesty of a youth," continued the Doctor, "who, in an eccentric manner, certainly, but with, I do not doubt, the best of motives, opened my eyes to the fell evil, I am enabled to cope with it at its birth. Richard Bultitude, I take this occasion of publicly thanking and commending you; your conduct was noble!"

Mr. Bultitude was too angry and disappointed to speak. He had thought his path was going to be made smooth, and now all this ridiculous fuss was being made about a few peppermint lozenges. He wished he had never mentioned them. It was not the last time he breathed that wish. "As for you, Coggs," said the Doctor, suddenly producing a lithe brown cane, "I shall make a public example of you."

Coggs stared idiotically and protested, but after a short and painful scene, was sent off up to his bedroom, yelping like a kicked puppy.

"One word more," said the Doctor, now almost calm again. "I know that you all think with me in your horror of the treachery I have just exposed. I know that you would scorn to participate in it." (A thrill and murmur, expressive of intense horror and scorn, went round the benches.) "You are anxious to prove that you do so beyond a doubt." (Again a murmur of assent.) "I give you all that opportunity. I have implicit trust and confidence in you—let every boarder go down into the box-room and fetch up his playbox, just as it is, and open it here before me."

There was a general fall of jaws at this very unexpected conclusion; but contriving to overcome their dismay, they went outside and down through the playground into the box-room, Paul amongst the rest, and amidst universal confusion, everyone opened his box, and, with a consideration especially laudable in heedless boyhood, thoughtfully and carefully removed from it all such dainties as might be calculated to shock or pain their preceptor.

Mr. Bultitude found a key which was labelled "playbox," and began to open a box which bore Dick's initials cut upon the lid; without any apprehensions, however, for he had given too strict orders to his daughter, to fear that any luxuries would be concealed there.

But no sooner had he raised the lid than he staggered back with disgust. It was crammed with cakes, butterscotch, hardbake, pots of jam, and even a bottle of ginger wine—enough to compromise a chameleon!

He set himself to pitch them all out as soon as possible with feverish haste, but Tipping was too quick for him. "Hallo!" he cried: "oh, I say, you fellows, come here! Just look at this! Here's this impudent young beggar, who sneaked of poor old Coggs for sucking jujubes, and very nearly got us all into a jolly good row, with his own box full all the time; butterscotch, if you please, and jam, and ginger wine! You'll just put 'em all back again, will you, you young humbug!"

"Do you use those words to me, sir?" said Paul angrily, for he did not like to be called a humbug.

"Yes, sir, please, sir," jeered Tipping; "I did venture to take such a liberty, sir."

"Then it was like your infernal impudence," growled Paul. "You be kind enough to leave my affairs alone. Upon my word, what boys are coming to nowadays!"

"Are you going to put that tuck back?" said Tipping impatiently.

"No, sir, I'm not. Don't interfere with what you're not expected to understand!"

"Well, if you won't," said Tipping easily, "I suppose we must. Biddlecomb, kindly knock him down, and sit on his head while I fill his playbox for him."

This was neatly and quickly done. Biddlecomb tripped Mr. Bultitude up, and sat firmly on him, while Tipping carefully replaced the good things in Dick's box, after which he locked it, and courteously returned the key. "As the box is heavy," he said, with a wicked wink, "I'll carry it up for you myself," which he did, Paul following, more dead than alive, and too shaken even to expostulate.

"Bultitude's box was rather too heavy for him, sir," he explained as he came in; and Dr. Grimstone, who had quite recovered his equanimity, smiled indulgently, and remarked that he "liked to see the strong assisting the weak."

All the boxes had by this time been brought up, and were ranged upon the tables, while the Doctor went round, making an almost formal inspection, like a Custom House officer searching compatriots, and becoming milder and milder as box after box opened to reveal a fair and innocent interior.

Paul's turn was coming very near, and his heart seemed to shrivel like a burst bladder. He fumbled with his key, and tried hard to lose it. It was terrible to have oneself to apply the match which is to blow one to the winds. If—if—the idea was almost too horrible—but if he, a blameless and respectable city merchant, were actually to find himself served like the miserable Coggs!

At last the Doctor actually stood by him. "Well, my boy," he said, not unkindly, "I'm not afraid of anything wrong here, at any rate."

Mr. Bultitude, who had the best reasons for not sharing his confidence, made some inarticulate sounds, and pretended to have a difficulty in turning the key.

"Eh? Come, open the box," said the Doctor with an altered manner. "What are you fumbling at it for in this—this highly suspicious manner? I'll open it myself."

He took the key and opened the lid, when the cakes and wine stood revealed in all their damning profusion. The Doctor stepped back dramatically. "Hardbake!" he gasped; "wine, pots of strawberry jam! Oh, Bultitude, this is a revelation indeed! So I have nourished one more viper in my bosom, have I? A crawling reptile which curries favour by denouncing the very crime it conceals in its playbox! Bultitude, I was not prepared for such duplicity as this!"

"I—I swear I never put them in!" protested the unhappy Paul. "I—I never touch such things: they would bring on my gout in half-an-hour. It's ridiculous to punish me. I never knew they were there!"

"Then why were you so anxious to avoid opening the box?" rejoined the Doctor. "No, sir, you're too ingenious; your guilt is clear. Go to your dormitory, and wait there till I come to you!"

Paul went upstairs, feeling utterly abandoned and helpless. Though a word as to his real character might have saved him, he could not have said it, and, worse still, knew now that he could not.

"I shall be caned," he told himself, and the thought nearly drove him mad. "I know I shall be caned! What on earth shall I do?"

He opened the door of his bedroom. Coggs was rocking and moaning on his bed in one corner of the room, but looked up with red furious eyes as Paul came in.

"What do you want up here?" he said savagely. "Go away, can't you!"

"I wish I *could* go away," said Paul dolefully; "but I'm—hum—I'm sent up here too," he explained, with some natural embarrassment.

"What!" cried Coggs, slipping off his bed and staring wildly: "you don't mean to say you're going to catch it too?"

"I've—ah—every reason to fear," said Mr. Bultitude stiffly, "that I am indeed going to 'catch it,' as you call it."

"Hooray!" shouted Coggs hysterically: "I don't care now. And I'll have some revenge on my own account as well. I don't mind an extra licking, and you're in for one as it is. Will you stand up to me or not?"

"I don't understand you," said Paul. "Don't come so near. Keep off, you young demon, will you!" he cried presently, as Coggs, exasperated by all his wrongs, was rushing at him with an evidently hostile intent. "There, don't be annoyed, my good boy," he pleaded, catching up a chair as a bulwark. "It was a misunderstanding. I wish you no harm. There, my dear young friend! Don't!"

The "dear young friend" was grappling with him and attempting to wrest the chair away by brute force. "When I get at you," he said, his hot breath hissing through the chair rungs, "I'll jolly well teach you to sneak of me!"

"Murder!" Paul gasped, feeling his hold on the chair relaxing. "Unless help comes this young fiend will have my blood!"

They were revolving slowly round the chair, watching each other's eyes like gladiators, when Paul noticed a sudden blankness and fixity in his antagonist's expression, and, looking round, saw Dr. Grimstone's awful form framed in the doorway, and gave himself up for lost.

6.
Learning and Accomplishments

> "I subscribe to Lucian: 'tis an elegant thing which cheareth up the mind, exerciseth the body, delights the spectators, which teacheth many comely gestures, equally affecting the ears, eyes and soul itself."—BURTON, *on Dancing*.

"What is this?" asked Dr. Grimstone in his most blood-curdling tone, after a most impressive pause at the dormitory door.

Mr. Bultitude held his tongue, but kept fast hold of his chair, which he held before him as a defence against either party, while Coggs remained motionless in the centre of the room, with crooked knees and hands dangling impotently.

"Will one of you be good enough to explain how you come to be found struggling in this unseemly manner? I sent you up here to meditate on your past behaviour."

"I should be most happy to meditate, sir," protested Paul, lowering his chair on discovering that there was no immediate danger, "if that—that bloodthirsty young ruffian there would allow me to do so. I am going about in bodily fear of him, Dr. Grimstone. I want him bound over to keep the peace. I decline to be left alone with him—he's not safe!"

"Is that so, Coggs? Are you mean and base enough to take this cowardly revenge on a boy who has had the moral courage to expose your deceit—for your ultimate good—a boy who is unable to defend himself against you?"

"He can fight when he chooses, sir," said Coggs; "he blacked my eye last term, sir!"

"I assure you," said Paul, with the convincing earnestness of truth, "that I never blacked anybody's eye in the whole course of my life. I am not—ah—a pugnacious man. My age, and—hum—my position, ought to protect me from these scandals——"

"You've come back this year, sir," said Dr. Grimstone, "with a very odd way of talking of yourself—an exceedingly odd way. Unless I see you abandoning it, and behaving like a reasonable boy again, I shall be forced to conclude you intend some disrespect and open defiance by it."

"If you would allow me an opportunity of explaining my position, sir," said Paul, "I would undertake to clear your mind directly of such a monstrous idea. I am trying to assert my rights, Dr. Grimstone—my rights as a citizen, as a householder! This is no place for me, and I appeal to you to set me free. If you only knew one tenth——"

"Let us understand one another, Bultitude," interrupted the Doctor. "You may think it an excellent joke to talk nonsense to me like this. But let me tell you there is a point where a jest becomes an insult. I've spared you hitherto out of consideration for the feelings of your excellent father, who is so anxious that you should become an object of pride and credit to him; but if you dare to treat me to any more of this bombast about 'explaining your rights,' you will force me to exercise one of mine—the right to inflict corporal punishment, sir—which you have just seen in operation upon another."

"Oh!" said Mr. Bultitude faintly, feeling utterly crestfallen—and he could say nothing more.

"As for those illicit luxuries in your playbox," continued the Doctor, "the fact that you brought the box up as it was is in your favour; and I am inclined on reflection to overlook the affair, if you can assure me that you were no party to their being put there?"

"On the contrary," said Paul, "I gave the strictest orders that there was to be no such useless extravagance. I objected to have the kitchen and housekeeper's room ransacked to make a set of rascally boys ill for a fortnight at my expense!"

The Doctor stared slightly at this creditable but unnatural view of the subject. However, as he could not quarrel with the sentiment, he let the manner of expressing it pass unrebuked for the present, and, after sentencing Coggs to two days' detention and the copying of innumerable French verbs, he sent the ill-matched pair down to the schoolroom to join their respective classes.

Paul went resignedly downstairs and into the room, where he found Mr. Blinkhorn at the head of one of the long tables, taking a class of about a dozen boys.

"Take your Livy and Latin Primer, Bultitude," said Mr. Blinkhorn mildly, "and sit down."

Mr. Blinkhorn was a tall angular man, with a long neck and slightly drooping head. He had thin wiry brown hair, and a plain face, with shortsighted kind brown eyes. In character he was mild and reserved, too conscientious to allow himself the luxury of either favourites or aversions among the boys, all of whom in his secret soul he probably disliked about equally, though he neither said nor did anything to show it.

Paul took a book—any book, for he did not know or care to know one from another—and sat down at the end furthest from the master, inwardly rebelling at having education thus forced upon him at his advanced years, but seeing no escape.

"At dinner time," he resolved desperately, "I will insist on speaking out, but just now it is simply prudent to humour them."

The rest of the class drew away from him with marked coldness and occasionally saluted him (when Mr. Blinkhorn's attention was called away) with terms and grimaces which Paul, although he failed thoroughly to understand them, felt instinctively were not intended as compliments.

Mr. Blinkhorn's notions of discipline were qualified by a sportsmanlike instinct which forbade him to harass a boy already in trouble, as he understood young Bultitude had been, and so he forbore from pressing him to take any share in the class work.

Mr. Bultitude therefore was saved from any necessity of betraying his total ignorance of his author, and sat gloomily on the hard form, impatiently watching the minute-hand skulk round the mean dull face of the clock above the chimney-piece, while around him one boy after another droned out a listless translation of the work before him, interrupted by mild corrections and comments from the master.

What a preposterous change from all his ordinary habits! At this very time, only twenty-four hours since, he was stepping slowly and majestically towards his accustomed omnibus, which was waiting with deference for him to overtake it; he was taking his seat, saluted respectfully by the conductor and cheerily by his fellow-passengers, as a man of recognised mark and position.

Now that omnibus would halt at the corner of Westbourne Terrace in vain, and go on its way Bankwards without him. He was many miles away—in the very last place where anyone would be likely to look for him, occupying the post of "whipping-boy" to his miserable son!

Was ever an inoffensive and respectable gentleman placed in a more false and ridiculous position?

If he had only kept his drawer locked, and hidden the abominable Garudâ Stone away from Dick's prying eyes; if he had let the moralising alone; if Boaler had not been so long fetching that cab, or if he had not happened to faint at the critical moment—what an immense difference any one of these apparent trifles would have made.

And now what was he to do to get out of this incongruous and distasteful place? It was all very well to say that he had only to insist upon a hearing from the Doctor, but what if, as he had very grave reason to fear, the Doctor should absolutely refuse to listen, should even proceed to carry out his horrible threat? Must he remain there till the holidays came to release him? Suppose Dick—as he certainly would unless he was quite a fool—declined to receive him during the holidays? It was absolutely necessary to return home at once; every additional hour he passed in imprisonment made it harder to regain his lost self.

Now and then he roused himself from all these gloomy thoughts to observe his companions. The boys at the upper end, near Mr. Blinkhorn, were fairly attentive, and he noticed one small smug-faced boy about half-way up, who, while a class-mate was faltering and blundering over some question, would cry "I know, sir. Let me tell him. Ask me, sir!" in a restless agony of superior information.

Down by Paul, however, the discipline was relaxed enough, as perhaps could only be expected on the first day of term. One wild-eyed long-haired boy had brought out a small china figure with which, and the assistance of his right hand draped in a pocket handkerchief, and wielding a penholder, he was busy enacting a drama based on the lines of Punch and Judy, to the breathless amusement of his neighbours.

Mr. Bultitude might have hoped to escape notice by a policy of judicious self-effacement, but unhappily his long, blank, uninterested face was held by his companions to bear an implied reproach; and being delicately sensitive on this point, they kicked his legs viciously, which made him extremely glad when dinnertime came, although he felt too faint and bilious to be tempted by anything but the lightest and daintiest luncheon.

But at dinner he found, with a shudder, that he was expected to swallow a thick ragged section of boiled mutton which had been carved and helped so long before he sat down to it, that the stagnant gravy was chilled and congealed into patches of greasy white. He managed to swallow it with many pauses of invincible disgust—only to find it replaced by a solid slab of pale brown suet pudding, sparsely bedewed with unctuous black treacle.

This, though a plentiful, and by no means unwholesome fare for growing boys, was not what he had been accustomed to, and feeling far too heavy and unwell after it to venture upon an encounter with the Doctor, he wandered slow and melancholy round the bare gravelled playground during the half-hour after dinner devoted to the inevitable "chevy," until the Doctor appeared at the head of the staircase.

It is always sad for the historian to have to record a departure from principle, and I have to confess with shame on Mr. Bultitude's account that, feeling the Doctor's eye upon him, and striving to propitiate him, he humiliated himself so far as to run about with an elaborate affection of zest, and his exertions were rewarded by hearing himself cordially encouraged to further efforts.

It cheered and emboldened him. "I've put him in a good temper," he told himself; "if I can only keep him in one till the evening, I really think I might be able to go up and tell him what a ridiculous mess I've got into. Why should I care, after all? At least I've done nothing to be ashamed of. It's an accident that might have happened to any man!"

It is a curious and unpleasant thing that, however reassuring and convincing the arguments may be with which we succeed in bracing ourselves to meet or disregard unpleasantness, the force of those arguments seldom or never outlasts the frame of mind in which they are composed, and when the unpleasantness is at hand, there we are, just as unreasonably alarmed at it as ever.

Mr. Bultitude's confidence faded away almost as soon as he found himself in the schoolroom again. He found himself assigned to a class at one end of the room, where Mr. Tinkler presently introduced a new rule in Algebra to them, in such a manner as to procure for it a lasting unpopularity with all those who were not too much engaged in drawing duels and railway trains upon their slates to attend.

Although Paul did not draw upon his slate, his utter ignorance of Algebra prevented him from being much edified by the cabalistic signs on the blackboard, which Mr. Tinkler seemed to chalk up dubiously, and rub out again as soon as possible, with an air of being ashamed of them. So he tried to nerve himself for the coming ordeal by furtively watching and studying the Doctor, who was taking a Xenophon class at the upper end of the room, and, being in fairly good humour, was combining instruction with amusement in a manner peculiarly his own.

He stopped the construing occasionally to illustrate some word or passage by an anecdote; he condescended to enliven the translation here and there by a familiar and colloquial paraphrase; he magnanimously refrained from pressing any obviously inconvenient questions; and his manner generally was marked by a geniality which was additionally piquant from its extreme uncertainty.

Mr. Bultitude could not help thinking it a rather ghastly form of gaiety, but he hoped it might last.

Presently, however, some one brought him a blue envelope on a tray. He read it, and a frown gathered on his face. The boy who was translating at the time went on again in his former slipshod manner (which had hitherto provoked only jovial criticism and correction) with complete self-complacency, but found himself sternly brought to book, and burdened by a heavy imposition, before he quite realised that his blunders had ceased to amuse.

Then began a season of sore trial and tribulation for the class. The Doctor suddenly withdrew the light of his countenance from them, and sunshine was succeeded by blackest thunderclouds. The wind was no longer tempered to the more closely shorn of the flock; the weakest vessels were put on unexpectedly at crucial passages, and, coming hopelessly to grief, were denounced as impostors and idlers, till half the class was dissolved in tears.

A few of the better grounded stood the fire, like a remnant of the Old Guard. With faces pale from alarm, and trembling voices, but perfect accuracy, they answered all the Doctor's searching inquiries after the paradigms of Greek verbs that seemed irregular to the verge of impropriety.

Paul saw it all with renewed misgiving. "If I were there," he thought, "I should have been run out and flogged long ago! How angry those stupid young idiots are making him! How can I go up and speak to him when he's like that? And yet I must. I'm sitting on dynamite as it is. The very first time they want me to answer any questions from some of their books, I shall be ruined! Why wasn't I better educated when I was a boy, or why didn't I make a better use of my opportunities! It will be a bitter thing if they thrash me for not knowing as much as Dick. Grimstone's coming this way now; it's all over with me!"

The Greek class had managed to repel the enemy, with some loss to themselves, and the Doctor now left his place for a moment, and came down towards the bench on which Paul sat trembling.

The storm, however, had passed over for the present, and he only said with restored calmness, "Who were the boys who learnt dancing last term?"

One or two of them said they had done so, and Dr. Grimstone continued: "Mr. Burdekin was unable to give you the last lesson of his course last term, and has arranged to take you to-day, as he will be in the neighbourhood. So be off at once to Mrs. Grimstone and change your shoes. Bultitude, you learnt last term, too. Go with the others."

Mr. Bultitude was too overcome by this unexpected attack to contradict it, though of course he was quite able to do so; but then, if he had, he must have explained all, and he felt strongly that just then was neither the time nor the place for particulars.

It would have been wiser perhaps, it would certainly have brought matters to a crisis, if he could have forced himself to tell everything—the whole truth in all its outrageous improbability—but he could not.

Let those who feel inclined to blame him for lack of firmness consider how difficult and delicate a business it must almost of necessity be for anyone to declare openly, in the teeth of common sense and plain facts, that there has been a mistake, and, in point of fact, he is not his own son, but his own father.

"I suppose I must go," he thought. "I needn't dance. Haven't danced since I was a young man. But I can't afford to offend him just now."

And so he followed the rest into a sort of cloak-room, where the tall hats which the boys wore on Sundays were all kept on shelves in white bandboxes; and there his hair was brushed, his feet were thrust into very shiny patent leather shoes, and a pair of kid gloves was given out to him to put on.

The dancing lesson was to be held in the "Dining Hall," from which the savour of mutton had not altogether departed. When Paul came in he found the floor cleared and the tables and forms piled up on one side of the room.

Biddlecomb and Tipping and some of the smaller boys were there already, their gloves and shiny shoes giving them a feeling of ceremony and constraint which they tried to carry off by an uncouth parody of politeness.

Siggers was telling stories of the dances he had been to in town, and the fine girls whose step had exactly suited his own, and Tipping was leaning gloomily against the wall listening to something Chawner was whispering in his ear.

There was a rustle of dresses down the stairs outside, and two thin little girls, looking excessively proper and prim, came in with an elderly gentlewoman who was their governess and wore a *pince-nez* to impart the necessary suggestion of a superior intellect. They were the Miss Mutlows, sisters of one of the day-boarders, and attended the course by special favour as friends of Dulcie's, who followed them in with a little gleam of shy anticipation in her eyes.

The Miss Mutlows sat stiffly down on a form, one on each side of her governess, and all three stared solemnly at the boys, who began to blush vividly under the inspection, to unbutton and rebutton their gloves with great care, and to shift from leg to leg in an embarrassed manner.

Dulcie soon singled out poor Mr. Bultitude, who, mindful of Tipping's warning, was doing his very best to avoid her.

She ran straight to him, laid her hand on his arm and looked into his face pleadingly. "Dick," she said, "you're not sulky still, are you?"

Mr. Bultitude had borne a good deal already, and, not being remarkably sweet-natured, he shook the little hand away, half petulant and half alarmed. "I do wish you wouldn't do this sort of thing in public. You'll compromise me, you know!" he said nervously.

Dulcie opened her grey eyes wide, and then a flush came into her cheeks, and she made a little disdainful upward movement of her chin.

"You didn't mind it once," she said. "I thought you might want to dance with me. You liked to last term. But I'm sure I don't care if you choose to be disagreeable. Go and dance with Mary Mutlow if you want to, though you did say she danced like a pair of compasses, and I shall tell her you said so, too. And you know you're not a good dancer yourself. *Are* you going to dance with Mary?"

Paul stamped. "I tell you I never dance," he said. "I can't dance any more than a lamp-post. You don't seem an ill-natured little girl, but why on earth can't you let me alone?"

Dulcie's eyes flashed. "You're a nasty sulky boy," she said in an angry undertone (all the conversation had, of course, been carried on in whispers). "I'll never speak to you or look at you again. You're the most horrid boy in the school—and the ugliest!"

And she turned proudly away, though anyone who looked might have seen the fire in her eyes extinguished as she did so. Perhaps Tipping did see it, for he scowled at them from his corner.

There was another sound outside, as of fiddlestrings being twanged by the finger, and, as the boys hastily formed up in two lines down the centre of the room and the Miss Mutlows and Dulcie prepared themselves for the curtsey of state, there came in a little fat man, with mutton-chop whiskers and a white face, upon which was written an unalterable conviction that his manner and deportment were perfection itself.

The two rows of boys bent themselves stiffly from the back, and Mr. Burdekin returned the compliment by an inclusive and stately inclination.

"Good afternoon, madam. Young ladies, I trust I find you well. (The curtsey just a leetle lower, Miss Mutlow—the right foot less drawn back. Beautiful! Feet closer at the recovery. Perfect!) Young gentlemen, good evening. Take your usual places, please, all of you, for our preliminary exercises. Now, the *chassée* round the room. Will you lead off, please, Dummer; the hands just lightly touching the shoulders, the head thrown negligently back to balance the figure; the whole deportment easy, but not careless. Now, please!"

And, talking all the time with a metrical fluency, he scraped a little jig on the violin, while Dummer led off a procession which solemnly capered round the room in sundry stages of conscious awkwardness. Mr. Bultitude shuffled along somehow after the rest, with rebellion at his heart and a deep sense of degradation. "If my clerks were to see me now!" he thought.

After some minutes of this, Mr. Burdekin stopped them and directed sets to be formed for "The Lancers."

"Bultitude," said Mr. Burdekin, "you will take Miss Mutlow, please."

"Thank you," said Paul, "but—ah—I don't dance."

"Nonsense, nonsense, sir, you are one of my most promising pupils. You mustn't tell me that. Not another word! Come, select your partners."

Paul had no option. He was paired off with the tall and rather angular young lady mentioned, while Dulcie looked on pouting, and snubbed Tipping, who humbly asked for the pleasure of dancing with her, by declaring that she meant to dance with Tom.

The dance began to a sort of rhythmical accompaniment by Mr. Burdekin, who intoned "Tops advance, retire and cross. Balance at corners. (Very nice, Miss Grimstone!) More '*abandon*,' Chawner! Lift the feet more from the floor. Not so high as that! Oh, dear me! that last figure over again. And slide the feet, oh, slide the feet! (Bultitude, you're leaving out all the steps!")

Paul was dragged, unwilling but unresisting, through it all by his partner, who jerked and pushed him into his place without a word, being apparently under strict orders from the governess not on any account to speak to the boys.

After the dance the couples promenaded in a stiff but stately manner round the room to a dirge-like march scraped upon the violin, the boys taking the parts of ladies jibbing away from their partners in a highly unlady-like fashion, and the boy burdened with the companionship of the younger Miss Mutlow walking along in a very agony of bashfulness.

"I suppose," thought Paul, as he led the way with Miss Mary Mutlow, "if Dick were ever to hear of this, he'd think it *funny*. Oh, if I ever get the upper hand of him again——. How much longer, I wonder, shall I have to play the fool to this infernal fiddle!"

But, if this was bad, worse was to come.

There was another pause, in which Mr. Burdekin said blandly, "I wonder now if we have forgotten our sailor's hornpipe. Perhaps Bultitude will prove the contrary. If I remember right, he used to perform it with singular correctness. And, let me tell you, there are a great number of spurious hornpipe steps in circulation. Come, sir, oblige me by dancing it alone!"

This was the final straw. It was not to be supposed for one moment that Mr. Bultitude would lower his dignity in such a preposterous manner. Besides, he did not know how to dance the hornpipe.

So he said, "I shall do nothing of the sort. I've had quite enough of this—ah—tomfoolery!"

"That is a very impolite manner of declining, Bultitude; highly discourteous and unpolished. I must insist now—really, as a personal matter—upon your going through the sailor's hornpipe. Come, you won't make a scene, I'm sure. You'll oblige me, as a gentleman?"

"I tell you I can't!" said Mr. Bultitude sullenly. "I never did such a thing in my life; it would be enough to kill me at my age!"

"This is untrue, sir. Do you mean to say you will not dance the hornpipe?"

"No," said Paul, "I'll be damned if I do!"

There was unfortunately no possible doubt about the nature of the word used—he said it so very distinctly. The governess screamed and called her charges to her. Dulcie hid her face, and some of the boys tittered.

Mr. Burdekin turned pink. "After that disgraceful language, sir, in the presence of the fairer sex, I have no more to do with you. You will have the goodness to stand in the centre of that form. Gentlemen, select your partners for the Highland schottische!"

Mr. Bultitude, by no means sorry to be freed from the irksome necessity of dancing with a heart ill-attuned for enjoyment, got up on the form and stood looking, sullenly enough, upon the proceedings. The governess glowered at him now and then as a monster of youthful depravity; the Miss Mutlows glanced up at him as they tripped past, with curiosity not unmixed with admiration, but Dulcie steadily avoided looking in his direction.

Paul was just congratulating himself upon his escape when the door opened wide, and the Doctor marched slowly and imposingly into the room.

He did this occasionally, partly to superintend matters, and partly as an encouraging mark of approbation. He looked round the class at first with benignant toleration, until his glance took in the bench upon which Mr. Bultitude was set up. Then his eye slowly travelled up to the level of Paul's head, his expression changing meanwhile to a petrifying glare.

It was not, as Paul instinctively felt, exactly the position in which a gentleman who wished to stand well with those in authority over him would prefer to be found. He felt his heart turn to water within him, and stared limp and helpless at the Doctor.

There was an awful silence (Dr. Grimstone was addicted to awful silences; and, indeed, if seldom strictly "golden," silence may often be called "iron"), but at last he inquired, "And pray what may you be doing up there, sir?"

"Upon my soul I can't say," said Mr. Bultitude feebly. "Ask that gentleman there with the fiddle—he knows."

Mr. Burdekin was a good-natured, easy-tempered little man, and had already forgotten the affront to his dignity. He was anxious not to get the boy into more trouble.

"Bultitude was a little inattentive and, I may say, wanting in respect, Dr. Grimstone," he said, putting it as mildly as he could with any accuracy; "so I ventured to place him there as a punishment."

"Quite right, Mr. Burdekin," said the Doctor: "quite right. I am sorry that any boy of mine should have caused you to do so. You are again beginning your career of disorder and rebellion, are you, sir? Go up into the schoolroom at once, and write a dozen copies before tea-time! A very little more eccentricity and insubordination from you, Bultitude, and you will reap a full reward—a full reward, sir!"

So Mr. Bultitude was driven out of the dancing class in dire disgrace—which would not have distressed him particularly, being only one more drop in his bitter cup—but that he recognised that now his hopes of approaching the Doctor with his burden of woe were fallen like a card castle. They were fiddled and danced away for at least twenty-four hours—perhaps for ever!

Bitterly did he brood over this as he slowly and laboriously copied out sundry vain repetitions of such axioms as, "Cultivate Habits of Courtesy and Self-control," and "True Happiness is to be sought in Contentment." He saw the prospect of a tolerably severe flogging growing more and more distinct, and felt that he could not present himself to his family with the consciousness of having suffered such an indelible disgrace. His family! What would become of them in his absence? Would he ever see his comfortable home in Bayswater again?

Tea-time came, and after it evening preparation, when Mr. Tinkler presided in a feeble and ineffective manner, perpetually suspecting that the faint sniggers he heard were indulged in at his own expense, and calling perfectly innocent victims to account for them.

Paul sat next to Jolland and, in his desperate anxiety to avoid further unpleasantness, found himself, as he could not for his life have written a Latin or a German composition, reduced to copy down his neighbour's exercises. This Jolland (who had looked forward to an arrangement of a very opposite kind) nevertheless cheerfully allowed him to do, though he expressed doubts as to the wisdom of a servile imitation—more, perhaps, from prudence than conscientiousness.

Jolland, in the intervals of study, was deeply engaged in the production of a small illustrated work of fiction, which he was pleased to call *The Adventures of Ben Buterkin at Scool*. It was in a great measure an autobiography, and the cuts depicting the hero's flagellations—which were frequent in the course of the narrative—were executed with much vigour and feeling.

He turned out a great number of these works in the course of the term, as well as faces in pen and ink with moving tongues and rolling eyes, and these he would present to a few favoured friends with a secretive and self-depreciatory giggle.

Amidst scenes and companions like these, Paul sat out the evening hours on his hard seat, which was just at the junction of two forms—an exquisitely uncomfortable position, as all who have tried it will acknowledge—until the time for going to bed came round again. He dreaded the hours of darkness, but there was no help for it—to protest would have been madness just then, and, once more, he was forced to pass a night under the roof of Crichton House.

It was even worse than the first, though this was greatly owing to his own obstinacy.

The boys, if less subdued, were in better temper than the evening before, and found it troublesome to keep up a feud when the first flush of resentment had died out. There was a general disposition to forget his departure from the code of schoolboy honour, and give him an opportunity of retrieving the past.

But he would not meet them half-way; his repeated repulses by the Doctor and all the difficulties that beset his return to freedom had made him very sulky and snappish. He had not patience or adaptability enough to respond to their advances, and only shrank from their rough good nature—which naturally checked the current of good feeling.

Then, when the lights were put out, some one demanded a story. Most of the bedrooms possessed a professional story-teller, and in one there was a young romancist who began a stirring history the very first night of the term, which always ran on until the night before the holidays, and, if his hearers were apt to yawn at the sixth week of it, he himself enjoyed and believed in it keenly from beginning to end.

Dick Bultitude had been a valued *raconteur*, it appeared, and his father found accordingly, to his disgust, that he was expected to amuse them with a story.

When he clearly understood the idea, he rejected it with so savage a snarl, that he soon found it necessary to retire under the bedclothes to escape the general indignation that followed.

Finding that he did not actively resent it (the real Dick would have had the occupant of the nearest bed out by the ears in a minute!), they profited by his prudence to come to his bedside, where they pillowed his weary head (with their own pillows) till the slight offered them was more than avenged.

After that, Mr. Bultitude, with the breath half beaten out of his body, lay writhing and spluttering on his hard, rough bed till long after silence had fallen over the adjoining beds, and the sleepy hum of talk in the other bedrooms had died away.

Then he, too, drifted off into wild and troubled dreams, which, at their maddest, were scattered into blankness by a sudden and violent shock, which jerked him, clutching and grasping at nothing, on to the cold, bare boards, where he rolled, shivering.

"An earthquake!" he thought, "an explosion ... gas—or dynamite! He must go and call the children ... Boaler ... the plate!"

But the reality to which he woke was worse still. Tipping and Coker had been patiently pinching themselves to keep awake until their enemy should be soundly asleep, in order to enjoy the exquisite pleasure of letting down the mattress; and, too dazed and frightened even to swear, Paul gathered up his bedclothes and tried to draw them about him as well as he might, and seek sleep, which had lost its security.

The Garudâ Stone had done one grim and cruel piece of work at least in its time.

7.
Cutting the Knot

"A Crowd is not Company; And Faces are but a Gallery of Pictures;
And Talke but a *Tinckling Cymball*, where there is no *Love*."

—Bacon.

Once more Mr. Bultitude rose betimes, dressed noiselessly, and stole down to the cold schoolroom, where one gas-jet was burning palely—for the morning was raw and foggy.

This time, however, he was not alone. Mr. Blinkhorn was sitting at his little table in the corner, correcting exercises, with his chilly hands cased in worsted mittens. He looked up as Paul came in, and nodded kindly.

Paul went straight to the fire, and stood staring into it with lack-lustre eye, too apathetic even to be hopeless, for the work of enlightening the Doctor seemed more terrible and impossible than ever, and he began to see that, if the only way of escape lay there, he had better make up his mind with what philosophy he could to adapt himself to his altered circumstances, and stay on for the rest of the term.

But the prospect was so doleful and so blank, that he drew a heavy sigh as he thought of it. Mr. Blinkhorn heard it, and rose awkwardly from the rickety little writing-table, knocking over a pile of marble-covered copy-books as he did so.

Then he crossed over to Paul and laid a hand gently on his shoulder. "Look here," he said: "why don't you confide in me? Do you think I'm blind to what has happened to you? I can see the change in you—if others cannot. Why not trust me?"

Mr. Bultitude looked up into his face, which had an honest interest and kindliness in it, and his heart warmed with a faint hope. If this young man had been shrewd enough to guess at his unhappy secret, might he not be willing to intercede with the Doctor for him? He looked good-natured—he would trust him.

"Do you mean to say really," he asked, with more cordiality than he had spoken for a long time, "that you—see—the—a—the difference?"

"I saw it almost directly," said Mr. Blinkhorn, with mild triumph.

"That's the most extraordinary thing," said Paul, "and yet it ought to be evident enough, to be sure. But no, you can't have guessed the real state of things!"

"Listen, and stop me if I'm wrong. Within the last few days a great change has been at work within you. You are not the idle, thoughtless, mischievous boy who left here for his holidays——"

"No," said Paul, "I'll swear I'm not!"

"There is no occasion for such strong expressions. But, at all events, you come back here an altogether different being. Am I right in saying so?"

"Perfectly," said Paul, overjoyed at being so thoroughly understood, "perfectly. You're a very intelligent young man, sir. Shake hands. Why, I shouldn't be surprised, after that, if you knew how it all happened?"

"That too," said Mr. Blinkhorn smiling, "I can guess. It arose, I doubt not, in a wish?"

"Yes," cried Paul, "you've hit it again. You're a conjurer, sir, by Gad you are!"

"Don't say 'by Gad,' Bultitude; it's inconsistent. It began, I was saying, in a wish, half unconscious perhaps, to be something other than what you had been——"

"I was a fool," groaned Mr. Bultitude, "yes, that was the way it began!"

"Then insensibly the wish worked a gradual transformation in your nature (you are old enough to follow me?)."

"Old enough for him to follow *me*!" thought Paul; but he was too pleased to be annoyed. "Hardly gradual I should say," he said aloud. "But go on, sir, pray go on. I see you know all about it."

"At first the other part of you struggled against the new feelings. You strove to forget them—you even tried to resume your old habits, your former way of life—but to no purpose; and when you came here, you found no fellowship amongst your companions——"

"Quite out of the question!" said Paul.

"Their pleasures give you no delight——"

"Not a bit!"

"They, on their side, perhaps misunderstand your lack of interest in their pursuits. They cannot see—how should they?—that you have altered your mode of life, and when they catch the difference between you and the Richard Bultitude they knew, why, they are apt to resent it."

"They are," agreed Mr. Bultitude: "they resent it in a confounded disagreeable way, you know. Why, I assure you, that only last night I was——"

"Hush," said Mr. Blinkhorn, holding up one hand, "complaints are unmanly. But I see you wonder at my knowing all this?"

"Well," said Paul, "I am rather surprised."

"What would you say if I told you I had undergone it myself in my time?"

"You don't mean to tell me there are *two* Garudâ Stones in this miserable world!" cried Paul, thoroughly astonished.

"I don't know what you mean now, but I can say with truth that I too have had my experiences—my trials. Months ago, from certain signs, I noticed, I foresaw that this was coming upon you."

"Then," said Mr. Bultitude, "I think, in common decency, you might have warned me. A post-card would have done it. I should have been better prepared to meet this, then!"

"It would have been worse than fruitless to attempt to hurry on the crisis. It might have even prevented what I fondly hoped would come to pass."

"Fondly hoped!" said Paul, "upon my word you speak plainly, sir."

"Yes," said Mr. Blinkhorn. "You see I knew the Dick Bultitude that was, so well; he was frolicksome, impulsive, mischievous even, but under it all there lay a nature of sterling worth."

"Sterling worth!" cried Paul. "A scoundrel, I tell you, a heartless, selfish young scoundrel. Call things by their right names, if you please."

"No, no," said Mr. Blinkhorn, "this extreme self-depreciation is morbid, very morbid. There was no actual vice."

"No actual vice! Why, God bless my soul, do you call ingratitude—the basest, most unfilial, most treacherous ingratitude—no vice, sir? You may be a very excellent young man, but if you gloss over things in that fashion, your moral sense must be perverted, sir—strangely perverted."

"There were faults on both sides, I fear," said Mr. Blinkhorn, growing a little scandalised by the boy's odd warmth of expression. "I have heard something of what you had to bear with. On the one hand, a father, undemonstrative, stern, easily provoked; on the other, a son, thoughtless, forgetful, and at times it may be even wilful. But you are too sensitive; you think too much of what seems to me a not unnatural (although of course improper) protest against coldness and injustice. I should be the last to encourage a child against a parent, but, to comfort your self-reproach, I think it right to assure you that, in my judgment, the outburst you refer to was very excusable."

"Oh," said Paul, "you do? You call that comfort? Excusable! Why, what the dooce do you mean, sir? You're taking the other side now!"

"This is not the language of penitence, Bultitude," said poor Mr. Blinkhorn, disheartened and bewildered. "Remember, you have put off the Old Man now!"

"I'm not likely to forget *that*," said Paul; "I only wish I could see my way to putting him on again!"

"You want to be your old self again?" gasped Mr. Blinkhorn.

"Why, of course I do," said Paul angrily; "I'm not an idiot!"

"You are weary of the struggle so soon?" said the other with reproach.

"Weary? I tell you I'm sick of it! If I had only known what was in store for me before I had made such a fool of myself!"

"This is horrible!" said Mr. Blinkhorn—"I ought not to listen to you."

"But you must," urged Paul; "I tell you I can't stand it any longer. I'm not fit for it at my age. You must see that yourself, and you must make Grimstone see it too!"

"Never!" said Mr. Blinkhorn firmly. "Nor do I see how that would help you. I will not let you go back in this deplorable way. You must nerve yourself to go on now in the path you have chosen; you must force your schoolfellows to love and respect you in your new character. Come, take courage! After all, in spite of your altered life, there is no reason why you should not be a frank and happy-hearted boy, you know."

"A frank and happy-hearted fiddlestick!" cried Paul rudely (he was so disgusted at the suggestion); "don't talk rubbish, sir! I thought you were going to show me some way out of all this, and instead of that, knowing the shameful way I've been treated, you can stand there and calmly recommend me to stay on here and be happy-hearted and frank!"

"You must be calm, Bultitude, or I shall leave you. Listen to reason. You are here for your good. Youth, it has been beautifully said, is the springtime of life. Though you may not believe it, you will never be happier than you are now. Our schooldays are——"

But Mr. Bultitude could not tamely be mocked with the very platitudes that had brought him all his misery—he cut the master short in a violent passion. "This is too much!" he cried—"you shall not palm off that miserable rubbish on me. I see through it. It's a plot to keep me here, and you're in it. It's false imprisonment, and I'll write to the *Times*. I'll expose the whole thing!"

"This violence is only ridiculous," said Mr. Blinkhorn. "If I were not too pained by it, I should feel it my duty to report your language to the Doctor. As it is, you have bitterly disappointed me; I can't understand it at all. You seemed so subdued, so softened lately. But until you come to me and say you regret this, I must decline to have anything more to say to you. Take your book and sit down in your place!"

And he went back to his exercises, looking puzzled and pained. The fact was, he was an ardent believer in the Good Boy of a certain order of school tales—the boy who is seized with a sudden conviction of the intrinsic baseness of boyhood, and does all in his power to get rid of the harmful taint; the boy who renounces his old comrades and his natural tastes (which after all seldom have any serious harm in them), to don a panoply of priggishness which is too often kick-proof.

This kind of boy is rare enough at most English schools, but Mr. Blinkhorn had been educated at a large Nonconformist College, where "Revivals" and "Awakenings" were periodical, and undoubtedly did produce changes of character violent enough, but sadly short in duration.

He was always waiting for some such boy to come to him with his confession of moral worthlessness and vows of unnatural perfection, and was too simple and earnest and good himself to realise that such states of the youthful mind are not unfrequently merely morbid and hysterical, and too often degenerate into Pharisaism, or worse still, hypocrisy.

So when he noticed Mr. Bultitude's silence and depression, his studied withdrawal from the others and his evident want of sympathy with them, he believed he saw the symptoms of a conscience at work, and that he had found his reformed boy at last.

It was a very unfortunate misunderstanding, for it separated Paul from, perhaps, the only person who would have had the guilelessness to believe his incredible story, and the good nature to help him to find escape from his misfortunes.

Mr. Bultitude on his part was more angry and disgusted than ever. He began to see that there was a muddle somewhere, and that his identity was unsuspected still. This young man, for all his fair speaking and pretended shrewdness, was no conjurer after all. He was left to rely on his own resources, and he had begun to lose all confidence in their power to extricate him.

As he brooded over this, the boys straggled down as before, and looked over their lessons for the day in a dull, lifeless manner. The cold, unsatisfying breakfast, and the half-hour assigned to "chevy," followed in due course, and after that Paul found himself set down with a class to await the German master, Herr Stohwasser.

He had again tried to pull himself together and approach the Doctor with his protest, but no sooner did he find himself near his presence than his heart began to leap wildly and then retired down towards his boots, leaving him hoarse, palpitating, and utterly blank of ideas.

It was no use—and he resigned himself for yet another day of unwelcome instruction.

The class was in a little room on the basement floor, with a linen-press taking up one side, some bare white deal tables and forms, and, on the walls, a few coloured German prints. They sat there talking and laughing, taking no notice of Mr. Bultitude, until the German master made his appearance.

He was by no means a formidable person, though stout and tall. He wore big round owlish spectacles, and his pale broad face and long nose, combined with a wild crop of light hair and a fierce beard, gave him the incongruous appearance of a sheep looking out of a gun-port.

He took his place with an air of tremendous determination to enforce a hard morning's work on the book they were reading—a play of Schiller's, of the plot of which, it is needless to say, no one of his pupils had or cared to have the vaguest notion, having long since condemned the whole subject, with insular prejudice, as "rot."

"Now, please," said Herr Stohwasser, "where we left off last term. Third act, first scene—Court before Tell's house. Tell is vid the carpenter axe, Hedwig vid a domestig labour occupied. Walter and Wilhelm in the depth sport with a liddle gross-bow. Biddlegom, you begin. Walter (sings)."

But Biddlecomb was in a conversational mood, and willing to postpone the task of translation, so he merely inquired, with an air of extreme interest, how Herr Stohwasser's German Grammar was getting on.

This was a subject on which (as he perhaps knew) the German never could resist enlarging, for in common with most German masters, he was giving birth to a new Grammar, which, from the daring originality of its plan, and its extreme simplicity, was destined to supersede all other similar works.

"Ach," he said, "it is brogressing. I haf just gompleted a gomprehensive table of ze irregular virps, vith ze eggserzizes upon zem. And zere is further an appendeeks which in itself gontains a goncise view of all ze vort-blays possible in the Charman tong. But, come, let us gontinue vith our Tell!"

"What are vort-blays?" persisted Biddlecomb insidiously, having no idea of continuing with his Tell just yet.

"A vort-blay," exclaimed Herr Stohwasser; "it is English, nicht so? A sporting vid vorts—a 'galembour'—a—Gott pless me, vat you call a 'pon.'"

"Like the one you made when you were a young man?" Jolland called out from the lower end of the table.

"Yes; tell us the one you made when you were a young man," the class entreated, with flattering eagerness.

Herr Stohwasser began to laugh with slow, deep satisfaction; the satisfaction of a successful achievement. "Hah, you remember dat!" he said, "ah, yes, I make him when a yong man; but, mind you, he was not a pon—he was a '*choke*.' I haf told you all about him before."

"We've forgotten it," said Biddlecomb: "tell it us again."

As a matter of fact this joke, in all its lights, was tolerably familiar to most of them by this time, but, either on its individual merits, or perhaps because it compared favourably with the sterner alternative of translating, it was periodically in request, and always met with evergreen appreciation.

Herr Stohwasser beamed with the pride of authorship. Like the celebrated Scotchman, he "jocked wi' deeficulty," and the outcome of so much labour was dear to him.

"I zent him into ze Charman *Kladderadatch* (it is a paper like your *Ponch*). It—mein choke—was upon ze Schleswig-Holstein gomplication; ze beginning was in this way——"

And he proceeded to set out in great length all the circumstances which had given materials for his "choke," with the successive processes by which he had shaped and perfected it, passing on to a recital of the masterpiece itself, and ending up by a philosophical analysis of the same, which must have placed his pupils in full possession of the point, for they laughed consumedly.

"I dell you zis," he said, "not to aggustom your minds vid frivolity and lightness, but as a lesson in ze gonstruction of ze langwitch. If you can choke in Charman, you will be able also to gonverse in Charman."

"Did the German what's-its-name print your joke?" inquired Coggs.

"It has not appeared yet," Herr Stohwasser confessed; "it takes a long time to get an imbortant choke like that out in brint. But I vait—I write to ze editor every week—and I vait."

"Why don't you put it in your Grammar?" suggested Tipping.

"I haf—ze greater part of it—(it vas a long choke, but I gompressed him). If I haf time, some day I will make anozer liddle choke to aggompany, begause I vant my Crammar to be a goot Crammar, you understandt. And now to our Tell. Really you beople do noding but chadder!"

All this, of course, had no interest for Mr. Bultitude, but it left him free to pursue his own thoughts in peace, and indeed this lesson would never have been recorded here, but for two circumstances which will presently appear, both of which had no small effect on his fortunes.

He sat nearest the window, and looked out on the pinched and drooping laurels in the enclosure, which were damp with frost melting in the sunshine. Over the wall he could see the tops of passing vehicles, the country carrier's cart, the railway parcels van, the fly from the station. He envied even the drivers; their lot was happier than his!

His thoughts were busy with Dick. Oddly enough, it had scarcely occurred to him before to speculate on what he might be doing in his absence; he had thought chiefly about himself. But now he gave his attention to the subject, what new horrors it opened up! What might not become of his well-conducted household under the rash rule of a foolish schoolboy! The office, too—who could say what mischief Dick might not be doing there, under the cover of his own respectable form?

Then it might seem good to him any day to smash the Garudâ Stone, and after that there would be no hope of matters being ever set right again!

And yet, miserable coward and fool that he was, with everything depending upon his losing no time to escape, he could not screw up his courage, and say the words that were to set him free.

All at once—and this is one of the circumstances that make the German lesson an important stage in this story—an idea suggested itself to him quite dazzling by its daring and brilliancy.

Some may wonder, when they hear what it was, why he never thought of it before, and it is somewhat surprising, but by no means without precedent. Artemus Ward has told us somewhere of a ferocious bandit who was confined for sixteen years in solitary captivity, before the notion of escape ever occurred to him. When it did, he opened the window and got out.

Perhaps a similar passiveness on Mr. Bultitude's part was due to a very natural and proper desire to do everything without scandal, and in a legitimate manner; to march out, as it were, with the honours of war. Perhaps it was simple dullness. The fact remains that it was not till then that he saw a way of recovering his lost position, without the disagreeable necessity of disclosing his position to anyone at Crichton House.

He had still—thank Heaven—the five shillings he had given Dick. He had not thrown them away with the other articles in his mad passion. Five shillings was not much, but it was more than enough to pay for a third-class fare to town. He had only to watch his opportunity, slip away to the station, and be at home again, defying the usurper, before anyone at Crichton House had discovered his absence.

He might go that very day, and the delight of this thought—the complete reaction from blank despair to hope—was so intense that he could not help rubbing his hands stealthily under the table, and chuckling with glee at his own readiness of resource.

When we are most elated, however, there is always a counteracting agent at hand to bring us down again to our proper level, or below it. The Roman general in the triumph never really needed the slave in the chariot to dash his spirits—he had his friends there already; the guests at an Egyptian dinner must have brought their own skeletons.

There was a small flaxen-haired little boy sitting next to Mr. Bultitude, seemingly a quite inoffensive being, who at this stage served to sober him by furnishing another complication.

"Oh, I say, Bultitude," he piped shrilly in Paul's ear, "I forgot all about it. Where's my rabbit?"

The unreasonable absurdity of such a question annoyed him excessively. "Is this a time," he said reprovingly, "to talk of rabbits? Mind your book, sir."

"Oh, I daresay," grumbled little Porter, the boy in question: "it's all very well, but I want my rabbit."

"Hang it, sir," said Paul angrily, "do you suppose I'm sitting on it?"

"You promised to bring me back a rabbit," persisted Porter doggedly; "you know you did, and it's a beastly shame. I mean to have that rabbit, or know the reason why."

At the other end of the table Biddlecomb had again dexterously allured Herr Stohwasser into the meshes of conversation; this time upon the question (*à propos de bottes*) of street performances. "I vill tell you a gurious thing," he was saying, "vat happened to me de oder day ven I vas valking down de Strandt. I saw a leedle gommon dirty boy with a tall round hat on him, and he stand in a side street right out in de road, and he take off his tall round hat, and he put it on de ground, and he stand still and look zo at it. So I shtop too, to see vat he vould do next. And bresently he take out a large sheet of baper and tear it in four pieces very garefully, and stick zem round de tall round hat, and put it on his head again, and zen he set it down on de grount and look at it vonce more, and all de time he never speak von vort. And I look and look and vonder vat he would do next. And a great growd of beoples com, and zey look and vonder too. And zen all at once de leedle dirty boy he take out all de paper and put on de hat, and he valk avay, laughing altogetter foolishly at zomzing I did not understand at all. I haf been thinking efer since vat in the vorldt he do all zat nonsence for. And zere is von ozer gurious thing I see in your London streets zat very same day. Zere vas a poor house cat dat had been by a cab overrun as I passed by, and von man vith a kind varm heart valk up and stamp it on de head for to end its pain. And anozer man vith anozer kind heart, he gom up directly and had not seen de cat overrun, but he see de first man stamping and he knock him down for ill-treating animals; it was quite gurious to see; till de policeman arrest dem both for fighting. Goggs, degline 'Katze,' and gif me ze berfect and bast barticiple of 'kampfen,' to fight." This last relapse into duty was caused by the sudden entrance of the Doctor, who stood at the door looking on for some time with a general air of being intimately acquainted with Schiller as an author, before suggesting graciously that it was time to dismiss the class.

Wednesday was a half-holiday at Crichton House, and so, soon after dinner, Paul found himself marshalled with the rest in a procession bound for the football field. They marched two and two, Chawner and three of the other elder boys leading with the ball and four goal-posts ornamented with coloured calico flags, and Mr. Blinkhorn and Mr. Tinkler bringing up the rear.

Mr. Bultitude was paired with Tom Grimstone, who, after eyeing him askance for some time, could control his curiosity no longer.

"I say, Dick," he began, "what's the matter with you this term?"

"My name is not Dick," said Paul stiffly.

"Oh, if you're so particular then," said Tom: "but, without humbug, what is the matter?"

"You see a change then," said Paul, "you do see a difference, eh?"

"Rather!" said Tom expressively. "You've come back what I call a beastly sneak, you know, this term. The other fellows don't like it; they'll send you to Coventry unless you take care."

"I wish they would," said Paul.

"You don't talk like the same fellow either," continued Tom; "you use such fine language, and you're always in a bait, and yet you don't stick up for yourself as you used to. Look here, tell me (we were always chums), is it one of your larks?"

"Larks!" said Paul. "I'm in a fine mood for larks. No, it's not one of my larks."

"Perhaps your old governor has been making a cad of himself then, and you're out of sorts about it."

"I'll thank you not to speak about him in that way," said Paul, "in my presence."

"Why," grumbled Tom, "I'm sure you said enough about him yourself last term. It's my belief you're imitating him now."

"Ah," said Paul, "and what makes you think that?"

"Why, you go about strutting and swelling just like he did when he came about sending you here. I say, do you know what Mums said about him after he went away?"

"No," said Paul, "your mother struck me as a very sensible and agreeable woman—if I may say so to her son."

"Well, Mums said your governor seemed to leave you here just like they leave umbrellas at picture galleries, and she believed he had a large-sized money-bag inside him instead of a heart."

"Oh!" said Paul, with great disgust, for he had thought Mrs. Grimstone a woman of better taste; "your mother said that, did she? Vastly entertaining to be sure—ha, ha! He would be pleased to know she thought that, I'm sure."

"Tell him, and see what he says," suggested Tom; "he is an awful brute to you though, isn't he?"

"If," growled Mr. Bultitude, "slaving from morning till night to provide education and luxury for a thankless brood of unprofitable young vipers is 'being a brute,' I suppose he is."

"Why, you're sticking up for him now!" said Tom. "I thought he was so strict with you. Wouldn't let you have any fun at home, and never took you to pantomimes?"

"And why should he, sir, why should he? Tell me that. Tell me why a man is to be hunted out of his comfortable chair after a well-earned dinner, to go and sit in a hot theatre and a thorough draught, yawning at the miserable drivel managers choose to call a pantomime? Now in my young days there *were* pantomimes. I tell you, sir, I've seen——"

"Oh, if you're satisfied, I don't care!" said Tom, astonished at this apparent change of front. "If you choose to come back and play the corker like this, it's your look-out. Only, if you knew what Sproule major said about you just now——"

"I don't want to know," said Paul; "it doesn't concern me."

"Perhaps it doesn't concern you what pa thinks either? Dad told Mums last night that he was altogether at a loss to know how to deal with you, you had come back so queer and unruly. And he said, let me see, oh, he said that 'if he didn't see an alteration very soon he should resort to more drastic measures'—drastic measures is Latin for a whopping."

"Good gracious!" thought Paul, "I haven't a moment to lose! he might 'resort to drastic measures' this very evening. I can't change my nature at my time of life. I must run for it, and soon."

Then he said aloud to Tom, "Can you tell me, my—my young friend, if, supposing a boy were to ask to leave the field—saying for instance that he was not well and thought he should be better at home—whether he would be allowed to go?"

"Of course he would," said Tom, "you ought to know that by this time. You've only to ask Blinkhorn or Tinkler; they'll let you go right enough."

Paul saw his course quite clearly now, and was overcome with relief and gratitude. He wrung the astonished Tom's hand warmly; "Thank you," he said, briskly and cheerfully, "thank you. I'm really uncommonly obliged to you. You're a very intelligent boy. I should like to give you sixpence."

But although Tom used no arguments to dissuade him, Mr. Bultitude remembered his position in time, and prudently refrained from such ill-judged generosity. Sixpences were of vital importance now, when he expected to be starting so soon on his perilous journey.

And so they reached the field where the game was to be played, and where Paul was resolved to have one desperate throw for liberty and home. He was more excited than anxious as he thought of it, and it certainly did seem as if all the chances were in his favour, and that fortune must have forsaken him indeed, if anything were allowed to prevent his escape.

8.
Unbending the Bow

"I pray you, give me leave to go from hence,

I am not well;"

Merchant of Venice.

"He will not blush, that has a father's heart,

To take in childish plays a childish part;

But bends his sturdy back to any toy

That youth takes pleasure in,—to please his boy."

The football field was a large one, bounded on two sides by tall wooden palings, and on the other two by a hedge and a new shingled road, separated from the field by a post and rails.

Two of the younger boys, proud of their office, raced down to the further end to set up the goal-posts. The rest lounged idly about without attempting to begin operations, except the new boy Kiffin, who was seen walking apart from the rest, diligently studying the "rules of the game of football," as laid down in a small *Boy's Own Pocket Book and Manual of Outdoor Sports*, with which he had been careful to provide himself.

At last Tipping suggested that they had better begin, and proposed that Mr. Blinkhorn and himself should toss up for the choice of sides, and this being done, Mr. Bultitude presently, to his great dismay, heard his name mentioned. "I'll have young Bultitude," said Tipping; "he used to play up decently. Look here, you young beggar, you're on my side, and if you don't play up it will be the worse for you!"

It was not worth while, however, to protest, since he would so soon be rid of the whole crew for ever, and so Paul followed Tipping and his train with dutiful submission, and the game began.

It was not a spirited performance. Mr. Tinkler, who was not an athlete, retired at once to the post and rails, on which he settled himself to enjoy a railway novel with a highly stimulating cover. Mr. Blinkhorn, who had more conscientious views of his office, charged about vigorously, performing all kinds of wonders with the ball, though evidently more from a sense of duty than with any idea of enjoyment.

Tipping occasionally took the trouble to oppose him, but as a concession merely, and with a parade of being under no necessity to do so; and these two, with a very small following of enthusiasts on either side, waged a private and confidential kind of warfare in different parts of the field, while the others made no pretence of playing for the present, but strolled about in knots, exchanging and bartering the treasures valuable in the sight of schoolboys, and gossiping generally.

As for Paul, he did not clearly understand what "playing up" might mean. He had not indulged in football since he was a genuine boy, and then only in a rudimentary and primitive form, and without any particular fondness for the exercise. But being now, in spirit at all events, a precise elderly person, with a decided notion of taking care of himself, he was resolved that not even Tipping should compel him to trust his person within range of that dirty brown globe, which whistled past his ear or seemed spinning towards his stomach with such a hideous suggestion of a cannon-ball about it.

All the ghastly instances, too, of accidents to life and limb in the football field came unpleasantly into his memory, and he saw the inadvisability of mingling with the crowd and allowing himself to be kicked violently on the shins.

So he trotted industriously about at a safe distance in order to allay suspicion, while waiting for a good opportunity to put his scheme of escape into execution.

At last he could wait no longer, for the fearful thought occurred to him, that if he remained there much longer, the Doctor—who, as he knew from Dick, always came to superintend, if not to share the sports of his pupils—might make his appearance, and then his chance would be lost for the present, for he knew too well that he should never find courage to ask permission from *him*.

With a beating heart he went up to Mr. Tinkler, who was still on the fence with his novel, and asked as humbly as he could bring himself to do:

"If you please, sir, will you allow me to go home? I'm—I'm not feeling at all well."

"Not well! What's the matter with you?" said Mr. Tinkler, without looking up.

Paul had not prepared himself for details, and the sudden question rather threw him off his guard.

"A slight touch of liver," he said at length. "It takes me after meals sometimes."

"Liver!" said Mr. Tinkler, "you've no right to such a thing at your age; it's all nonsense, you know. Run in and play, that'll set you up again."

"It's fatal, sir," said Paul. "My doctor expressly warned me against taking any violent exercise soon after luncheon. If you knew what liver is, you wouldn't say so!"

Mr. Tinkler stared, as well he might, but making nothing of it, and being chiefly anxious not to be interrupted any longer, only said, "Oh, well, don't bother me; I daresay it's all right. Cut along!"

So Mr. Bultitude was free; the path lay open to him now. He knew he would have little difficulty in finding his way to the station, and, once there, he would have the whole afternoon in which to wait for a train to town.

"I've managed that excellently," he thought, as he ran blithely off, almost like the boy he seemed. "Not the slightest hitch. I defy the fates themselves to stop me now!"

But the fates are ladies, and—not of course that it follows—occasionally spiteful. It is very rash indeed to be ungallant enough to defy them—they have such an unpleasant habit of accepting the challenge.

Mr. Bultitude had hardly got clear of the groups scattered about the field, when he met a small flaxen-haired boy, who was just coming down to join the game. It was Porter, his neighbour of the German lesson.

"There you are, Bultitude, then," he said in his squeaky voice: "I want you."

"I can't stop," said Paul, "I'm in a hurry—another time."

"Another time won't do," said little Porter, laying hold of him by his jacket. "I want that rabbit."

This outrageous demand took Mr. Bultitude's breath away. He had no idea what rabbit was referred to, or why he should be required to produce such an animal at a moment's notice. This was the second time an inconvenient small boy had interfered between him and liberty. He would not be baffled twice. He tried to shake off his persecutor.

"I tell you, my good boy, I haven't such a thing about me. I haven't indeed. I don't even know what you're talking about."

This denial enraged Porter.

"I say, you fellows," he called out, "come here! Do make Bultitude give me my rabbit. He says he doesn't know anything about it now!"

At this several of the loungers came up, glad of a distraction.

"What's the matter?" some of them asked.

"Why," whined Porter, "he promised to bring me back a rabbit this term, and now he pretends he does not know anything about it. Make him say what he's done with it!"

Mr. Bultitude was not usually ready of resource, but now he had what seemed a happy thought.

"Gad!" he cried, pretending to recollect it, "so I did—to be sure, a rabbit, of course, how could I forget it? It's—it's a splendid rabbit. I'll go and fetch it!"

"Will you?" cried Porter, half relieved. "Where is it, then?"

"Where?" said Paul sharply (he was growing positively brilliant). "Why, in my playbox to be sure; where should it be?"

"It isn't in your playbox, I know," put in Siggers: "because I saw it turned out yesterday and there was no rabbit then. Besides, how could a rabbit live in a playbox? He's telling lies. I can see it by his face. He hasn't any rabbit!"

"Of course I haven't!" said Mr. Bultitude. "How should I? I'm not a conjurer. It's not a habit of mine to go about with rabbits concealed on my person. What's the use of coming to me like this? It's absurd, you know; perfectly absurd!"

The crowd increased until there was quite a ring formed round Mr. Bultitude and the indignant claimant, and presently Tipping came bustling up.

"What's the row here, you fellows?" he said. "Bultitude again, of course. What's he been doing now?"

"He had a rabbit he said he was keeping for me," explained little Porter: "and now he won't give it up or tell me what he's done with it."

"He has some mice he ought to give us, too," said one or two new-comers, edging their way to the front.

Mr. Bultitude was of course exceedingly annoyed by this unlooked-for interruption, and still more by such utterly preposterous claims on him for animals; however, it was easy to explain that he had no such things in his possession, and after that of course no more could be said. He was beginning to disclaim all liability, when Siggers stopped him.

"Keep that for the present," he said. "I say, we ought to have a regular trial over this, and get at the truth of it properly. Let's fetch him along to the goal-posts and judge him!"

He fixed upon the goal-posts as being somehow more formal, and, as his proposal was well received, two of them grasped Mr. Bultitude by the collar and dragged him along in procession to the appointed spot between the two flags, while Siggers followed in what he conceived to be a highly judicial manner, and evidently enjoying himself prodigiously.

Paul, though highly indignant, allowed himself to be led along without resistance. It was safest to humour them, for after all it would not last long, and when they were tired of baiting him he could watch his time and slip quietly away.

When they reached the goal-posts Siggers arranged them in a circle, placing himself, the hapless Paul, and his accusers in the centre. "You chaps had better all be jurymen," he said. "I'll be judge, and unless he makes a clean breast of it," he added with judicial impartiality, "the court will jolly well punch his ugly young head off."

Siggers' father was an Old Bailey barrister in good and rather sharp practice, so that it was clearly the son's mission to preside on this occasion. But unfortunately his hour of office was doomed to be a brief one, for Mr. Blinkhorn, becoming aware that the game was being still more scantily supported, and noticing the crowd at the goal, came up to know the reason of it at a long camel-like trot, his hat on the back of his head, his mild face flushed with exertion, and his pebble glasses gleaming in the winter sunshine.

"What are you all doing here? Why don't you join the game? I've come here to play football with you, and how can I do it if you all slink off and leave me to play by myself?" he asked with pathos.

"Please, sir," said Siggers, alarmed at the threatened loss of his dignity, "it's a trial, and I'm judge."

"Yes, sir," the whole ring shouted together. "We're trying Bultitude, sir."

On the whole, perhaps, Mr. Bultitude was glad of this interference. At least justice would be done now, although this usher had blundered so unpardonably that morning.

"This is childish, you know," said Mr. Blinkhorn, "and it's not football. The Doctor will be seriously angry if he comes and sees you trifling here. Let the boy go."

"But he's cheated some of the fellows, sir," grumbled Tipping and Siggers together.

"Well, *you*'ve no right to punish him if he has. Leave him to me."

"Will you see fair play between them, sir? He oughtn't to be let off without being made to keep his word."

"If there is any dispute between you and Bultitude," said Mr. Blinkhorn, "I have no objection to settle it—provided it is within my province."

"Settle it without me," said Paul hurriedly. "I've leave to go home. I'm ill."

"Who gave you leave to go home?" asked the master.

"That young man over there on the rails," said Paul.

"I am the proper person to apply to for leave; you know that well enough," said Mr. Blinkhorn, with a certain coldness in his tone. "Now then, Porter, what is all this business about?"

"Please, sir," said Porter, "he told me last term he had a lot of rabbits at home, and if I liked he would bring me back a lop-eared one and let me have it cheap, and I gave him two shillings, sir, and sixpence for a hutch to keep it in; and now he pretends he doesn't know anything about it!"

To Paul's horror two or three other boys came forward with much the same tale. He remembered now that during the holidays he had discovered that Dick was maintaining a sort of amateur menagerie in his bedroom, and that he had ordered the whole of the livestock to be got rid of or summarily destroyed.

Now it seemed that the wretched Dick had already disposed of it to these clamorous boys, and, what was worse, had stipulated with considerable forethought for payment in advance. For the first time he repented his paternal harshness. Like the netted lion, a paltry white mouse or two would have set him free; but, less happy than the beast in the fable, he had not one!

He tried to stammer out excuses. "It's extremely unfortunate," he said, "but the fact is I'm not in a position to meet this—this sudden call upon me. Some other day, perhaps——"

"None of your long words, now," growled Tipping. (Boys hate long words as much as even a Saturday Reviewer.) "Why haven't you brought the rabbits?"

"Yes," said Mr. Blinkhorn. "Why, having promised to bring the rabbits with you, haven't you kept your word? You must be able to give some explanation."

"Because," said Mr. Bultitude, wriggling with embarrassment, "I—that is my father—found out that my young rascal of a son—I mean his young rascal of a son (*me*, you know) was, contrary to my express orders, keeping a couple of abominable rabbits in his bedroom, and a quantity of filthy little white mice which he tried to train to climb up the banisters. And I kept finding the brutes running about my bath-room, and—well, of course, I put a stop to it;

and—no, what am I saying?—my father, of course, he put a stop to it; and, in point of fact, had them all drowned in a pail of water."

It might be thought that he had an excellent opportunity here of avowing himself, but there was the risk that Mr. Blinkhorn would disbelieve him, and, with the boys, he felt that the truth would do anything but increase his popularity. But dissembling fails sometimes outside the copy-books, and Mr. Bultitude's rather blundering attempt at it only landed him in worse difficulties.

There was a yell of rage and disappointment from the defrauded ones, who had cherished a lingering hope that young Bultitude had those rabbits somewhere, but (like Mr. Barkis and his wooden lemon) found himself unable to part with them when the time came to fulfil his contract. And as contempt is a frame of mind highly stimulating to one's self-esteem, even those who had no personal interest in the matter joined in the execrations with hearty goodwill and sympathy.

"Why did you let him do it? They were ours, not his. What right had your governor to go and drown our rabbits, eh?" they cried wrathfully.

"What right?" said Paul. "Mustn't a man do as he pleases in his own house, then? I—he was not obliged to see the house overrun with vermin, I suppose?"

But this only made them angrier, and they resented his defence with hoots, and groans, and hisses.

Mr. Blinkhorn meanwhile was pondering the affair conscientiously. At last he said, "But you know the Doctor would never allow animals to be kept in the school, if Bultitude had brought them. The whole thing is against the rules, and I shall not interfere."

"Ah, but," said Chawner, "he promised them all to day-boarders. The Doctor couldn't object to that, could he, sir?"

"True," said Mr. Blinkhorn, "true. I was not aware of that. Well then, Bultitude, since you are prevented from performing what you promised to do, I'm sure you won't object to do what is fair and right in the matter?"

"I don't think I quite follow you," said Mr. Bultitude. But he dreaded what was coming next.

"It's very simple. You have taken money from these boys, and if you can't give them value for it, you ought to return all you took from them. I'm sure you see that yourself."

"I don't admit that I owe them anything," said Paul; "and at all events it is highly inconvenient to pay them now."

"If your own sense of honour isn't enough," said Mr. Blinkhorn, "I must take the matter into my own hands. Let every boy who has any claim upon him tell me exactly what it is."

One boy after another brought forward his claim. One had entrusted Dick, it appeared, with a shilling, for which he was to receive a mouse with a "plum saddle," and two others had invested ninepence each in white mice. With Porter's half-crown, the total came to precisely five shillings—all Paul had in the world, the one rope by which he could ever hope to haul himself up to his lost pinnacle!

Mr. Blinkhorn, naturally enough, saw no reason why the money, being clearly due, should not be paid at once. "Give me any money you have about you, Bultitude," he said, "and I'll satisfy your debts with it, as far as it goes."

Paul clasped his arm convulsively. "No!" he cried hoarsely, "not that! Don't make me do that! I—I can't pay them—not now. They don't understand. If they only give me time they shall have double their money back—waggon-loads of rabbits, the best rabbits money can buy—if they'll wait. Tell them to wait. My dear sir, don't see me wronged! I won't pay now!"

"They have waited long enough," said Mr. Blinkhorn; "you must pay them."

"I tell you I won't!" cried Paul; "do you hear? Not one sixpence. Oh, if you knew! That infernal Garudâ Stone! What fools people are!"

Then in his despair he did the most fatal thing possible. He tried to save himself by flight, and with a violent plunge broke through the circle and made for the road which led towards the station.

Instantly the whole school, only too glad of the excitement, was at his heels. The unhappy Colonial Produce merchant ran as he had not run for a quarter of a century, faster even than he had on his first experience of Coggs' and Coker's society on that memorable Monday night. But in spite of his efforts the chase was a short one. Chawner and Tipping very soon had him by the collar, and brought him back, struggling and kicking out viciously, to Mr. Blinkhorn, whose good opinion he had now lost for ever.

"Please, sir," said Chawner, "I can feel something like a purse in his pocket. Shall I take it out, sir?"

"As he refuses to act with common honesty—yes," said Mr. Blinkhorn.

It was Dick's purse, of course; and in spite of Paul's frantic efforts to retain it, it was taken from him, its contents equitably divided amongst the claimants, and the purse itself returned to him—empty.

"Now, Bultitude," said Mr. Blinkhorn, "if you really wish to leave the field, you may."

Mr. Bultitude lost what little temper he had yet to lose; he flung the useless purse from him and broke away from them all in a condition little removed from insanity.

Leave the field! What a mockery the permission was now. How was he to get home, a distance of more than fifty miles, without a penny in his pocket? Ten minutes before, and freedom was within his grasp, and now it had eluded him and was as hopelessly out of reach as ever!

No one pitied him; no one understood the real extent of his loss. Mr. Blinkhorn and the few enthusiasts went back to their unobtrusive game, while the rest of the school discussed the affair in groups, the popular indignation against young Bultitude's hitherto unsuspected meanness growing more marked every instant.

It might have even taken some decided and objectionable form before long, but when it was at its height there was a sudden cry of alarm. "*Cave*, you fellows, here's Grim!" and indeed in the far distance the Doctor's portly and imposing figure could be seen just turning the corner into the field.

Mr. Bultitude felt almost cheered. This coming to join his pupils' sports showed a good heart; the Doctor would almost certainly be in a good humour, and he cheated himself into believing that, at some interval in the game, he might perhaps find courage to draw near and seek to interest him in his incredible woes.

It was quite extraordinary to see how the game, which had hitherto decidedly languished and hung fire, now quickened into briskness and became positively spirited. Everyone developed a hearty interest in it, and it would almost seem as if the boys, with more delicacy than they are generally credited with, were unwilling to let their master guess how little his indulgence was really appreciated. Even Mr. Tinkler, whose novel had kept him spell-bound on his rail all through the recent excitement, now slipped it hurriedly into his pocket and rushed energetically into the fray, shouting encouragement rather indiscriminately to either side, till he had an opportunity of finding out privately to which leader he had been assigned.

Dr. Grimstone came down the field at a majestic slow trot, calling out to the players as he came on—"Well done, Mutlow! Finely played, sir! Dribble it along now. Ah, you're afraid of it! Run into it, sir, run into it! No running with the ball now, Siggers; play without those petty meannesses, or leave the game! There, leave the ball to me, will you—leave it to me!"

And, as the ball had rolled in his direction, he punted it up in an exceedingly dignified manner, the whole school keeping respectfully apart, until he had brought it to a reasonable distance from the goal, when he kicked it through with great solemnity, amidst faint, and it is to be feared somewhat sycophantic applause, and turned away with the air of a man surfeited of success.

"For which side did I win that?" he asked presently, whereupon Tipping explained that his side had been the favoured one. "Well then," he said, "you fellows must all back me up, or I shall not play for you any more;" and he kicked off the ball for the next game.

It was noticeable that the party thus distinguished did not seem precisely overwhelmed with pleasure at the compliment, which, as they knew from experience, implied considerable exertion on their part, and even disgrace if they were unsuccessful.

The other side too looked unhappy, feeling themselves in a position of extreme delicacy and embarrassment. For if they played their best, they ran some risk of offending the Doctor, or, what was worse, drawing him over into their ranks; while if, on the other hand, they allowed themselves to be too easily worsted, they might be suspected of sulkiness and temper—offences which he was very ready to discover and resent.

Dr. Grimstone for his part enjoyed the exercise, and had no idea that he was not a thoroughly welcome and valued playmate. But though it was pleasant to outsiders to see a schoolmaster permitting himself to share in the recreation of his pupils, it must be owned that to the latter the advantages of the arrangement seemed something more than dubious.

Mr. Bultitude, being on the side adopted by the Doctor, found too soon that he was expected to bestir himself. More than ever anxious now to conciliate, he did his very best to conquer his natural repugnance and appear more interested than alarmed as the ball came in his way; but although (in boating slang) he "sugared" with some adroitness, he was promptly found out, for his son had been a dashing and plucky player.

It was bitter for him to run meekly about while scathing sarcasms and comments on his want of courage were being hurled at his head. It shattered the scanty remnants of his self-respect, but he dared not protest or say a single word to open the Doctor's eyes to the injustice he was doing him.

He was unpleasantly reminded, too, of the disfavour he had acquired amongst his companions, by some one or other of them running up to him every moment when the Doctor's attention was called elsewhere, and startling his nerves by a sly jog or pinch, or an abusive epithet hissed viciously into his ears—Chawner being especially industrious in this respect.

And in this unsatisfactory way the afternoon dragged along until the dusk gathered and the lamps were lighted, and it became too dark to see goal-posts or ball.

By the time play was stopped and the school reformed for the march home, Mr. Bultitude felt that he was glad even to get back to labour as a relief from such a form of enjoyment. It was perhaps the most miserable afternoon he had ever spent in his whole easy-going life. In the course of it he had passed from brightest hope to utter despair; and now nothing remained to him but to convince the Doctor, which he felt quite unequal to do, or to make his escape without money—which would inevitably end in a recapture.

May no one who reads this ever be placed upon the horns of such a dilemma!

9.
A Letter from Home

"Here are a few of the unpleasantest words

That ever blotted paper....

                               A letter,

And every word in it a gaping wound."

Merchant of Venice.

If it were not that it was so absolutely essential to the interest of this story, I think I should almost prefer to draw a veil over the sufferings of Mr. Bultitude during the rest of that unhappy week at Crichton House; but it would only be false delicacy to do so.

Things went worse and worse with him. The real Dick in his most objectionable moods could never have contrived to render himself one quarter so disliked and suspected as his substitute was by the whole school—masters and boys.

It was in a great measure his own fault, too; for to an ordinary boy the life there would not have had any intolerable hardships, if it held out no exceptional attractions. But he would not accommodate himself to circumstances, and try, during his enforced stay, to get as much instruction and enjoyment as possible out of his new life.

Perhaps, in his position, it would be too much to expect such a thing and, at all events, it never even occurred to him to attempt it. He consumed himself instead with inward raging and chafing at his hard lot, and his utter powerlessness to break the spell which bound him.

Sometimes, indeed, he would resolve to bear it no longer, and would start up impulsively to impart his misfortunes to some one in minor authority—not the Doctor, he had given that up in resigned despair long since. But as surely as ever he found himself coming to the point, the words would stick fast in his throat, and he was only too thankful to get away, with his tale untold, on any frivolous pretext that first suggested itself.

This, of course, brought him into suspicion, for such conduct had the appearance of a systematic course of practical joking, and even the most impartial teachers will sometimes form an unfavourable opinion of a particular boy on rather slender grounds, and then find fresh confirmation of it in his most insignificant actions.

As for the school generally, his scowls and his sullenness, his deficiency in the daring and impudence that had warmed their hearts towards Dick, and, above all, his strange knack of getting them into trouble—for he seldom received what he considered an indignity without making a formal complaint—all this brought him as much hearty dislike and contempt as, perhaps, the most unsympathetic boy ever earned since boarding-schools were first invented.

The only boy who still seemed to retain a secret tenderness for him, as the Dick he had once looked up to and admired, was Jolland, who persisted in believing, and in stating his belief, that this apparent change of demeanour was a perverted kind of joke on Bultitude's part, which he would condescend to explain some day when it had gone far enough, and he wearied and annoyed Paul beyond endurance by perpetually urging him to abandon his ill-judged experiment and discover the point of the jest.

But for Jolland's help, which he persevered in giving in spite of the opposition and unpopularity it brought upon himself, Mr. Bultitude would have found it impossible to make any pretence of performing the tasks required of him.

He found himself expected, as a matter of course, to have a certain familiarity with Greek paradigms and German conversation scraps, propositions in Euclid and Latin gerunds, of all of which, having had a strict commercial education in his young days, he had not so much as heard before his metamorphosis. But by carefully copying Jolland's exercises, and introducing enough mistakes of his own to supply the necessary local colour, he was able to escape to a great degree the discovery of his blank ignorance on all these subjects—an ignorance which would certainly have been put down as mere idleness and obstinacy.

But it will be readily believed that he lived in constant fear of such discovery, and as it was, his dependence on a little scamp like his son's friend was a sore humiliation to one who had naturally supposed hitherto that any knowledge he had not happened to acquire could only be meretricious and useless.

He led a nightmare sort of existence for some days, until something happened which roused him from his state of passive misery into one more attempt at protest.

It was Saturday morning, and he had come down to breakfast, after being knocked about as usual in the dormitory over night, with a dull wonder how long this horrible state of things could possibly be going to last, when he saw on his plate a letter with the Paddington post-mark, addressed in a familiar hand—his daughter Barbara's.

For an instant his hopes rose high. Surely the impostor had been found out at last, and the envelope would contain an urgent invitation to him to come back and resume his rights—an invitation which he might show to the Doctor as his best apology.

But when he looked at the address, which was "Master Richard Bultitude," he felt a misgiving. It was unlikely that Barbara would address him thus if she knew the truth; he hesitated before tearing it open.

Then he tried to persuade himself that of course she would have the sense to keep up appearances for his own sake on the outside of the letter, and he compelled himself to open the envelope with fingers that trembled nervously.

The very first sentences scattered his faint expectations to the winds. He read on with staring eyes, till the room seemed to rock with him like a packet-boat and the sprawling school-girl handwriting, crossed and recrossed on the thin paper, changed to letters of scorching flame. But perhaps it will be better to give the letter in full, so that the reader may judge for himself whether it was calculated or not to soothe and encourage the exiled one.

Here it is:

> "MY DEAREST DARLING DICK,—I hope you have not been expecting a letter from me before this, but I had such lots to tell you that I waited till I had time to tell it all at once. For I have such news for you! You can't think how pleased you will be when you hear it. Where shall I begin? I hardly know, for it still seems so funny and strange—almost like a dream—only I hope we shall never wake up.
>
> "I think I must tell you anyhow, just as it comes. Well, ever since you went away, dear Father has been completely changed; you would hardly believe it unless you saw him. He is quite jolly and boyish—only fancy! and we are always telling him he is the biggest baby of us all, but it only makes him laugh. Once, you know, he would have been awfully angry if we had even hinted at it.
>
> "Do you know, I really think that the real reason he was so cross and sharp with us that last week was because you were going away; for now the wrench of parting is over, he is quite light-hearted again. You know how he always hates showing his feelings.
>
> "He is so altered now, you can't think. He has actually only once been up to the city since you left, and then he came

home at four o'clock, and he seems to quite like to have us all about him. Generally he stays at home all the morning and plays at soldiers with baby in the dining-room. You would laugh to see him loading the cannons with real powder and shot, and he didn't care a bit when some of it made holes in the sideboard and smashed the looking-glass.

"We had such fun the other afternoon; we played at brigands—papa and all of us. Papa had the upper conservatory for a robber-cave, and stood there keeping guard with your pop-gun; and he wouldn't let the servants go by without a kiss, unless they showed a written pass from us! Miss McFadden called in the middle of it, but she said she wouldn't come in, as papa seemed to be enjoying himself so. Boaler has given warning, but we can't think why. We have been out nearly every evening—once to Hengler's and once to the Christy Minstrels, and last night to the Pantomime, where papa was so pleased with the clown that he sent round afterwards and asked him to dine here on Sunday, when Sir Benjamin and Lady Bangle and Alderman Fishwick are coming. Won't it be jolly to see a clown close to? Should you think he'd come in *his* evening dress? Miss Mangnall has been given a month's holiday, because papa didn't like to see us always at lessons. Think of that!

"We are going to have the whole house done up and refurnished at last. Papa chose the furniture for the drawing-room yesterday. It is all in yellow satin, which is rather bright, I think. I haven't seen the carpet yet, but it is to match the furniture; and there is a lovely hearthrug, with a lion-hunt worked on it.

"But that isn't the best of it; we are going to have the big children's party after all! No one but children invited, and everyone to do exactly what they like. I wanted so much to have you home for it, but papa says it would only unsettle you and take you away from your work.

"Had Dulcie forgotten you? I should like to see her so much. Now I really must leave off, as I am going to the Aquarium with papa. Mind you write me as good a letter as this is, if that old Doctor lets you. Minnie and Roly send love and kisses, and papa sends his kind regards, and I am to say he hopes you are settling down steadily to work.

"With best love, your affectionate sister,
"BARBARA BULTITUDE."

"P.S.—I nearly forgot to say that Uncle Duke came the other day and has stayed here ever since. He is going to make papa's fortune! I believe by a gold mine he knows about somewhere, and a steam tramway in Lapland. But I don't like him very much—he is so polite."

It would be nothing short of an insult to the reader's comprehension, if I were to enter into an elaborate explanation of the effect this letter had upon Mr. Bultitude. He took it in by degrees, trying to steady his nerves at each additional item of poor Barbara's well-meant intelligence by a sip at his tin-flavoured coffee. But when he came to the postscript, in spite of its purport being mercifully broken to him gradually by the extreme difficulty of making it out from two undercurrents of manuscript, he choked convulsively and spilt his coffee.

Dr. Grimstone visited this breach of etiquette with stern promptness. "This conduct at table is disgraceful, sir—perfectly disgraceful—unworthy of a civilised being. I have been a teacher of youth for many years, and never till now did I have the pain of seeing a pupil of mine choke in his breakfast-cup with such deplorable ill-breeding. It's pure greediness, sir, and you will have the goodness to curb your indecent haste in consuming your food for the future. Your excellent father has frequently complained to me, with tears in his eyes, of the impossibility of teaching you to behave at meals with common propriety!"

There was a faint chuckle along the tables, and several drank coffee with studied elegance and self-repression either as a valuable example to Dick, or as a personal advertisement. But Paul was in no mood for reproof and instruction. He stood up in his excitement, flourishing his letter wildly.

"Dr. Grimstone!" he said; "never mind my behaviour now. I've something to tell you. I can't bear it any longer. I must go home at once—at once, sir!"

There was a general sensation at this, for his manner was peremptory and almost dictatorial. Some thought he would get a licking on the strength of it, and most hoped so. But the Doctor dismissed them to the playground, keeping Paul back to be dealt with in privacy.

Mrs. Grimstone played nervously with her dry toast at the end of the table, for she could not endure to see the boys in trouble and dreaded a scene, while Dulcie looked on with wide bright eyes.

"Now, sir," said the Doctor, looking up from his marmalade, "why must you go home at once?"

"I've just had a letter," stammered Paul.

"No one ill at home, I hope?"

"No, no," said Paul. "It's not that; it's worse! She doesn't know what horrible things she tells me!"

"Who is 'she'?" said the Doctor—and Dulcie's eyes were larger still and her face paled.

"I decline to say," said Mr. Bultitude. It would have been absurd to say 'my daughter,' and he had not presence of mind just then to transpose the relationships with neatness and success. "But indeed I am wanted most badly!"

"What are you wanted for, pray?"

"Everything!" declared Paul; "it's all going to rack and ruin without me!"

"That's absurd," said the Doctor; "you're not such an important individual as all that, Bultitude. But let me see the letter."

Show him the letter—lay bare all those follies of Dick's, the burden of which he might have to bear himself very shortly—never! Besides, what would be the use of it? It would be no argument in favour of sending him home—rather the reverse—so Paul was obliged to say, "Excuse me, Dr. Grimstone, it is—ah—of a private nature. I don't feel at liberty to show it to anyone."

"Then, sir," said the Doctor, with some reason, "if you can't tell me who or what it is that requires your presence at home, and decline to show me the letter which would presumably give me some idea on the subject, how do you expect that I am to listen to such a preposterous demand—eh? Just tell me that!"

Once more would Paul have given worlds for the firmness and presence of mind to state his case clearly and effectively; and he could hardly have had a better opportunity, for schoolmasters cannot always be playing the tyrant, and the Doctor was, in spite of his attempts to be stern, secretly more amused than angry at what seemed a peculiarly precocious piece of effrontery.

But Paul felt the dismal absurdity of his position. Nothing he had said, nothing he could say, short of the truth, would avail him, and the truth was precisely what he felt most unable to tell. He hung his head resignedly, and held his tongue in confusion.

"Pooh!" said the Doctor at last; "let me have no more of this tomfoolery, Bultitude. It's getting to be a positive nuisance. Don't come to me with any more of these ridiculous stories, or some day I shall be annoyed. There, go away, and be contented where you are, and try to behave like other people."

"'Contented!'" muttered Paul, when out of hearing, as he went upstairs and through the empty schoolroom into the playground. "'Behave like other people!' Ah, yes, I suppose I shall have to come to that in time. But that letter—— Everything upside down—— Bangle asked to meet a common clown! That fellow Duke letting me in for gold-mines and tramways! It's all worse than I ever dreamed of; and I must stay here and be 'contented!' It's—it's perfectly damnable!"

All through that morning his thoughts ran in the same doleful groove, until the time for work came to an end, and he found himself in the playground, and free to indulge his melancholy for a few minutes in solitude; for the others were still loitering about in the schoolroom, and a glass outhouse originally intended for a conservatory, but now devoted to boots and slates, and the books liberally besmeared with gilt, and telling of the exploits of boy-heroes so beloved of boys.

Mr. Bultitude, only too delighted to get away from them for a little while, was leaning against the parallel bars in dull despondency, when he heard a rustling in the laurel hedge which cut off the house garden from the gravelled playground, and looking up, saw Dulcie slip through the shrubs and come towards him with an air of determination in her proud little face.

She looked prettier and daintier than ever in her grey hat and warm fur tippet; but of course Paul was not of the age or in the mood to be much affected by such things—he turned his head pettishly away.

"It's no use doing that, Dick," she said: "I'm tired of sulking. I shan't sulk any more till I have an explanation."

Paul made the sound generally written "Pshaw!"

"You ought to tell me everything. I will know it. Oh, Dick, you might tell me! I always told you anything you wanted to know; and I let mamma think it was I broke the clock-shade last term, and you know you did it. And I want to know something so very badly!"

"It's no use coming to *me*, you know," said Paul. "I can't do anything for you."

"Yes, you can; you know you can!" said Dulcie impulsively. "You can tell me what was in that letter you had at breakfast—and you shall too!"

"What an inquisitive little girl you are," said Paul sententiously. "It's not nice for little girls to be so inquisitive—it doesn't look well."

"I knew it!" cried Dulcie; "you don't want to tell me—because—because it's from that other horrid girl you like better than me. And you promised to belong to me for ever and ever, and now it's all over! Say it isn't! Oh, Dick, promise to give the other girl up. I'm sure she's not a nice girl. She's written you an unkind letter; now hasn't she?"

"Upon my word," said Paul, "this is very forward; at your age too. Why, my Barbara——"

"Your Barbara! you dare to call her that? Oh, I knew I was right; I *will* see that letter now. Give it me this instant!" said Dulcie imperiously; and Paul really felt almost afraid of her.

"No, no," he said, retreating a step or two, "it's all a mistake; there's nothing to get into such a passion about—there isn't indeed! And—don't cry—you're really a pretty little girl. I only wish I could tell you everything; but you'd never believe me!"

"Oh, yes, I would, Dick!" protested Dulcie, only too willing to be convinced of her boy-lover's constancy; "I'll believe anything, if you'll only tell me. And I'm sorry I was so angry. Sit down by me and tell me from the very beginning. I promise not to interrupt."

Paul thought for a moment. After all, why shouldn't he? It was much pleasanter to tell his sorrows to her little ear and hear her childish wonder and pity than face her terrible father—he had tried that. And then she might tell her mother; and so his story might reach the Doctor's ears after all, without further effort on his part.

"Well," he said at last, "I think you're a good-natured little girl; you won't laugh. Perhaps I will tell you!"

So he sat down on the bench by the wall, and Dulcie, quite happy again now at this proof of good faith, nestled up against him confidingly, waiting for his first words with parted lips and eager sparkling eyes.

"Not many days ago," began Paul, "I was somebody very different from——"

"Oh, indeed," said a jarring, sneering voice close by; "was you?" And he looked up and saw Tipping standing over him with a plainly hostile intent.

"Go away, Tipping," said Dulcie; "we don't want you. Dick is telling me a secret."

"He's very fond of telling, I know," retorted Tipping. "If you knew what a sneak he was you'd have nothing to do with him, Dulcie. I could tell you things about him that——"

"He's not a sneak," said Dulcie. "Are you, Dick? Why don't you go, Tipping. Never mind what he says, Dick; go on as if he wasn't there. I don't care what he says!"

It was a most unpleasant situation for Mr. Bultitude, but he did not like to offend Tipping. "I—I think—some other time, perhaps," he said nervously. "Not now."

"Ah, you're afraid to say what you were going to say now I'm here," said the amiable Tipping, nettled by Dulcie's little air of haughty disdain. "You're a coward; you know you are. You pretend to think such a lot of Dulcie here, but you daren't fight!"

"Fight!" said Mr. Bultitude. "Eh, what for?"

"Why, for her, of course. You can't care much about her if you daren't fight for her. I want to show her who's the best man of the two!"

"I don't want to be shown," wailed poor Dulcie piteously, clinging to the reluctant Paul; "I know. Don't fight with him, Dick. I say you're not to."

"Certainly not!" said Mr. Bultitude with great decision. "I shouldn't think of such a thing!" and he rose from the bench and was about to walk away, when Tipping suddenly pulled off his coat and began to make sundry demonstrations of a martial nature, such as dancing aggressively towards his rival and clenching his fists.

By this time most of the other boys had come down into the playground, and were looking on with great interest. There was an element of romance in this promised combat which gave it additional attractions. It was like one of the struggles between knightly champions in the Waverley novels. Several of them would have fought till they couldn't see out of their eyes if it would have given them the least chance of obtaining favour in Dulcie's sight, and they all envied Dick, who was the only boy that was not unmercifully snubbed by their capricious little princess.

Paul alone was blind to the splendour of his privileges. He examined Tipping carefully, as the latter was still assuming a hostile attitude and chanting a sort of war-cry supposed to be an infallible incentive to strife.

"Yah, you're afraid!" he sang very offensively. "I wouldn't be a funk!"

"Pooh!" said Paul at last; "go away, sir, go away!"

"Go away, eh?" jeered Tipping. "Who are you to tell me to go away? Go away yourself!"

"Certainly," said Paul, only too happy to oblige. But he found himself prevented by a ring of excited backers.

"Don't funk it, Dick!" cried some, forgetting recent ill-feeling in the necessity for partisanship. "Go in and settle him as you did that last time. I'll second you. You can do it!"

"Don't hit each other in the face," pleaded Dulcie, who had got upon a bench and was looking down into the ring—not, if the truth must be told, without a certain pleasurable excitement in the feeling that it was all about her.

And now Mr. Bultitude discovered that he was seriously expected to fight this great hulking boy, and that the sole reason for any disagreement was an utterly unfounded jealousy respecting this little girl Dulcie. He had not a grain of chivalry in his disposition—chivalry being an eminently unpractical virtue—and naturally he saw no advantage in letting himself be mauled for the sake of a child younger than his own daughter.

Dulcie's appeal enraged Tipping, who took it as addressed solely to himself. "You ought to be glad to stick up for her," he said between his teeth. "I'll mash you for this—see if I don't!"

Paul thought he saw his way clear to disabuse Tipping of his mistaken idea. "Are you proposing," he asked politely, "to—to 'mash' me on account of that little girl there on the seat?"

"You'll soon see," growled Tipping. "Shut your head, and come on!"

"No, but I want to know," persisted Mr. Bultitude. "Because," he said with a sickly attempt at jocularity which delighted none, "you see, I don't want to be mashed. I'm not a potato. If I understand you aright, you want to fight me because you think me likely to interfere with your claim to that little girl's—ah—affections?"

"That's it," said Tipping gruffly; "so you'd better waste no more words about it, and come on."

"But I don't care about coming on," protested Paul earnestly. "It's all a mistake. I've no doubt she's a very nice little girl, but I assure you, my good boy, I've no desire to stand in your way for one instant. She's nothing to me—nothing at all! I give her up to you. Take her, young fellow, with my blessing! There, now, that's all settled comfortably—eh?"

He was just looking round with a self-satisfied and relieved air, when he began to be aware that his act of frank unselfishness was not as much appreciated as it deserved. Tipping, indeed, looked baffled and irresolute for one moment, but a low murmur of disgust arose from the bystanders, and even Jolland declared that it was "too beastly mean."

As for Dulcie, she had been looking on incredulously at her champion's unaccountable tardiness in coming to the point. But this public repudiation was too much for her. She gave a little low wail as she heard the shameless words of recantation, and then, without a word, jumped lightly down from her bench and ran away to hide herself somewhere and cry.

Even Paul, though he knew that he had done nothing but what was strictly right, and had acted purely in self-protection, felt unaccountably ashamed of himself as he saw this effect of his speech. But it was too late now.

10.
The Complete Letter-Writer

> "Accelerated by ignominious shovings—nay, as it is written, by smitings, twitchings, spurnings *à posteriori* not to be named."—*French Revolution.*

> "This letter being so excellently ignorant will breed no terror in the youth."—*Twelfth Night.*

Mr. Bultitude had meant to achieve a double stroke of diplomacy—to undeceive Dulcie and conciliate the lovesick Tipping. But whatever his success may have been in the former respect, the latter object failed conspicuously.

"You shan't get off by a shabby trick like that," said Tipping, exasperated by the sight of Dulcie's emotion; "you've made her cry now, and you shall smart for it. So, now, are you going to stand up to me like a man, or will you take a licking?"

"I'm not going to help you to commit a breach of the peace," said Paul with great dignity. "Go away, you quarrelsome young ruffian! Get one of your schoolfellows to fight you, if you must fight. I don't want to be mixed up with you in any way."

But at this Tipping, whose blood was evidently at boiling point, came prancing down on him in a Zulu-like fashion, swinging his long arms like a windmill, and finding that his enemy made no attempt at receiving him, but only moved away apprehensively, he seized him by the collar as a prelude to dealing him a series of kicks behind.

Although Mr. Bultitude, as we have seen, was opposed to fighting as a system he could not submit to this sort of thing without at least some attempt to defend himself; and judging it of the highest importance to disable his adversary in the most effectual manner before the latter had time to carry out his offensive designs, he turned sharply round and hit him a very severe blow in the lower part of his waistcoat.

The result fulfilled his highest expectations. Tipping collapsed like a pocket-rule, and staggered away speechless, and purple with pain, while Paul stood calm and triumphant. He had shown these fellows that he wasn't going to stand any nonsense. They would leave him alone after this, perhaps.

But once more there were cries and murmurs of "Shame!" "No hitting below the belt!" "Cad—coward!"

It appeared that, somehow, he had managed to offend their prejudices even in this. "It's very odd," he thought; "when I didn't fight they called me a coward, and now, when I do, I don't seem to have pleased them much. I don't care, though. I've settled *him*."

But after a season of protracted writhing by the parallel bars, Tipping came out, still gasping and deadly pale, leaning on Biddlecomb's shoulder, and was met with universal sympathy and condolence.

"Thanks!" he said with considerable effort. "Of course—I'm not going—to fight him after a low trick like that; but perhaps you fellows will see that he doesn't escape quite as easily as he fancies?"

There was a general shout. "No; he shall pay for it! We'll teach him to fight fair! We'll see if he tries that on again!"

Paul heard it with much uneasiness. What new devilry were they about to practise upon him? He was not left long in doubt.

"I vote," suggested Biddlecomb, as if he were proposing a testimonial, "we make him run the gauntlet. Grim won't come out and catch us. I saw him go out for a drive an hour ago." And the idea was very favourably entertained.

Paul had heard of "running the gauntlet," and dimly suspected that it was not an experience he was likely to enjoy, particularly when he saw everyone busying himself with tying the end of his pocket-handkerchief into a hard knot. He tried in vain to excuse himself, declaring again and again that he had never meant to injure the boy. He had only defended himself, and was under the impression that he was at perfect liberty to hit him wherever he could, and so on. But they were in no mood for excuses.

With a stern magisterial formality worthy of a Vehm-Gericht, they formed in two long lines down the centre of the playground; and while Paul was still staring in wonder at what this strange manœuvre might mean, somebody pounced upon him and carried him up to one end of the ranks, where Tipping had by this time sufficiently recovered to be able to "set him going," as he chose to call it, with a fairly effective kick.

After that he had a confused sense of flying madly along the double line of avengers under a hail of blows which caught him on every part of his head, shoulders, and back till he reached the end, where he was dexterously turned and sent spinning up to Tipping again, who in his turn headed him back on his arrival, and forced him to brave the terrible lane once more.

Never before had Mr. Bultitude felt so sore and insulted. But they kept it up long after the thing had lost its first freshness—until at last exhaustion made them lean to mercy, and they cuffed him ignominiously into a corner, and left him to lament his ill-treatment there till the bell rang for dinner, for which, contrary to precedent, his recent violent exercise had excited little appetite.

"I shall be killed soon if I stay here," he moaned; "I know I shall. These young brigands would murder me cheerfully, if they were not afraid of being caned for it. I'm a miserable man, and I wish I was dead!"

Although that afternoon, being Saturday, was a half-holiday, Mr. Bultitude was spared the ordeal of another game at football; for a smart storm of rain and sleet coming on about three o'clock kept the school—not altogether unwilling prisoners—within doors for the day.

The boys sat in their places in their schoolroom, amusing themselves after their several fashions—some reading, some making libellous copies of drawings that took their fancy in the illustrated papers, some playing games; others, too listless to play and too dull to find pleasure in the simplest books, filled up the time as well as they could by quarrelling and getting into various depths of hot water. Paul sat in a corner pretending to read a story relating the experiences of certain infants of phenomenal courage and coolness in the Arctic regions. They killed bears and tamed walruses all through the book; but for the first time, perhaps, since their appearance in print their exploits fell flat. Not, however, that this reflected any discredit upon the author's powers, which are justly admired by all healthy-minded boys; but it was beyond the power of literature just then to charm Mr. Bultitude's thoughts from the recollection of his misfortunes.

As he took in all the details of his surroundings—the warm close room; the raw-toned desks and tables at which a rabble of unsympathetic boys were noisily whispering and chattering, with occasional glances in his direction, from which, taught by experience, he augured no good; the high uncurtained windows, blurred with little stars of half-frozen rain, and the bare, bleak branches of the trees outside tossing drearily against a low leaden sky—he tried in vain to cheat himself into a dreamy persuasion that all this misery could not be real, but would fade away as suddenly and mysteriously as it had stolen upon him.

Towards the close of the afternoon the Doctor came in and took his place at the writing-table, where he was apparently very busy with the composition of some sort of document, which he finished at last with evident satisfaction at the result of his labour. Then he observed that, according to their custom of a Saturday afternoon, the hour before tea-time should be devoted to "writing home."

So the books, chess-boards, and dominoes were all put away, and a new steel pen and a sheet of notepaper, neatly embossed with the heading "Crichton House School" in old English letters, having been served out to everyone, each boy prepared himself to write down such things as filial affection, strict truthfulness, and the desire of imparting information might inspire between them.

Paul felt, as he clutched his writing materials, much as a shipwrecked mariner might be expected to do at finding on his desolate island a good-sized flag and a case of rockets. His hopes revived once more; he forgot the smarts left by the knots in the handkerchiefs, he had a whole hour before him—it was possible to set several wires in motion for his release in an hour.

Yes, he must write several letters. First, one to his solicitor detailing, as calmly and concisely as his feelings would allow, the shameful way in which he had been treated, and imploring him to take measures of some sort for getting him out of his false and awkward position; one to his head clerk, to press upon him the necessity of prudence and caution in dealing with the impostor; notes to Bangle and Fishwick putting them off—they should not be outraged by an introduction to a vulgar pantomime clown under his roof; and lastly (this was an outburst he could not deny himself), a solemn impressive appeal to the common humanity, if not to the ordinary filial instincts, of his undutiful son.

His fingers tingled to begin. Sentences of burning, indignant eloquence crowded confusedly into his head—he would write such letters as would carry instant conviction to the most practical and matter-of-fact minds. The pathos and dignity of his remonstrances should melt even Dick's selfish, callous heart.

Perhaps he overrated the power of his pen—perhaps it would have required more than mere ink to persuade his friends to disbelieve their own senses, and see a portly citizen of over fifty packed into the frame of a chubby urchin of fourteen. But, at all events, no one's faith was put to so hard a test—those letters were never written.

"Don't begin to write yet, any of you," said the Doctor; "I have a few words to say to you first. In most cases, and as a general rule, I think it wisest to let every boy commit to paper whatever his feelings may dictate to him. I wish to claim no censorship over the style and diction of your letters. But there have been so many complaints lately from the parents of some of the less advanced of you, that I find myself obliged to make a change. Your father particularly, Richard Bultitude," he added, turning suddenly upon the unlucky Paul, "has complained bitterly of the slovenly tone and phrasing of your correspondence; he said very justly that they would disgrace a stable-boy, and unless I could induce you to improve them, he begged he might not be annoyed by them in future."

It was by no means the least galling part of Mr. Bultitude's trials, that former forgotten words and deeds of his in his original condition were constantly turning up at critical seasons, and plunging him deeper into the morass just when he saw some prospect of gaining firm ground.

So, on this occasion, he did remember that, being in a more than usually bad temper one day last year, he had, on receiving a sprawling, ill-spelt application from Dick for more pocket-money, to buy fireworks for the 5th of November, written to make some such complaint to the schoolmaster. He waited anxiously for the Doctor's next words; he might want to read the letters before they were sent off, in which case Paul would not be displeased, for it would be an easier and less dangerous way of putting the Doctor in possession of the facts.

But his complaints were to be honoured by a much more effectual remedy, for it naturally piqued the Doctor to be told that boys instructed under his auspices wrote like stable-boys. "However," he went on, "I wish your people at home to be assured from time to time of your welfare, and to prevent them from being shocked and distressed in future by the crudity of your communications, I have drawn up a short form of letter for the use of the lower boys in the second form—which I shall now proceed to dictate. Of course all boys in the first form, and all in the second above Bultitude and Jolland, will write as they please, as usual. Richard, I expect you to take particular pains to write this out neatly. Are you all ready? Very well then, ... now;" and he read out the following letter, slowly—

"My dear Parents (or parent according to circumstances) comma" (all of which several took down most industriously)—"You will be rejoiced to hear that, having arrived with safety at our destination, we have by this time fully resumed our customary regular round of earnest work relieved and sweetened by hearty play. ('Have you all got "hearty play" down?'" inquired the Doctor rather suspiciously, while Jolland observed in an undertone that it would take some time to get *that* down.) "I hope, I trust I may say without undue conceit, to have made considerable progress in my school-tasks before I rejoin the family circle for the Easter vacation, as I think you will admit when I inform you of the programme we intend" ('D.V. in brackets and capital letters'—as before, this was taken down verbatim by Jolland, who probably knew very much better), "intend to work out during the term.

"In Latin, the class of which I am a member propose to thoroughly master the first book of Virgil's magnificent Epic, need I say I refer to the soul-moving story of the Pious Æneas?" (Jolland was understood by his near neighbours to remark that he thought the explanation distinctly advisable), "whilst, in Greek, we have already commenced the thrilling account of the 'Anabasis' of Xenophon, that master of strategy! nor shall we, of course, neglect in either branch of study the syntax and construction of those two noble languages"—("noble languages," echoed the writers mechanically, contriving to insinuate a touch of irony into the words).

"In German under the able tutelage of Herr Stohwasser, who, as I may possibly have mentioned to you in casual conversation, is a graduate of the University of Heidelberg" ("and a silly old hass," added Jolland parenthetically), "we have resigned ourselves to the spell of the Teutonian Shakespeare" (there was much difference of opinion as to the manner of spelling the "Teutonian Shakespeare"), "as, in my opinion, Schiller may be not inaptly termed, and our French studies comprise such exercises, and short poems and tales, as are best calculated to afford an insight into the intricacies of the Gallic tongue.

"But I would not have you imagine, my dear parents (or parent, as before), that, because the claims of the intellect have been thus amply provided for, the requirements of the body are necessarily overlooked!

"I have no intention of becoming a mere bookworm, and, on the contrary, we have had one excessively brisk and pleasant game at football already this season, and should, but for the unfortunate inclemency of the weather, have engaged again this afternoon in the mimic warfare.

"In the playground our favourite diversion is the game of 'chevy,' so called from the engagement famed in ballad and history (I allude to the battle of Chevy Chase), and indeed, my dear parents, in the rapid alternations of its fortunes and the diversity of its incident, the game (to my mind) bears a striking resemblance to the accounts of that ever-memorable contest.

"I fear I must now relinquish my pen, as the time allotted for correspondence is fast waning to its close, and tea-time is approaching. Pray give my kindest remembrance to all my numerous friends and relatives, and accept my fondest love and affection for yourselves, and the various other members of the family circle.

"I am, I am rejoiced to say, in the enjoyment of excellent health, and surrounded as I am by congenial companions, and employed in interesting and agreeable pursuits, it is superfluous to add that I am happy.

"And now, my dear parents, believe me, your dutiful and affectionate son, so and so."

The Doctor finished his dictation with a roll in his voice, as much as to say, "I think that will strike your respective parents as a chaste and classical composition; I think so!"

But unexceptionable as its tone and sentiments undoubtedly were, it was far from expressing the feelings of Mr. Bultitude. The rest accepted it not unwillingly as an escape from the fatigue of original composition, but to him the neat, well-balanced sentences seemed a hollow mockery. As he wrote down each successive phrase, he wondered what Dick would think of it, and when at last it was finished, the precious hour had gone for another week!

In speechless disgust but without protest, for his spirit was too broken by this last cruel disappointment, he had to fold, put into an envelope and direct this most misleading letter under the Doctor's superintending eye, which of course allowed him no chance of introducing a line or even a word to counteract the tone of self-satisfaction and contentment which breathed in every sentence of it.

He saw it stamped, and put into the postbag, and then his last gleam of hope flickered out; he must give up struggling against the Inevitable; he must resign himself to be educated, and perhaps flogged here, while Dick was filling his house with clowns and pantaloons, destroying his reputation and damaging his credit at home. Perhaps, in course of time, he would grow accustomed to it, and, meanwhile, he would be as careful as possible to do and say nothing to make himself remarkable in any way, by which means he trusted, at least, to avoid any fresh calamity.

And with this resolution he went to bed on Saturday night, feeling that this was a dreary finish to a most unpleasant week.

11.
A Day of Rest

"There was a letter indeed to be intercepted by a man's father to do him good with him!"—*Every Man in his Humour.*

"I cannot lose the thought yet of this letter,

Sent to my son; nor leave t' admire the change

Of manners, and the breeding of our youth

Within the kingdom, since myself was one."—*Ibid.*

Sunday came—a day which was to begin a new week for Mr. Bultitude, and, of course, for the rest of the Christian world as well. Whether that week would be better or worse than the one which had just passed away he naturally could not tell—it could hardly be much worse.

But the Sunday itself, he anticipated, without, however, any very firm grounds for such an assumption, would be a day of brief but grateful respite; a day on which he might venture to claim much the same immunity as was enjoyed in former days by the insolvent; a day, in short, which would glide slowly by with the rather drowsy solemnity peculiar to the British sabbath as observed by all truly respectable persons.

And yet that very Sunday, could he have foreseen it, was destined to be the most eventful day he had yet spent at Crichton House, where none had proved wanting in incident. During the next twelve hours he was to pass through every variety of unpleasant sensation. Embarrassment, suspense, fear, anxiety, dismay, and terror were to follow each other in rapid succession, and to wind up, strangely enough, with a delicious ecstasy of pure relief and happiness—a fatiguing programme for any middle-aged gentleman who had never cultivated his emotional faculties.

Let me try to tell how this came about. The getting-up bell rang an hour later than on week-days, but the boys were expected to prepare certain tasks suitable for the day before they rose. Mr. Bultitude found that he was required to learn by heart a hymn in which the rhymes "join" and "divine," "throne" and "crown," were so happily wedded that either might conform to the other—a graceful concession to individual taste which is not infrequent in this class of poetry. Trivial as such a task may seem in these days of School Boards, it gave him infinite trouble and mental exertion, for he had not been called upon to commit anything of the kind to memory for many years, and after mastering that, there still remained a long chronological list (the dates approximately computed) of the leading events before and immediately after the Deluge, which was to be repeated "without looking at the book."

While he was wrestling desperately with these, for he was determined, as I have said before, to do all in his power to keep himself out of trouble, Mrs. Grimstone, in her morning wrapper, paid a visit to the dormitories and, in spite of all Paul's attempts to excuse himself, insisted upon pomatuming his hair—an indignity which he felt acutely.

"When she knows who I really am," he thought, "she'll be sorry she made such a point of it. If there's one thing upon earth I loathe more than another, it's marrow-oil pomade!"

Then there was breakfast, at which Dr. Grimstone appeared, resplendent in glossy broadcloth, and dazzling shirt-front and semi-clerical white tie, and after breakfast, an hour in the schoolroom, during which the boys (by the aid of repeated references to the text) wrote out "from memory" the hymn they had learnt, while Paul managed somehow to stumble through his dates and events to the satisfaction of Mr. Tinkler, who, to increase his popularity, made a point of being as easily satisfied with such repetitions as he decently could.

After that came the order to prepare for church. There was a general rush to the little room with the shelves and bandboxes, where church books were procured, and great-coats and tight kid gloves put on.

When they were almost ready the Doctor came in, wearing his blandest and most paternal expression.

"A—it's a collection Sunday to-day, boys," he said. "Have you all got your threepenny-bits ready? I like to see my boys give cheerfully and liberally of their abundance. If any boy does not happen to have any small change, I can accommodate him if he comes to me."

And this he proceeded to do from a store he had with him of that most convenient coin—the chosen expression of a congregation's gratitude—the common silver threepence, for the school occupied a prominent position in the church, and had acquired a great reputation amongst the churchwardens for the admirable uniformity with which one young gentleman after another "put into the plate"; and this reputation the Doctor was naturally anxious that they should maintain.

I am sorry to say that Mr. Bultitude, fearing lest he should be asked if he had the required sum about him, and thus his penniless condition might be discovered and bring him trouble, got behind the door at the beginning of the money-changing transactions and remained there till it was over—it seemed to him that it would be too paltry to be disgraced for want of threepence.

Now, being thus completely furnished for their devotions, the school formed in couples in the hall and filed solemnly out for the march to church.

Mr. Bultitude walked nearly last with Jolland, whose facile nature had almost forgotten his friend's shortcomings on the previous day. He kept up a perpetual flow of chatter which, as he never stopped for an answer, permitted Paul to indulge his own thoughts unrestrained.

"Are you going to put your threepenny-bit in?" said Jolland; "I won't if you don't. Sometimes, you know, when the plate comes round, old Grim squints down the pews to see we don't shirk. Then I put in sixpence. Have you done your hymn? I do hate a hymn. What's the use of learning hymns? They won't mark you for them, you know, in any exam. I ever heard of, and it can't save you the expense of a hymnbook unless you learnt all the hymns in it, and that would take you years. Oh, I say, look! there's young Mutlow and his governor and mater. I wonder what Mutlow's governor does? Mutlow says he's a 'gentleman' if you ask him, but I believe he lies. See that fly driving past? Mother Grim" (the irreverent youth always spoke of Mrs. Grimstone in this way) "and Dulcie are in it. I saw Dulcie look at you, Dick. It's a shame to treat her as you did yesterday. There's young Tom on the box; don't his ears stick out rummily? I wonder if the 'ugly family' will be at church to-day? You know the ugly family; all with their mouths open and their eyes goggling, like a jolly old row of pantomime heads. And oh, Dick, suppose Connie Davenant's people have changed their pew—that'll be a sell for you rather, won't it?"

"I don't understand you," said Mr. Bultitude stiffly; "and, if you don't object, I prefer not to be called upon to talk just now."

"Oh, all right!" said Jolland, "there aren't so many fellows who will talk to you; but just as you please—I don't want to talk."

And so the pair walked on in silence; Jolland with his nose in the air, determined that after this he really must cut his former friend as the other fellows had done, since his devotion was appreciated so little, and Paul watching the ascending double line of tall chimney-pot hats as they surged before him in regular movement, and feeling a dull wonder at finding himself setting out to church in such ill-assorted company.

They entered the church, and Paul was sent down to the extreme end of a pew next to the one reserved for the Doctor and his family. Dulcie was sitting there already on the other side of the partition; but she gave no sign of having noticed his arrival, being apparently absorbed in studying the rose-window over the altar.

He sat down in his corner with a sense of rest and almost comfort, though the seat was not a cushioned one. He had the inoffensive Kiffin for a neighbour, his chief tormentors were far away from him in one of the back pews, and here at least he thought no harm could come to him. He could allow himself safely to do what I am afraid he generally did do under the circumstances—snatch a few intermittent but sweet periods of dreamless slumber.

But, while the service was proceeding, Mr. Bultitude was suddenly horrified to observe that a young lady, who occupied a pew at right angles to and touching that in which he sat, was deliberately making furtive signals to him in a most unmistakable manner.

She was a decidedly pretty girl of about fifteen, with merry and daring blue eyes and curling golden hair, and was accompanied by two small brothers (who shared the same book and dealt each other stealthy and vicious kicks throughout the service), and by her father, a stout, short-sighted old gentleman in gold spectacles, who was perpetually making the wrong responses in a loud and confident tone.

To be signalled to in a marked manner by a strange young lady of great personal attractions might be a coveted distinction to other schoolboys, but it simply gave Mr. Bultitude cold thrills.

"I suppose *that's* 'Connie Davenant,'" he thought, shocked beyond measure as she caught his eye and coughed demurely for about the fourth time. "A very forward young person! I think somebody ought to speak seriously to her father."

"Good gracious! she's writing something on the flyleaf of her prayer-book," he said to himself presently. "I hope she's not going to send it to *me*. I won't take it. She ought to be ashamed of herself!"

Miss Davenant was indeed busily engaged in pencilling something on a blank sheet of paper; and, having finished, she folded it deftly into a cocked-hat, wrote a few words on the outside, and placed it between the leaves of her book.

Then, as the congregation rose for the Psalms, she gave a meaning glance at the blushing and scandalised Mr. Bultitude and by dexterous management of her prayer-book shot the little cocked-hat, as if unconsciously, into the next pew.

By a very unfortunate miscalculation, however, the note missed its proper object, and, clearing the partition, fluttered deliberately down on the floor by Dulcie's feet.

Paul saw this with alarm; he knew that at all hazards he must get that miserable note into his own possession and destroy it. It might have his name somewhere about it; it might seriously compromise him.

So he took advantage of the noise the congregation made in repeating a verse aloud (it was not a high church) to whisper to Dulcie: "Little Miss Grimstone, excuse me, but there's a—a note in the pew down by your feet. I believe it's intended for me."

Dulcie had seen the whole affair and had been not a little puzzled by it, a clandestine correspondence being a new thing in her short experience; but she understood that in this golden-haired girl, her elder by several years, she saw her rival, for whom Dick had so basely abandoned her yesterday, and she was old enough to feel the slight and the sweetness of revenge.

So she held her head rather higher than usual, with her firm little chin projecting wilfully, and waited for the next verse but one before retorting, "Little Master Bultitude, I know it is."

"Could you—can you manage to reach it?" whispered Paul entreatingly.

"Yes," said Dulcie, "I could."

"Then will you—when they sit down?"

"No," said Dulcie firmly, "I shan't."

The other girl, she noticed with satisfaction, had become aware of the situation and was evidently uneasy. She looked as imploringly as she dared at remorseless little Dulcie, as if appealing to her not to get her into trouble; but Dulcie bent her eyes obstinately on her book and would not see her.

If the letter had been addressed to any other boy in the school, she would have done her best to shield the culprits; but this she could not bring herself to do here. She found a malicious pleasure in remaining absolutely neutral, which of course was very wrong and ill-natured of her.

Mr. Bultitude began now to be seriously alarmed. The fatal paper must be seen by some one in the Doctor's pew as soon as the congregation sat down again; and, if it reached the Doctor's hands, it was impossible to say what misconstruction he might put upon it or what terrible consequences might not follow.

He was innocent, perfectly innocent; but though the consciousness of innocence is frequently a great consolation, he felt that unless he could imbue the Doctor with it as well, it would not save him from a flogging.

So he made one more desperate attempt to soften Dulcie's resolution: "Don't be a naughty little girl," he said, very injudiciously for his purpose, "I tell you I must have it. You'll get me into a terrible mess if you're not careful!"

But although Dulcie had been extremely well brought up, I regret to say that the only answer she chose to make to this appeal was that slight contortion of the features, which with a pretty girl is euphemised as a "*moue*," and with a plain one is called "making a face." When he saw it he knew that all hope of changing her purpose must be abandoned.

Then they all sat down, and, as Paul had foreseen, there the white cocked-hat lay on the dark pew-carpet, hideously distinct, with *billet doux* in every fold of it!

It could only be a question of time now. The curate was reading the first lesson for the day, but Mr. Bultitude heard not a verse of it. He was waiting with bated breath for the blow to fall.

It fell at last. Dulcie, either with the malevolent idea of hastening the crisis, or (which I prefer to believe for my own part) finding that her ex-lover's visible torments were too much for her desire of vengeance, was softly moving a heavy hassock towards the guilty note. The movement caught her mother's eye, and in an instant the compromising paper was in her watchful hands.

She read it with incredulous horror, and handed it at once to the Doctor.

The golden-haired one saw it all without betraying herself by any outward confusion. She had probably had some experience in such matters, and felt tolerably certain of being able, at the worst, to manage the old gentleman in the gold spectacles. But she took an early opportunity of secretly conveying her contempt for the traitress Dulcie, who continued to meet her angry glances with the blandest unconsciousness.

Dr. Grimstone examined the cocked-hat through his double eyeglasses, with a heavy thunder-cloud gathering on his brows. When he had mastered it thoroughly, he bent forward and glared indignantly past his wife and daughter for at least half a minute into the pew where Mr. Bultitude was cowering, until he felt that he was coming all to pieces under the piercing gaze.

The service passed all too quickly after that. Paul sat down and stood up almost unconsciously with the rest; but for the first time in his life he could have wished the sermon many times longer.

The horror of his position quite petrified him. After all his prudent resolutions to keep out of mischief and to win the regard and confidence of his gaoler by his good conduct, like the innocent convict in a melodrama, this came as nothing less than a catastrophe. He walked home in a truly dismal state of limp terror.

Fortunately for him none of the others seemed to have noticed his misfortune, and Jolland made no further advances. But even the weather tended to increase his depression, for it was a bleak, cheerless day, with a bitter and searching wind sweeping the gritty roads where yesterday's rain was turned to black ice in the ruts, and the sun shone with a dull coppery glitter that had no warmth or geniality about it.

The nearer they came to Crichton House the more abjectly miserable became Mr. Bultitude's state of mind. It was as much as he could do to crawl up the steps to the front door, and his knees positively clapped together when the Doctor, who had driven home, met them in the hall and said in a still grave voice, "Bultitude, when you have taken off your coat, I want you in the study."

He was as long about taking off his coat as he dared, but at last he went trembling into the study, which he found empty. He remembered the room well, with its ebony-framed etchings on the walls, bookcases and blue china over the draped mantelpiece, even to a large case of elaborately carved Indian chessmen in bullock-carts and palanquins, on horses and elephants, which stood in the window-recess. It was the very room to which he had been shown when he first called about sending his son to the school. He had little thought then that the time would come when he would attend there for the purpose of being flogged; few things would have seemed less probable. Yet here he was.

But his train of thought was abruptly broken by the entrance of the Doctor. He marched solemnly in, holding out the offending missive. "Look at this, sir!" he said, shaking it angrily before Paul's eyes. "Look at this! what do you mean by receiving a flippant communication like this in a sacred edifice? What do you mean by it?"

"I—I didn't receive it," said Paul, at his wits' end.

"Don't prevaricate with me, sir; you know well enough it was intended for you. Have the goodness to read it now, and tell me what you have to say for yourself!"

Paul read it. It was a silly little school-girl note, half slang and half sentiment, signed only with the initials C.D. "Well, sir?" said the Doctor.

"It's very forward and improper—very," said Paul; "but it's not my fault—I can't help it. I gave the girl no encouragement. I never saw her before in all my life!"

"To my own knowledge, Bultitude, she has sat in that pew regularly for a year."

"Very probably," said Paul, "but I don't notice these matters. I'm past that sort of thing, my dear sir."

"What is her name? Come, sir, you know that."

"Connie Davenant," said Paul, taken unawares by the suddenness of the question. "At least, I—I heard so to-day." He felt the imprudence of such an admission as soon as he had made it.

"Very odd that you know her name if you never noticed her before," said the Doctor.

"That young fellow—what's-his-name—Jolland told me," said Paul.

"Ah, but it's odder still that she knows yours, for I perceive it is directed to you by name."

"It's easily explained, my dear sir," said Paul; "easily explained. I've no doubt she's heard it somewhere. At least, I never told her; it is not likely. I do assure you I'm as much distressed and shocked by this affair as you can be yourself. I am indeed. I don't know what girls are coming to nowadays."

"Do you expect me to believe that you are perfectly innocent?" said the Doctor.

"Yes, I do," said Mr. Bultitude. "I can't prevent fast young ladies from sending me notes. Why, she might have sent *you* one!"

"We won't go into hypothetical cases," said the Doctor, not relishing the war being carried into his own country; "she happened to prefer you. But, although your virtuous indignation seems to me a trifle overdone, sir, I don't see my way clear to punishing you on the facts, especially as you tell me you never encouraged these—these overtures, and my Dulcie, I am bound to say, confirms your statement that it was all the other young lady's doing. But if I had had any proof that you had begun or responded to her—hem—advances, nothing could have saved you from a severe flogging at the very least—so be careful for the future."

"Ah!" said Paul rather feebly, quite overwhelmed by the narrowness of his escape. Then with a desperate effort he found courage to add, "May I—ah—take advantage of this—this restored cordiality to—to—in fact to make a brief personal explanation? It—it's what I've been trying to tell you for a long time, ever since I first came, only you never will hear me out. It's highly important. You've no notion how serious it is!"

"There's something about you this term, Richard Bultitude," said the Doctor slowly, "that I confess I don't understand. This obstinacy is unusual in a boy of your age, and if you really have a mystery it may be as well to have it out and have done with it. But I can't be annoyed with it now. Come to me after supper to-night, and I shall be willing to hear anything you may have to say."

Paul was too overcome at this unexpected favour to speak his thanks. He got away as soon as he could. His path was smoothed at last!

That afternoon the boys, or all of them who had disposed of the work set them for the day, were sitting in the schoolroom, after a somewhat chilly dinner of cold beef, cold tarts, and cold water, passing the time with that description of literature known as "Sunday reading."

And here, at the risk of being guilty of a digression, I must pause to record my admiration for this exceedingly happy form of compromise, which is, I think, peculiar to the British and, to a certain extent, the American nations.

It has many developments; ranging from the mild Transatlantic compound of cookery and camp-meetings, to the semi-novel, redeemed and chastened by an arrangement which sandwiches a sermon or a biblical lecture between each chapter of the story—a great convenience for the race of skippers.

Then there are one or two illustrated magazines which it is always allowable to read on the Sabbath without fear of rebuke from the strictest—though it is not quite easy to see why.

Open any one of the monthly numbers, and the chances are that you may possibly find at one part a neat little doctrinal essay by a literary bishop; the rest of the contents will consist of nothing more serious than a paper upon "cockroaches and their habits" by an eminent savant; a description of foreign travel, done in a brilliant and wholly secular vein; and, further on again, an article on æsthetic furniture—while the balance of the number will be devoted to instalments of two thrilling novels by popular authors, whose theology is seldom their strongest point.

Oddly enough, too, when these very novels come out later in three-volume form, with the "mark of the beast" in the shape of a circulating library ticket upon them, they will be fortunate if they are not interdicted altogether by some of the serious families who take in the magazines as being "so suitable for Sundays."

Mr. Bultitude, at all events, had reason to be grateful for this toleration, for in one of the bound volumes supplied to him he found a most interesting and delightfully unsectarian novel, which appealed to his tastes as a business man, for it was all about commerce and making fortunes by blockade-running; and though he was no novel reader as a rule, his mind was so relieved and set at rest by the prospect of seeing the end of his trouble at last, that he was able to occupy his mind with the fortunes of the hero.

He naturally detected technical errors here and there. But that pleased him, and he was becoming so deeply absorbed in the tale that he felt seriously annoyed when Chawner came softly up to the desk at which he was sitting, and sat down close to him, crossing his arms before him, and leaning forward upon them with his sallow face towards Paul.

"Dickie," he began, in a cautious, oily tone, "did I hear the Doctor say before dinner that he would hear anything you have to tell him after supper? Did I?"

"I really can't say, sir," said Paul; "if you were near the keyhole at the time, very likely you did."

"The door was open," said Chawner, "and I was in the cloak-room, so I heard, and I want to know. What is it you're going to tell the Doctor?"

"Mind your own business, sir," said Paul sharply.

"It is my own business," said Chawner; "but I don't want to be told what you're going to tell him. I know."

"Good heavens!" said Mr. Bultitude, annoyed to find his secret in possession of this boy of all others.

"Yes," repeated Chawner. "I know, and I tell you what—I won't have it!"

"Won't have it! and why?"

"Never mind why. Perhaps I don't choose that the Doctor shall be told just yet; perhaps I mean to go up and tell him myself some other day. I want to have a little more fun out of it before I've done."

"But—but," said Paul, "you young ghoul, do you mean to say that all you care for is to see other people's sufferings?"

Chawner grinned maliciously. "Yes," he said suavely; "it amuses me."

"And so," said Paul, "you want to hold me back a little longer—because it's so funny; and then, when you're quite tired of your sport, you'll go up and tell the Doctor my—my unhappy story yourself, eh? No, my friend; I'd rather not tell him myself—but I'll be shot if I let *you* have a finger in it. I know my own interests better than that!"

"Don't get in a passion, Dickie," said Chawner; "it's Sunday. You'll have to let me go up instead of you—when I've frightened them a little more."

"Who do you mean by them, sir?" said Paul, growing puzzled.

"As if you didn't know! Oh, you're too clever for me, Dickie, I can see," sniggered Chawner.

"I tell you I don't know!" said Mr. Bultitude. "Look here, Chawner—your confounded name is Chawner, isn't it?—there's a mistake somewhere, I'm sure of it. Listen to me. I'm not going to tell the Doctor what you think I am!"

"What do I think you are going to tell him?"

"I haven't the slightest idea; but, whatever it is, you're wrong."

"Ah, you're too clever, Dickie; you won't betray yourself; but other people want to pay Coker and Tipping out as well as you, and I say you must wait."

"I shan't say anything to affect anyone but myself," said Paul; "if you know all about it, you must know that—it won't interfere with your amusement that I can see."

"Yes, it will," said Chawner irritably, "it will—you mayn't mean to tell of anyone but yourself; but directly Grimstone asks you questions, it all comes out. I know all about it. And, anyway, I forbid you to go up till I give you leave."

"And who the dooce are you?" said Mr. Bultitude, nettled at this assumption of authority. "How are you going to prevent me, may I ask?"

"S'sh! here's the Doctor," whispered Chawner hurriedly. "I'll tell you after tea. What am I doing out of my place, sir? Oh, I was only asking Bultitude what was the collect for to-day, sir. Fourth Sunday after the Epiphany? thank you, Bultitude."

And he glided back to his seat, leaving Paul in a state of vague uneasiness. Why did this fellow, with the infernal sly face and glib tongue, want to prevent him from righting himself with the world, and how could he possibly prevent him? It was absurd; he would take no notice of the young scoundrel—he would defy him.

But he could not banish the uneasy feeling; the cup had slipped so many times before at the critical moment that he could not be sure whose hand would be the next to jog his elbow. And so he went down to tea with renewed misgivings.

12.
Against Time

> "There is a kind of Followers likewise, which are dangerous, being indeed Espials; which enquire the Secrets of the House and beare Tales of them."—BACON.

> "Then give me leave that I may turn the key,
>
> That no man enter till my tale be done."

Very possibly Chawner's interference in Mr. Bultitude's private affairs has surprised others besides the victim of it; but the fact is that there was a most unfortunate misunderstanding between them from the very first, which prevented the one from seeing, the other from explaining, the real state of the case.

Chawner, of course, no more guessed Paul's true name and nature than anyone else who had come in contact with him in his impenetrable disguise, and his motive for attempting to prevent an interview with the Doctor can only, I fear, be explained by another slight digression.

The Doctor, from a deep sense of his responsibility for the morals of those under his care, was perhaps a trifle over-anxious to clear his moral garden of every noxious weed, and too constant in his vigilant efforts to detect the growing shoot of evil from the moment it showed above the surface.

As he could not be everywhere, however, it is evident that many offences, trivial or otherwise, must have remained unsuspected and unpunished, but for a theory which he had originated and took great pains to propagate amongst his pupils.

The theory was that every right-minded boy ought to feel himself in such a fiduciary position towards his master, that it became a positive duty to acquaint him with any delinquencies he might happen to observe among his fellows; and if, at the same time, he was oppressed by a secret burden on his own conscience, it was understood that he might hope that the joint revelation would go far to mitigate his own punishment.

It is doubtful whether this system, though I believe it is found successful in Continental colleges, can be usefully applied to English boys; whether it may not produce a habit of mutual distrust and suspicion, and a tone the reverse of healthy.

For myself, I am inclined to think that a schoolmaster will find it better in the long run, for both the character and morals of his school, if he is not too anxious to play the detective, and refrains from encouraging the more weak-minded or cowardly boys to save themselves by turning "schoolmaster's evidence."

Dr. Grimstone thought otherwise; but it must be allowed that the system, as in vogue at Crichton House, did not work well.

There were boys, of course, who took a sturdier view of their own rights and duties, and despised the talebearers as they deserved; there were others, also, too timid and too dependent on the good opinion of others to risk the loss of it by becoming informers; but there were always one or two whose consciences were unequal to the burden of their neighbour's sin, and could only be relieved by frank and full confession.

Unhappily they had, as a general rule, contributed largely to the sum of guilt themselves, and did not resort to disclosure until detection seemed reasonably imminent.

Chawner was the leader of this conscientious band; he revelled in the system. It gave him the means at once of gratifying the almost universal love of power and of indulging a catlike passion for playing with the feelings of others, which, it is to be hoped, is more uncommon.

He knew he was not popular, but he could procure most of the incidents of popularity; he could have his little court of cringing toadies; he could levy his tribute of conciliatory presents, and vent many private spites and hatreds into the bargain—and he generally did.

Having himself a tendency to acts of sly disobedience, he found it a congenial pastime to set the fashion from time to time in some one of the peccadilloes to which boyhood is prone, and to which the Doctor's somewhat restrictive code added a large number, and as soon as he saw a sufficient number of his companions satisfactorily implicated, his opportunity came.

He would take the chief culprits aside, and profess, in strict confidence, certain qualms of conscience which he feared could only be appeased by unburdening his guilt-laden soul.

To this none would have had any right to object—had it not necessarily, or at least from Chawner's point of view, involved a full, true, and particular account of the misdoings of each and every one; and consequently, for some time after these professions of misgivings, Chawner would be surrounded by a little crowd of anxiously obsequious friends, all trying hard to overcome his scruples or persuade him at least to omit their names from his revelations.

Sometimes he would affect to be convinced by their arguments and send them away reassured; at others his scruples would return in an aggravated form; and so he would keep them on tenterhooks of suspense for days and weeks, until he was tired of the amusement—for this practising on the fears of weaker natures is a horribly keen delight to some—or until some desperate little dog, unable to bear his torture any longer, would threaten to give himself up and make an end of it.

Then Chawner, to do him justice, always relieved him from so disagreeable a necessity, and would go softly into the Doctor's study, and, in a subdued and repentant tone, pour out his general confession for the public good.

Probably the Doctor did not altogether respect the instruments he saw fit to use in this way; some would have declined to hear the informer out, flogged him well, and forgotten it; but Dr. Grimstone—though he was hardly likely to be impressed by these exhibitions of noble candour, and did not fail to see that the prospect of obtaining better terms for the penitent himself had something to do with them—yet encouraged the system as a matter of policy, went thoroughly into the whole affair, and made it the cause of an explosion which he considered would clear the moral atmosphere for some time to come.

I hope that, after this explanation, Chawner's opposition to Mr. Bultitude's plans will be better understood.

After tea, he made Paul a little sign to follow him, and the two went out together into the little glass-house beyond the schoolroom; it was dark, but there was light enough from the room inside for them to see each other's face.

"Now, sir," began Paul, with dignity, when he had closed the glass door behind him, "perhaps you'll be good enough to tell me how you mean to prevent me from seeing Dr. Grimstone, and telling him—telling him what I have to tell him?"

"I'll tell you, Dickie," said Chawner, with an evil smirk. "You shall know soon enough."

"Don't stand grinning at me like that, sir," said the angry Mr. Bultitude; "say it out at once; it will make no difference to me, I give you warning!"

"Oh, yes it will, though. I think it will. Wait. I heard all you said to Grimstone in the study to-day about that girl—Connie Davenant, you know."

"I don't care; I am innocent. I have nothing to reproach myself with."

"What a liar you are!" said Chawner, more in admiration than rebuke. "You told him you never gave her any encouragement, didn't you? And he said if he ever found you had, nothing could save you from a licking, didn't he?"

"He did," said Paul, "he was quite right from his point of view—what then?"

"Why, this," said Chawner: "Do you remember giving Jolland, the last Sunday of last term, a note for that very girl?"

"I never did!" said poor Mr. Bultitude, "I never saw the wretched girl before."

"Ah!" said Chawner, "but I've got the note in my pocket! Jolland was seedy and asked me to take it for you, and I read it, and it was so nicely written that I thought I should like to keep it myself, and so I did—and here it is!"

And he drew out with great caution a piece of crumpled paper and showed it to the horrified old gentleman. "Don't snatch ... it's rude; there it is, you see: 'My dear Connie' ... 'yours ever, Dick Bultitude.' No, you don't come any nearer ... there, now it's safe.... Now what do you mean to do?"

"I—I don't know," said Paul, feeling absolutely checkmated. "Give me time."

"I tell you what I mean to do; I shall keep my eye on you, and directly I see you making ready to go to Grimstone, I shall get up first and take him this ... then you'll be done for. You'd better give in, really, Dickie!"

The note was too evidently genuine; Dick must have written it (as a matter of fact he had; in a moment of pique, no doubt, at some caprice of his real enslaver Dulcie's—but his fickleness brought fatal results on his poor father's undeserving head)—if this diabolical Chawner carried out his threats he would indeed be "done for"; he did not yet fully understand the other's motive, but he thought that he feared lest Paul, in declaring his own sorrows, might also accuse Tipping and Coker of acts of cruelty and oppression, which Chawner proposed to denounce himself at some more convenient opportunity; he hesitated painfully.

"Well?" said Chawner, "make up your mind; are you going to tell him, or not?"

"I must!" said Paul hoarsely. "I promise you I shall not bring any other names in ... I don't want to ... I only want to save myself—and I can't stand it any longer. Why should you stand between me and my rights in this currish way? I didn't know there were boys like you in the world, sir; you're a young monster!"

"I don't mean you to tell the Doctor anything at all," said Chawner. "I shall do what I said."

"Then do your worst!" said Paul, stung to defiance.

"Very well, then," returned Chawner meekly, "I will—and we'll see who wins!"

And they went back to the schoolroom again, where Mr. Bultitude, boiling with rage and seriously alarmed as well, tried to sit down and appear as if nothing had happened.

Chawner sat down too, in a place from which he could see all Paul's movements, and they both watched one another anxiously from the corners of their eyes till the Doctor came in.

"It's a foggy evening," he said as he entered: "the younger boys had better stay in. Chawner, you and the rest of the first form can go to church; get ready at once."

Paul's heart leaped with triumph; with his enemy out of the way, he could carry out his purpose unhindered. The same thing apparently occurred to Chawner, for he said mildly, "Please, sir, may Richard Bultitude come too?"

"Can't Bultitude ask leave for himself?" said the Doctor.

"I, sir!" said the horrified Paul, "it's a mistake—I don't want to go. I—I don't feel very well this evening!"

"Then you see, Chawner, you misunderstood him. By the way, Bultitude, there was something you were to tell me, I think?"

Chawner's small glittering eyes were fixed on Paul menacingly as he managed to stammer that he did want to say something in private.

"Very well, I am going out to see a friend for an hour or so—when I come back I will hear you," and he left the room abruptly.

Chawner would very probably have petitioned to stay in that evening as well, had he had time and presence of mind to do so; as it was, he was obliged to go away and get ready for church, but when his preparations were made he came back to Paul, and leaning over him said with an unpleasant scowl, "If I get back in time, Bultitude, we'll see whether you baulk me quite so easily. If I come back and find you've done it—I shall take in that letter!"

"You may do what you please then," said Paul, in a high state of irritation, "I shall be well out of your reach by that time. Now have the goodness to take yourself off."

As he went, Mr. Bultitude thought, "I never in all my life saw such a fellow as that, never! It would give me real pleasure to hire someone to kick him."

The evening passed quietly; the boys left at home sat in their places, reading or pretending to read. Mr. Blinkhorn, left in charge of them, was at his table in the corner noting up his diary. Paul was free for a time to think over his position.

At first he was calm and triumphant; his dearest hopes, his long-wished-for opportunity of a fair and unprejudiced hearing, were at last to be fulfilled—Chawner was well out of the way for the best part of two hours—the Doctor was very unlikely to be detained nearly so long over one call; his one anxiety was lest he might not be able, after all, to explain himself in a thoroughly effective manner—he planned out a little scheme for doing this.

He must begin gradually of course, so as not to alarm the schoolmaster or raise doubts of his sincerity or, worse still, his sanity. Perhaps a slight glance at instances of extraordinary interventions of the supernatural from the earliest times, tending to show the extreme probability of their survival on rare occasions even to the present day, might be a prudent and cautious introduction to the subject—only he could not think of any, and, after all, it might weary the Doctor.

He would start somewhat in this manner: "You cannot, my dear sir, have failed to observe since our meeting this year, a certain difference in my manner and bearing"—one's projected speeches are somehow generally couched in finer language than, when it comes to the point, the tongue can be prevailed upon to utter. Mr. Bultitude learned this opening sentence by heart, he thought it taking and neat, the sort of thing to fix his hearer's attention from the first.

After that he found it difficult to get any further; he knew himself that all he was about to describe was plain, unvarnished fact—but how would it strike a stranger's ear? He found himself seeking ways in which to tone down the glaring improbability of the thing as much as possible, but in vain; "I don't know how I shall ever get it all out," he told himself at last; "if I think about it much longer I shall begin to disbelieve in it myself."

Here Biddlecomb came up in a confidential manner and sat down by Paul; "Dick," he began, in rather a trembling voice, "did I hear the Doctor say something about your having something to tell him?"

"Oh Lord, here's another of them now!" thought Paul. "You are right, young sir," he said: "have you any objection? mention it, you know, if you have, pray mention it. It's a matter of life and death to me, but if you at all disapprove, of course that ought to be final!"

"No, but," protested Biddlecomb, "I, I daresay I've not treated you very well lately, I——"

"You were kind enough to suggest several very uncommonly unpleasant ways of annoying me, sir," said Paul resentfully, "if you mean that. You've kicked me more than once, and your handkerchief, unless I am very much mistaken, had the biggest and the hardest knot in it yesterday. If that gives you the right to interfere and dictate to me now, like your amiable friend, Master Chawner, I suppose you have it."

"Now you're angry," said Biddlecomb humbly; "I don't wonder at it. I've behaved like a cad, I know, but, and this is what I wanted to say, I was sorry for you all the time."

"That's very comforting," said Paul drily; "thank you. I'm vastly obliged to you."

"I was, though," said Biddlecomb. "I, I was led away by the other fellows—I always liked you, you know, Bultitude."

"You've a very odd way of showing your affection," remarked Mr. Bultitude; "but go on, let me hear all you have to say."

"It isn't much," said Biddlecomb, quite broken down; "only don't sneak of me this time, Dick, let me off, there's a good fellow. I'll stick up for you after this, I will really. You used not to be a fellow for sneaking once. It's caddish to sneak!"

"Don't be alarmed, my good friend," said Paul; "I won't poach on that excellent young man Chawner's preserves. What I am going to tell the Doctor has nothing to do with you."

"On your honour?" said Biddlecomb eagerly.

"Yes," said Paul testily, "on my honour. Now, perhaps, you'll let me alone. No, I won't shake hands, sir. I've had to accept your kicks, but I don't want your friendship."

Biddlecomb went off, looking slightly ashamed of himself but visibly relieved from a haunting fear. "Thank goodness!" thought Paul, "he wasn't as obstinate as the other fellow. What a set they are! I knew it, there's another boy coming up now!"

And indeed one boy after another came up in the same way as Biddlecomb had done, some cringing more than others, but all vowing that they had never intended to do any harm, and entreating him to change his mind about complaining of his ill-treatment. They brought little offerings to propitiate him and prove the depth of their unaltered regard—pencil-cases and pocket-knives, and so forth, until they drove Paul nearly to desperation. However, he succeeded in dispelling their fears after some hot arguments, and had just sent away the last suppliant, when he saw Jolland too rise and come towards him.

Jolland leaned across Paul's desk with folded arms and looked him full in the face with his shallow light green eyes. "I don't know what you've said to all those chaps," he began; "they've come back looking precious glum, but they won't tell me what you said," (Mr. Bultitude had in satisfying their alarm taken care to let them know his private opinion of them, which was not flattering), "but I've got something to say to you, and it's this. I never thought you would quite come down to this sort of thing!"

"What sort of thing?" said Paul, who was beginning to have enough of it.

"Why, going up and letting on against all of us—it's mean, you know. If you have got bashed about pretty well since you came back, it's been all your own fault, and you know it. Last term you got on well enough—this time you began to be queer and nasty the very first day you came. I thought it was one of your larks at first, but I don't know what it is now, and I don't care. I stood up for you as long as I could, till you acted like a funk yesterday. Then I took my share in lamming you, and I'd do it again. But if you are cad enough to pay us all out in this way, I'll have no more to do with you—mind that. That's all I came to say."

This was an unpalatable way of putting things, but Paul could not help seeing that there was some truth in it. Jolland had been kind to him, too, in a careless sort of way, and at some cost to himself; so it was with more mildness than temper that he answered him.

"You're on the wrong tack, my boy, the wrong tack. I've no wish to tell tales of anyone, as I've been trying to explain to your friends. There's something the matter with me which you wouldn't understand if I told you."

"Oh, I didn't know," said Jolland, mollified; "if it's only physic you want."

"Whatever it is," said Paul, not caring to undeceive him, "it won't affect you or anyone here, but myself. You're not a bad young fellow, I believe. I don't want to get you into trouble, sir; you don't want much assistance, I'm afraid, in that department. So be off, like a good fellow, and leave me in peace."

All these interviews had taken time. He was alarmed on looking at the clock to see that it was nearly eight; the Doctor was a long time over that call—for the first time he began to feel uneasy—he made hurried mental calculations as to the probability of the Doctor or Chawner being the first to return.

The walk to church took about twenty minutes; say the service took an hour, allowing for the return, he might expect Chawner by about half-past eight; it was striking the hour now—half an hour only in which he could hope for any favourable result from the interview!

For he saw this plainly, that if Chawner were once permitted to get the Doctor's ear first and show him that infamous love-note, no explanation of his (even if he had nerve to make it then, which he doubted) could possibly seem anything more than a desperate and far-fetched excuse; if he could anticipate Chawner, on the other hand, and once convince the Doctor of the truth of his story, the informer's malice would fall flat.

And still the long hand went rapidly on, as Mr. Bultitude sat staring stupidly at it with a faint sick feeling—it had passed the quarter now—why did the Doctor delay in this unwarrantable manner? What a farce social civilities were—if he had allowed himself to be prevailed on to stay to supper! Twenty minutes past; Chawner and the others might return at any moment—a ring at the bell; they were there! all was over now—no, he was saved, that was Dr. Grimstone's voice in the hall—what an unconscionable time he was taking off his greatcoat and gloves.

But all comes to the man who waits. In another moment the Doctor looked in, singled out Mr. Bultitude with a sharp glance, and a, "Now, Bultitude, I will hear you!" and led the way to his study.

Paul staggered rather than walked after him: as usual at the critical moment his carefully prepared opening had deserted him—his head felt heavy and crowded—he wanted to run away, but forced himself to overcome such a suicidal proceeding and follow to the study.

There was a lighted reading-lamp with a green glass shade upon the table. The Doctor sat down by it in an armchair by the fire, crossed his legs, and joined the tops of his fingers together. "Now, Bultitude," he said again.

"Might I—might I sit down?" said poor Mr. Bultitude in a thick voice; it was all that occurred to him to say.

"Sit by all means," said the Doctor blandly.

So Paul drew a chair opposite the Doctor and sat down. He tried desperately to clear his head and throat and begin; but the only distinct thought in his mind just then was that the green lamp-shade lent a particularly ghastly hue to the Doctor's face.

"Take your time, Bultitude," said the latter, after a long minute, in which a little skeleton clock on the mantelpiece ticked loudly—"there's no hurry, my boy."

But this only reminded Paul that there was every need for hurry—Chawner might come in, and follow him here, unless he made haste.

Still, he could only say, "You see me in a very agitated state, Dr. Grimstone—a very agitated state, sir."

The Doctor gave a short, dry cough. "Well, Bultitude," he said.

"The fact is, sir, I'm in a most unfortunate position, and—and the worst of it is, I don't know how to begin." Here he made another dead stop, while the Doctor raised his heavy eyebrows, and looked at the clock.

"Do you see any prospect of your finding yourself able to begin soon?" he inquired at last, with rather suspicious suavity. "Perhaps if you came to me later on——"

"Not for the world!" said Paul, in a highly nervous condition. "I shall begin very soon, Doctor, I shall begin directly. Mine is such a very singular case; it's difficult, as you see, to, to open it!"

"Have you anything on your mind?" asked the Doctor suddenly.

Paul could hear steps and voices in the adjoining cloakroom—the churchgoers had returned. "Yes—no!" he answered, losing his head completely now.

"That's a somewhat extraordinary, not to say an ambiguous, reply," said the Doctor; "what am I to understand by——"

There was a tap at the door. Paul started to his feet in a panic. "Don't let him in!" he shrieked, finding his voice at last. "Hear me first—you shall hear me first! Say that other rascal is not to come in. He wants to ruin me!"

"I was going to say I was engaged," said the Doctor; "but there's something under this I must understand. Come in, whoever you are."

And the door opened softly, and Chawner stepped meekly in; he was rather pale and breathed hard, but was otherwise quite composed.

"Now, then, Chawner," said the Doctor impatiently, "what is it? Have you something on your mind, too?"

"Please, sir," said Chawner, "has Bultitude told you anything yet?"

"No, why? Hold your tongue, Bultitude. I shall hear Chawner now—not you!"

"Because, sir," explained Chawner, "he knew I had made up my mind to tell you something I thought you ought to know about him, and so he threatened to come first and tell some falsehood (I'm sure I don't know what) about me, sir. I think I ought to be here too."

"It's a lie!" shouted Paul, "What a villain that boy is! Don't believe a word he says, Dr. Grimstone; it's all false—all!"

"This is very suspicious," said the Doctor; "if your conscience were good, Bultitude, you could have no object in preventing me from hearing Chawner. Chawner, in spite of some obvious defects in his character," he went on, with a gulp (he never could quite overcome a repulsion to the boy), "is, on the whole, a right-minded and, ah, conscientious boy. I hear Chawner first."

"Then, sir, if you please," said Chawner, with an odious side smirk of triumph at Paul, who, quite crushed by the horror of the situation, had collapsed feebly on his chair again, "I thought it was my duty to let you see this. I found it to-day in Bultitude's prayerbook, sir." And he handed Dick's unlucky scrawl to the Doctor, who took it to the lamp and read it hurriedly through.

After that there was a terrible moment of dead silence; then the Doctor looked up and said shortly, "You did well to tell me of this, Chawner; you may go now."

When they were alone once more he turned upon the speechless Paul with furious scorn and indignation. "Contemptible liar and hypocrite," he thundered, pacing restlessly up and down the room in his excitement, till Paul felt very like Daniel, without his sense of security, "you are unmasked—unmasked, sir! You led me to believe that you were as much shocked and pained at this girl's venturing to write to you as I could be myself. You called it, quite correctly, 'forward and improper'; you pretended you had never given her the least encouragement—had not heard her name even—till to-day. And here is a note, written, as I should imagine, some time since, in which you address her as 'Connie Davenant,' and have the impudence to admire the hat she wore the Sunday before! I shudder, sir, to think of such duplicity, such precocious and shameless depravity. It astounds me. It deprives me of all power to think!"

Paul made some faint and inarticulate remark about being a family man—always most particular, and so forth—luckily it passed unheard.

"What shall I do with you?" continued the Doctor; "how shall I punish such monstrous misconduct?"

"Don't ask *me*, sir," said Paul, desperately—"only, for heaven's sake, get it over as soon as possible."

"If I linger, sir," retorted the Doctor, "it is because I have grave doubts whether your offence can be expiated by a mere flogging—whether that is not altogether too light a retribution."

"He can't want to *torture* me," thought Paul.

"Yes," said the Doctor again, "the doubt has prevailed. On a mind so hardened the cane would leave no lasting impression. I cannot allow your innocent companions to run the risk of contamination from your society. I must not permit this serpent to glide uncrushed, this cockatrice to practise his epistolary wiles, within my peaceful fold. My mind is made up—at whatever cost to myself—however it may distress and grieve your good father, who is so pathetically anxious for you to do him credit, sir. I must do my duty to the parents of the boys entrusted to my care. I shall not flog you, sir, for I feel it would be useless. I shall expel you."

"What!" Paul leaped up incredulous. "Expel me? Do I hear you aright, Dr. Grimstone? Say it again—you will expel me?"

"I have said it," the Doctor said sternly; "no expostulations can move me now" (as if Mr. Bultitude was likely to expostulate!) "Mrs. Grimstone will see that your boxes are packed the first thing to-morrow morning, and I shall take you myself to the station and consign you to the home you have covered with blushes and shame, by the 9.15 train, and I shall write a letter to-night explaining the causes for your dismissal."

Mr. Bultitude covered his face with his hands, to hide, not his shame and distress, but his indecent rapture. It seemed almost too good to be true! He saw himself about to be provided with every means of reaching home in comfort and safety. He need dread no pursuit now. There was no chance, either, of his being forced to return to the prison-house—the Doctor's letter would convince even Dick of the impossibility of that. And, best of all, this magnificent stroke of good luck had been obtained without the ignominy and pain of a flogging, without even the unpleasant necessity of telling his strange secret.

But (having gained some experience during his short stay at the school) he had the duplicity to pretend to sob bitterly.

"But one night more, sir," continued the Doctor, "shall you pass beneath this roof, and that apart from your fellows. You will occupy the spare bedroom until the morning, when you quit the school in disgrace—for ever."

I said in another chapter that this Sunday would find Paul, at its close, after a trying course of emotions, in a state of delicious ecstasy of pure relief and happiness—and really that scarcely seems too strong an expression for his feelings.

When he found himself locked securely into a comfortable, warm bedroom, with curtains and a carpet in it, safe from the persecutions of all those terrible boys, and when he remembered that this was actually the last night of his stay here—that he would certainly see his own home before noon next day, the reaction was so powerful that he could not refrain from skipping and leaping about the room in a kind of hysterical gaiety.

And as he laid his head down on a yielding lavender-scented pillow, his thoughts went back without a pang to the varied events of the day; they had been painful, very painful, but it was well worth while to have gone through them to appreciate fully the delightful intensity of the contrast. He freely forgave all his tormentors, even Chawner—for had not Chawner procured his release?—and he closed his eyes at last with a smile of Sybaritic satisfaction and gentle longing for the Monday's dawn to break.

And yet some, after his experiences, would have had their misgivings.

13.
A Respite

"Discipulorum inter jubeo plorare cathedras."

Blithe and gay was Mr. Bultitude when he opened his eyes on Monday morning and realised his incredible good fortune; in a few hours he would be travelling safely and comfortably home, with every facility for regaining his rights. He chuckled—though his sense of humour was not large—he chuckled, as he lay snugly in bed, to think of Dick's discomfiture on seeing him return so unexpectedly; he began to put it down, quite unwarrantably, to his own cleverness, as having conceived and executed such a stroke of genius as procuring his own expulsion.

He remained in bed until long after the getting-up bell had rung, feeling that his position ensured him perfect impunity in this, and when he rose at length it was in high spirits, and he dressed himself with a growing toleration for things in general, very unlike his ordinary frame of mind. When he had finished his toilet, the Doctor entered the room.

"Bultitude," he said gravely, "before sending you from us, I should like to hear from your own lips that you are not altogether without contrition for your conduct."

Mr. Bultitude considered that such an acknowledgment could not possibly do any harm, so he said—as, indeed, he might with perfect truth—that "he very much regretted what had passed."

"I am glad to hear that," said the Doctor, more briskly, "very glad; it relieves me from a very painful responsibility. It may not impossibly induce me to take a more lenient view of your case."

"Oh!" gasped Mr. Bultitude, feeling very uncomfortable all at once.

"Yes; it is a serious step to ruin a boy's career at its outset by unnecessary harshness. Nothing, of course, can palliate the extreme baseness of your behaviour. Still from certain faint indications in your character of better things, I do not despair even yet (after you have received a public lesson at my hands, which you will never forget) of rearing you to become in time an ornament to the society in which it will be your lot to move. I will not give up in despair—I will persevere a little longer."

"Thank you!" Paul faltered, with a sudden sinking sensation.

"Mrs. Grimstone, too," said the Doctor, "has been interceding for you; she has represented to me that a public expression of my view of your conduct, together with a sharp, severe dose of physical pain, would be more likely to effect a radical improvement in your character, and to soften your perverted heart, than if I sent you away in hopeless disgrace, without giving you an opportunity of showing a desire to amend."

"It's—very kind of Mrs. Grimstone," said Paul faintly.

"Then I hope you will show your appreciation of her kindness. Yes, I will not expel you. I will give you one more chance to retrieve your lost reputation. But, for your own sake, and as a public warning, I shall take notice of your offence in public. I shall visit it upon you by a sound flogging before the whole school at eleven o'clock. You need not come down till then—your breakfast will be sent up to you."

Paul made a frantic attempt to dissuade him from his terrible determination. "Dr. Grimstone," he said, "I—I should much prefer being expelled, if it is all the same to you."

"It is not all the same to me," said the Doctor. "This is mere pride and obstinacy, Bultitude; I should do wrong to take any notice of it."

"I—I tell you I have great objection to—to being flogged," said Paul eagerly; "it wouldn't improve me at all; it would harden me, sir,—harden me. I—I cannot allow you to flog me, Dr. Grimstone. I have strong prejudices against the system of corporal punishment. I object to it on principle. Expulsion would make me quite a different being, I assure you; it would reform me—save me—it would indeed."

"So, to escape a little personal inconvenience, you would be content to bring sorrow upon your worthy father's grey head, would you, sir?" said the Doctor. "I shall not oblige you in this. Nor, I may add, will your cowardice induce me to spare you in your coming chastisement. I leave you, sir—we shall meet again at eleven!"

And he stalked out of the room. Perhaps, though he did not admit this even to himself, there were more considerations for commuting the sentence of expulsion than those he had mentioned. Boys are not often expelled from private schools, except for especially heinous offences, and in this case there was no real reason why the Doctor should be Quixotic enough to throw up a portion of his income—particularly if he could produce as great a moral effect by other means.

But his clemency was too much for Mr. Bultitude; he threw himself on the bed and raved at the hideous fate in store for him; ten short minutes ago, and he had been so happy—so certain of release—and now, not only was he as far from all hope of escape as ever, but he had the certainty before him of a sound flogging in less than two hours!

Just after something has befallen us which, for good or ill, will make a great change in our lives, what a totally new aspect the common everyday things about us are apt to wear—the book we were reading, the letter we had begun, the picture we knew—what a new and tender attraction they may have for us, or what a grim and terrible irony!

Something of this Paul felt dimly, as he finished dressing, in a dazed, unconscious manner. The comfortable bedroom, with its delicately-toned wall-paper and flowery cretonnes, had become altogether hateful in his eyes now. Instead of feeling grateful (as he surely ought to have been) for the one night of perfect security and comfort he had passed there, he only loathed it for the delusive peace it had brought him.

There was a gentle tap at the door, and Dulcie came in, bearing a tray with his breakfast, and looking like a little Royalist bearing food to a fugitive Cavalier; though Paul did not quite carry out his share of the simile.

"There!" she said, almost cheerfully; "I got Mummy to let me take up your breakfast; and there's an egg for you, and muffins."

Mr. Bultitude sat on a chair and groaned.

"You might say 'thank you,'" said Dulcie, pouting. "That other girl wouldn't have brought you up much breakfast if she'd been in my place. I was going to tell you that I'd forgiven you, because very likely you never meant her to write to you" (Dulcie had not been told the sequel to the Davenant episode, which was quite as well for Paul). "But you don't seem to care whether I do or not."

"I feel so miserable!" sighed Paul.

"Then you must drink some coffee," prescribed Dulcie decidedly; "and you must eat some breakfast. I brought an egg on purpose; it's so strengthening, you know."

"Don't!" cried Paul, with a short howl of distress at this suggestion. "Don't talk about the—the flogging, I can't bear it."

"But it's not papa's *new* cane, you know, Dick," said Dulcie consolingly. "I've hidden that; it's only the old one, and you always said that didn't hurt so very much, after a little while. It isn't as if it was the horsewhip, either. Daddy lost that out riding in the holidays."

"Oh, the horsewhip's worse, is it?" said Paul, with a sickly smile.

"Tom says so," said Dulcie. "After all, Dick, it will be all over in five minutes, or, perhaps, a little longer, and I do think you oughtn't to mind that so much, now, after mamma and I have begged you off from being expelled. We might never have seen one another again, Dick!"

"You begged me off!" cried Paul.

"Yes," said Dulcie; "Daddy wouldn't change his mind for ever so long—till I coaxed him. I couldn't bear to let you go."

"You've done a very cruel thing," said Paul. "For such a little girl as you are, you've done an immense amount of mischief. But for you, that letter would not have been found out. You need not have spoilt my only chance of getting out of this horrible place!"

Dulcie set down the tray, and, putting her hands behind her, leaned against a corner of a wardrobe.

"And is that all you say to me!" she said, with a little tremble in her voice.

"That is all," said Paul. "I've no doubt you meant well, but you shouldn't have interfered. All this has come upon me through that. Take away the breakfast. It makes me ill even to look at it."

Dulcie shook out her long brown hair, and clenched her small fist in an undeniable passion, for she had something of her father's hot temper when roused. "Very well, then," she said, moving with great dignity towards the door. "I'm very sorry I ever did interfere. I wish I'd let you be sent home to your papa, and see what he'd do to you. But I'll never, never interfere one bit with you again. I won't say one single word to you any more.... I'll never even look at you if you want me to ever so much.... I shall tell Tipping he can hit you as much as ever he likes, and I shall show Tom where I put the new cane—and I only hope it will hurt!" And with this parting shot she was gone.

Mr. Bultitude wandered disconsolately about the upper part of the house after this, not daring to go down, and not able to remain in any one place. The maids who came up to make the beds looked at him with pitiful interest, but he was too proud to implore help from them. To hide would only make matters worse, for, as he had not a penny in his pocket, and no probability of being able to borrow one, he must remain in the house till hunger forced him from his hiding-place—supposing they did not hunt him out long before that time.

The shouts of the boys in the playground during their half-hour's play had long since died away; he heard the clock in the hall strike eleven—time for him to seek his awful rendezvous. The Doctor had not forgotten him, he found, for presently the butler came up and ceremoniously announced that the Doctor "would see him now, if he pleased."

He stumbled downstairs in a half-unconscious condition, the butler threw open the two doors which led to the schoolroom, and Paul tottered in, more dead than alive with shame and fear.

The whole school were at their places, with no books before them, and arranged as if to hear a lecture. Mr. Blinkhorn alone was absent, for, not liking these exhibitions, he had taken an opportunity of slipping out into the playground, round which he was now solemnly trotting at the "double" with elbows squared and head up; an exercise which he said was an excellent thing for the back and lungs. He had a habit of suddenly leaving the class he was taking to indulge in it for a few minutes, returning breathless but refreshed.

Mr. Tinkler was at his seat, wearing that faint grin on his face with which he might have prepared to see a pig killed or a bull-fight, and all the boys fixed their eyes expectantly on Mr. Bultitude as he appeared at the doorway.

"Stand there, sir," said the Doctor, who was standing at his writing-table in an attitude; "out there in the middle, where your schoolfellows can see you." Paul obeyed and stood where he was told, looking, as he felt, absolutely boneless.

"Some of those here," began the Doctor in an impressive bass, "may wonder why I have called you all together on this, the first day of the week; most of those who reside under my roof are acquainted with, and I trust execrate, the miserable cause of my doing so.

"If there is one virtue which I have striven to implant more than any other in your breasts," he continued, "it is the cultivation of a modest and becoming reserve in your intercourse with those of the opposite sex.

"With the majority I have, I hope, been successful, and it is as painful for me to tell as for you to hear, that there exists in your midst a youthful reprobate, trained in all the arts of ensnaring the vagrant fancies of innocent but giddy girlhood.

"See him as he cowers there before your gaze, in all the bared hideousness of his moral depravity" (the Doctor on occasions like these never spared his best epithets, and Paul soon began to feel himself a very villain); "a libertine, young in years, but old in—in everything else, who has not scrupled to indite an amatory note, so appalling in its familiarity, and so outrageous in the warmth of its sentiments, that I cannot bring myself to shock your ears with its contents.

"You do well to shun him as a moral leper; but how shall I tell you that, not satisfied with pressing his effusions upon the shrinking object of his precocious affections, the impious wretch has availed himself of the shelter of a church to cloak his insidious advances, and even force a response to them from a heedless and imprudent girl!

"If," continued the Doctor, now allowing his powerful voice to boom to its full compass—"if I can succeed in bringing this coward, this unmanly dallier in a sentiment which the healthy mind of boyhood rejects as premature, to a sense of his detestable conduct; if I can score the lesson upon his flesh so that some faint notion of its force and purport may be conveyed to what has been supplied to him as a heart, then I shall not have lifted this hand in vain!

"He shall see whether he will be allowed to trail the fair name of the school for propriety and correctness of deportment in the dust of a pew-floor, and spurn my reputation as a preceptor like a church hassock beneath his feet!

"I shall say no more; I will not prolong these strictures, deserved though they be, beyond their proper limits.... I shall now proceed to act. Richard Bultitude, remain there till I return to mete out to you with no sparing hand the punishment you have so richly merited."

With these awful words the Doctor left the room, leaving Paul in a state of abject horror and dread which need not be described. Never, never again would he joke, as he had been wont to do with Dick in lighter moods, on the subject of corporal punishment under any circumstances—it was no fit theme for levity; if this—this outrage were really done to him, he could never be able to hold up his head again. What if it were to get about in the city!

The boys, who had sunk, as they always did, into a state of torpid awe under the Doctor's eloquence, now recovered spirits enough to rally Paul with much sprightly humour.

"He's gone to fetch his cane," said some, and imitated for Paul's instruction the action of caning by slapping a ruler upon a copy-book with a dreadful fidelity and resonance; others sought to cross-examine him upon the love-letter, it appearing from their casual remarks that not a few had been also honoured by communications from the artless Miss Davenant.

It is astonishing how unfeeling even ordinary good-natured boys can be at times.

Chawner sat at his desk with raised shoulders, rubbing his hands, and grinning like some malevolent ape: "I told you, Dickie, you know," he murmured, "that it was better not to cross me."

And still the Doctor lingered. Some kindly suggested that he was "waxing the cane." But the more general opinion was that he had been detained by some visitor; for it appeared that (though Paul had not noticed it) several had heard a ring at the bell. The suspense was growing more and more unbearable.

At last the door opened in a slow ominous manner, and the Doctor appeared. There was a visible change in his manner, however. The white heat of his indignation had died out: his expression was grave but distinctly softened—and he had nothing in his hand.

"I want you outside, Bultitude," he said; and Paul, still uncertain whether the scene of his disgrace was only about to be shifted, or what else this might mean, followed him into the hall.

"If anything can strike shame and confusion into your soul, Richard," said the Doctor, when they were outside, "it will be what I have to tell you now. Your unhappy father is here, in the dining-room."

Paul staggered. Had Dick the brazen effrontery to come here to taunt him in his slavery? What was the meaning of it? What should he say to him? He could not answer the Doctor but by a vacant stare.

"I have not seen him yet," said the Doctor. "He has come at a most inopportune moment" (here Mr. Bultitude could *not* agree with him). "I shall allow you to meet him first, and give you the opportunity of breaking your conduct to him. I know how it will wring his paternal heart!" and the Doctor shook his head sadly, and turned away.

With a curious mixture of shame, anger, and impatience, Paul turned the handle of the dining-room door. He was to meet Dick face to face once more. The final duel must be fought out between them here. Who would be the victor?

It was a strange sensation on entering to see the image of what he had so lately been standing by the mantelpiece. It gave a shock to his sense of his own identity. It seemed so impossible that that stout substantial frame could really contain Dick. For an instant he was totally at a loss for words, and stood pale and speechless in the presence of his unprincipled son.

Dick on his side seemed at least as much embarrassed. He giggled uneasily, and made a sheepish offer to shake hands, which was indignantly declined.

As Paul looked he saw distinctly that his son's fraudulent imitation of his father's personal appearance had become deteriorated in many respects since that unhappy night when he had last seen it. It was then a copy, faultlessly accurate in every detail. It was now almost a caricature, a libel!

The complexion was nearly sallow, with the exception of the nose, which had rather deepened in colour. The skin was loose and flabby, and the eyes dull and a little bloodshot. But perhaps the greatest alteration was in the dress. Dick wore an old light tweed shooting-coat of his, and a pair of loose trousers of blue serge; while, instead of the formally tied black neckcloth his father had worn for a quarter of a century, he had a large scarf round his neck of some crude and gaudy colour; and the conventional chimney-pot hat had been discarded for a shabby old wide-brimmed felt wideawake.

Altogether, it was by no means the costume which a British merchant, with any self-respect whatever, would select, even for a country visit.

And thus they met, as perhaps never, since this world was first set spinning down the ringing grooves of change, met father and son before!

14.
An Error of Judgment

"The Survivorship of a worthy Man in his Son is a Pleasure scarce inferior to the Hopes of the Continuance of his own Life." *Spectator.*

"Du bist ein Knabe—sei es immerhin

Und fahre fort, den Fröhlichen zu spielen."

SCHILLER, *Don Carlos.*

Paul was the first to break a very awkward silence. "You young scoundrel!" he said, with suppressed rage. "What the devil do you mean by laughing like that? It's no laughing matter, let me tell you, sir, for one of us!"

"I can't help laughing," said Dick; "you do look so queer!"

"Queer! I may well look queer. I tell you that I have never, never in my whole life, spent such a perfectly infernal week as this last!"

"Ah!" observed Dick, "I thought you wouldn't find it *all* jam! And yet you seemed to be enjoying yourself, too," he said with a grin, "from that letter you wrote."

"What made you come here? Couldn't you be content with your miserable victory, without coming down to crow and jeer at me?"

"It isn't that," said Dick. "I—I thought I should like to see the fellows, and find out how you were getting on, you know." These, however, were not his only and his principal motives. He had come down to get a sight of Dulcie.

"Well, sir," said Mr. Bultitude, with ponderous sarcasm, "you'll be delighted to hear that I'm getting on uncommonly well—oh, uncommonly! Your high-spirited young friends batter me to sleep with slippers on most nights, and, as a general thing, kick me about during the day like a confounded football! And last night, sir, I was going to be expelled; and this morning I'm forgiven, and sentenced to be soundly flogged before the whole school! It was just about to take place as you came in; and I've every reason to believe it is merely postponed!"

"I say, though," said Dick, "you must have been going it rather, you know. I've never been expelled. Has Chawner been sneaking again? What have you been up to?"

"Nothing. I solemnly swear—nothing! They're finding out things you've done, and thrashing *me*."

"Well," said Dick soothingly, "you'll work them all off during the term, I daresay. There aren't many really bad ones. I suppose he's seen my name cut on his writing-table?"

"No; not that I'm aware of," said Paul.

"Oh, he'd let you hear of it if he had!" said Dick. "It's good for a swishing, that is. But, after all, what's a swishing? I never cared for a swishing."

"But I do care, sir. I care very much, and, I tell you, I won't stand it. I can't! Dick," he said abruptly as a sudden hope seized him. "You, you haven't come down here to say you're tired of your folly, have you? Do you want to give it up?"

"Rather not," said Dick. "Why should I? No school, no lessons, nothing to do but amuse myself, eat and drink what I like, and lots of money. It's not likely, you know."

"Have you ever thought that you're bringing yourself within reach of the law, sir?" said Paul, trying to frighten him. "Perhaps you don't know that there's an offence known as 'false personation with intent to defraud,' and that it's a felony. That's what you're doing at this moment, sir!"

"Not any more than you are!" retorted Dick. "I never began it. I had as much right to wish to be you as you had to wish to be me. You're just what you said you wanted to be, so you can't complain."

"It's useless to argue with you, I see," said Paul. "And you've no feelings. But I'll warn you of one thing. Whether that is my body or not you've fraudulently taken possession of, I don't know; if it is not, it is very like mine, and I tell you this about it. The sort of life you're leading it, sir, will very soon make an end of you, if you don't take care. Do you think that a constitution at my age can stand sweet wines and pastry, and late hours? Why, you'll be laid up with gout in another day or two. Don't tell me, sir. I know you're suffering from indigestion at this very minute. I can see your liver (it may be *my* liver for anything I know) is out of order. I can see it in your eyes."

Dick was a little alarmed at this, but he soon said: "Well, and if I am seedy, I can get Barbara to take the stone and wish me all right again, can't I? That's easy enough, I suppose."

"Oh, easy enough!" said Paul, with a suppressed groan. "But, Dick, you don't go up to Mincing Lane in that suit and that hat? Don't tell me you do that!"

"When I do go up, I wear them," said Dick composedly. "Why not? It's a roomy suit, and I hate a great topper on my head; I've had enough of that here on Sundays. But it's slow up at your office. The chaps there aren't half up to any larks. I made a first-rate booby-trap, though, one day for an old yellow buffer who came in to see you. He *was* in a bait when he found the waste-paper basket on his head!"

"What was his name?" said Paul, with forced calm.

"Something like 'Shells.' He said he was a very old friend of mine, and I told him he lied."

"Shellack—my Canton correspondent—a man I was anxious to be of use to when he came over!" moaned Mr. Bultitude. "Miserable young cub, you don't know what mischief you've done!"

"Well, it won't matter much to you now," said Dick; "you're out of it all."

"Do you—do you mean to keep me out of it for ever, then?" asked Paul.

"As long as ever I can!" returned Dick frankly. "It will be rather interesting to see what sort of a fellow you'll grow into—if you ever do grow. Perhaps you will always be like that, you know. This magic is a rum thing to meddle with."

This suggestion almost maddened Paul. He made one stride forward, and faced his son with blazing eyes. "Do you think I will put up with it?" he said, between his teeth. "Do you suppose I shall stand calmly by and see you degrading and ruining me? I may never be my old self again, but I don't mean to play into your hands for all that. You can't always keep me here, and wherever I go I'll tell my tale. I know you, you clumsy rogue, you haven't the sense to play your part with common intelligence now. You would betray yourself directly I challenged you to deny my story.... You know you would.... You couldn't face me for five minutes. By Gad! I'll do it now. I'll expose you before the Doctor—before the whole school. You shall see if you can dispose of me quite so easily as you imagine!"

Dick had started back at first in unmistakable alarm at this unexpected defiance, probably feeling his self-possession unequal to such a test; but, when Paul had finished, he said doggedly: "Well, you can do it if you choose, I suppose. I can't stop you. But I don't see what good it would do."

"It would show people you were an impudent impostor, sir," said Paul sternly, going to the door as if to call the Doctor, though he shrank secretly from so extreme and dangerous a measure.

There was a hesitation in his manner, in spite of the firmness of his words, which Dick was not likely to miss. "Stop!" he said. "Before you call them in, just listen to me for a minute. Do you see this?" And, opening his coat, he pulled out from his waistcoat pocket one end of his watch-chain. Hanging to it, attached by a cheap gilt fastening of some sort, was a small grey tablet. Paul knew it at once—it was the Garudâ Stone. "You know it, I see," said Dick, as Paul was about to move towards him—with what object he scarcely knew himself. "Don't trouble to come any closer. Well, I give you fair warning. You can make things very nasty for me if you like. I can't help that—but, if you do—if you try to score off me in any way, now or at any time—if you don't keep it up when the Doctor comes in—I tell you what I shall do. I shall go straight home and find young Roly. I shall give him this stone, and just tell him to say some wish after me. I don't believe there are many things it can't do, and all I can say is—if you find yourself and all this jolly old school (except Dulcie) taken off somewhere and stuck down all at once thousands of miles away on a desolate island, or see yourself turned into a Red Indian, or, or a cabhorse, you'll have yourself to thank for it—that's all. Now you can have them all up and fire away."

"No," said Paul, in a broken voice, for, wild as the threat was, he could not afford to despise it after his experiences of the stone's power, "I—I was joking, Dick; at least I didn't mean it. I know of course I'm helpless. It's a sad thing for a father to say, but you've got the best of it.... I give in ... I won't interfere with you. There's only one thing I ask. You won't try any more experiments with that miserable stone.... You'll promise me that, at least?"

"Yes," said Dick: "it's all right. I'll play fair. As long as you behave yourself and back me up I won't touch it. I only want to stay as I am. I don't want to hurt you."

"You won't lose it?" said Paul anxiously. "Couldn't you lock it up? that fastening doesn't look very safe."

"It will do well enough," said Dick. "I got it done at the watchmaker's round the corner, for sixpence. But I'll have a stronger ring put in somewhere, if I think of it."

There was a pause, in which the conversation seemed about to flag hopelessly, but at last Dick said, almost as if he felt some compunction for his present unfilial attitude: "Now, you know, it's much better to take things quietly. It can't be altered now, can it? And it's not such bad fun being a boy after all—for some things. You'll get into it by-and-by, you see if you don't, and be as jolly as a sandboy. We shall get along all right together, too. I shan't be hard on you. It isn't my fault that you happen to be at this particular school—you chose it! And after this term you can go to any other school you like—Eton or Rugby, or anywhere. I don't mind the expense. Of, if you'd rather, you can have a private tutor. And I'll buy you a pony, and you can ride in the Row. You shall have a much better time of it than I ever had, as long as you let me go on my own way."

But these dazzling bribes had no influence upon Mr. Bultitude; nothing short of complete restitution would ever satisfy him, and he was too proud and too angry at his crushing defeat to even pretend to be in the least pacified.

"I don't want your pony," he said bitterly; "I might as well have a white elephant, and I don't suppose I should enjoy myself much more at a public school than I do here. Let's have no humbug, sir. You're up and I'm down—there's no more to be said—I shall tell the Doctor nothing, but I warn you, if ever the time comes———"

"Oh, of course," said Dick, feeling tolerably secure, now he had disposed of the main difficulty. "If you can turn me out, I suppose you will—that's only fair. I shall take care not to give you the chance. And, oh, I say, do you want any tin? How much have you got left?"

Paul turned away his head, lest Dick should see the sudden exultation he knew it must betray, as he said, with an effort to appear unconcerned, "I came away with exactly five shillings, and I haven't a penny now!"

"I say," said Dick, "you are a fellow; you must have been going it. How did you get rid of it all in a week?"

"It went, as far as I can understand," said Mr. Bultitude, "in rabbits and mice. Some boys claimed it as money they paid you to get them, I believe."

"All your own fault," said Dick, "you would have them drowned. But you'd better have some tin to get along with. How much do you want? Will half-a-crown do?"

"Half-a-crown is not much, Dick," said his father, almost humbly.

"It's—ahem—a handsome allowance for a young fellow like you," said Dick, rather unkindly; "but I haven't any half-crowns left. I must give you this, I suppose."

And he held out a sovereign, never dreaming what it signified to Paul, who clutched it with feelings too great for words, though gratitude was not a part of them, for was it not his own money?

"And now look out," said Dick, "I hear Grim. Remember what I told you; keep it up."

Dr. Grimstone came in with the air of a man who has a painful duty to perform; he started slightly as his eye noted the change in his visitor's dress and appearance. "I hope," he began gravely, "that your son has spared me the pain of going into the details of his misbehaviour; I wish I could give you a better report of him."

Dick was plainly, in spite of his altered circumstances, by no means at ease in the schoolmaster's presence; he stood, shifting from foot to foot on the hearth-rug, turning extremely red and obstinately declining to raise his eyes from the ground.

"Oh, ah," he stammered at last, "you were just going to swish him, weren't you, when I turned up, sir?"

"I found myself forced," said the Doctor, slightly shocked at this coarse way of putting things, "forced to contemplate administering to him (for his ultimate benefit) a sharp corrective in the presence of his schoolfellows. I distress you, I see, but the truth must be told. He has no doubt confessed his fault to you?"

"No," said Dick, "he hasn't though. What's he been up to now?"

"I had hoped he would have been more open, more straightforward, when confronted with the father who has proved himself so often indulgent and anxious for his improvement; it would have been a more favourable symptom, I think. Well, I must tell you myself. I know too well what a shock it will be to your scrupulously sensitive moral code, my dear Mr. Bultitude" (Dick showed a painful inclination to giggle here); "but I have to break to you the melancholy truth that I detected this unhappy boy in the act of conducting a secret and amorous correspondence with a young lady in a sacred edifice!"

Dick whistled sharply: "Oh, I say!" he cried, "that's bad" (and he wagged his head reprovingly at his disgusted father, who longed to denounce his hypocrisy, but dared not); "that's bad ... he shouldn't do that sort of thing you know, should he? At his age too ... the young dog!"

"This horror is what I should have expected from you," said the Doctor (though he was in truth more than scandalised by the composure with which his announcement was received). "Such boldness is indeed characteristic of the dog, an animal which, as you are aware, was with the ancients a synonym for shamelessness. No boy, however abandoned, should hear such words of unequivocal condemnation from a father's lips without a pang of shame!"

Paul was only just able to control his rage by a great effort.

"You're right there, sir," said Dick; "he ought to be well ragged for it ... he'll break my heart, if he goes on like this, the young beggar. But we mustn't be too hard on him, eh? After all, it's nature, you know, isn't it?"

"I beg your pardon?" said Dr. Grimstone very stiffly.

"I mean," explained Dick, with a perilous approach to digging the other in the ribs, "we did much the same sort of thing in our time, eh? I'm sure I did—lots of times!"

"I can't reproach myself on that head, Mr. Bultitude; and permit me to say, that such a tone of treating the affair is apt to destroy the effect, the excellent moral effect, of your most impressively conveyed indignation just now. I merely give you a hint, you understand!"

"Oh, ah," said Dick, feeling that he had made a mistake, "yes, I didn't mean that. But I say, you haven't given him a—a whopping yet, have you?"

"I had just stepped out to procure a cane for that purpose," said the Doctor, "when your name was announced."

"Well, look here, you won't want to start again when I'm gone, will you?"

"An ancient philosopher, my dear sir, was accustomed to postpone the correction of his slaves until the first glow of his indignation had passed away. He found that he could——"

"Lay it on with more science," suggested Dick, while Paul writhed where he stood. "Perhaps so, but you might forgive him now, don't you think? he won't do it again. If he goes writing any more love-letters, tell me, and I'll come and talk to him; but he's had a lesson, you know. Let him off this time."

"I have no right to resist such an entreaty," said the Doctor, "though I may be inclined myself to think that a few strokes would render the lesson more permanent. I must ask you to reconsider your plea for his pardon."

Paul heard this with indescribable anxiety; he had begun to feel tolerably sure that his evil hour was postponed *sine die*, but might not Dick be cruel and selfish enough to remain neutral, or even side with the enemy, in support of his assumed character?

Luckily he was not. "I'd rather let him off," he said awkwardly; "I don't approve of caning fellows myself. It never did me any good, I know, and I got enough of it to tell."

"Well, well, I yield. Richard, your father has interceded for you; and I cannot disregard his wishes, though I have my own view in the matter. You will hear no more of this disgraceful conduct, sir, unless you do something to recall it to my memory. Thank your father for his kindness, which you so little deserved, and take your leave of him."

"Oh, there, it's all right!" said Dick; "he'll behave himself after this, I know. And oh! I say, sir," he added hastily, "is—is Dulcie anywhere about?"

"My daughter?" asked the Doctor. "Would you like to see her?"

"I shouldn't mind," said Dick, blushing furiously.

"I'm sorry to say she has gone out for a walk with her mother," said the Doctor. "I'm afraid she cannot be back for some time. It's unfortunate."

Dick's face fell. "It doesn't matter," he muttered awkwardly. "She's all right, I hope?"

"She is very seldom ailing, I'm happy to say; just now she is particularly well, thank you."

"Oh, is she?" said Dick gloomily, probably disappointed to find that he was so little missed, and not suspecting that his father had been accepted as a substitute.

"Well, do you mind—could I see the fellows again for a minute or two—I mean I should rather like to inspect the school, you know."

"See my boys? Certainly, my dear sir, by all means; this way," and he took Dick out to the schoolroom—Paul following out of curiosity. "You'll find us at our studies, you see," said the Doctor, as he opened the first baize door. There was a suspicious hubbub and hum of voices from within; but as they entered every boy was bent over his books with the rapt absorption of the devoted student—an absorption that was the direct effect of the sound the door-handle made in turning.

"Our workshop," said the Doctor airily, looking round. "My first form, Mr. Bultitude. Some good workers here, and some idle ones."

Dick stood in the doorway, looking (if the truth must be told) uncommonly foolish. He had wanted, in coming there, to enjoy the contrast between the past and present—which accounts for a good many visits of "old boys" to the scene of their education. But, confronted with his former schoolfellows, he was seized at first with an utterly unreasonable fear of detection.

The class behaved as classes usually do on such occasions. The good boys smirked and the bad ones stared—the general expression being one of uneasy curiosity. Dick said never a word, feeling strangely bashful and nervous.

"This is Tipping, my head boy," touching that young gentleman on the shoulder, and making him several degrees more uncomfortable. "I expect solid results from Tipping some day."

"He looks as if his head was pretty solid," said Dick, who had once cut his knuckles against it.

"My second boy, Biddlecomb. If he applies himself, he too will do me credit in the world."

"How do, Biddlecomb?" said Dick. "I owe you ninepence—I mean—oh hang it, here's a shilling for you! Hallo, Chawner!" he went on, gradually overcoming his first nervousness, "how are you getting on, eh? Doing much in the sneaking way lately?"

"You know him!" exclaimed the Doctor with naive surprise.

"No, no; I don't know him. I've heard of him, you know—heard of him!" Chawner looked down his nose with a feeble attempt at a gratified simper, while his neighbours giggled with furtive relish.

"Well," said Dick at last, after a long look at all the old familiar objects, "I must be off, you know. Got some important business at home this evening to look after. The fellows look very jolly and contented, and all that sort of thing. Enough to make one want to be a boy again almost, eh? Good-bye, you chaps—ahem, young gentlemen, I wish you good morning!"

And he went out, leaving behind him the impression that "young Bultitude's governor wasn't half such a bad old buffer."

He paused at the open front door, to which Paul and the Doctor had accompanied him. "Good-bye," he said; "I wish I'd seen Dulcie. I should like to see your daughter, sir; but it can't be helped. Good-bye; and you," he added in a lower tone to his father, who was standing by, inexpressibly pained and disgusted by his utter want of dignity, "you mind what I told you. Don't try any games with me!"

And, as he skipped jauntily down the steps to the gateway, the Doctor followed his unwieldy, oddly-dressed form with his eyes, and, inclining his head gravely to Dick's sweeping wave of the hand, asked with a compassionate tone in his voice. "You don't happen to know, Richard, my boy, if your father has had any business troubles lately—anything to disturb him?"

And Mr. Bultitude's feelings prevented him from making any intelligible reply.

15.
The Rubicon

"My three schoolfellows,

Whom I will trust—as I will adders fanged;

They bear the mandate."

Paul never quite knew how the remainder of that day passed at Crichton House. He was ordered to join a class which was more or less engaged with some kind of work: he had a hazy idea that it was Latin, though it may have been Greek; but he was spared the necessity of taking any active part in the proceedings, as Mr. Blinkhorn was not disposed to be too exacting with a boy who in one short morning had endured a sentence of expulsion, a lecture, the immediate prospect of a flogging, and a paternal visit, and, as before, mercifully left him alone.

His classmates, however, did not show the same chivalrous delicacy; and Paul had to suffer many unmannerly jests and gibes at his expense, frequent and anxious inquiries as to the exact nature of his treatment in the dining-room, with sundry highly imaginative versions of the same, while there was much candid and unbiassed comment on the appearance and conduct of himself and his son.

But he bore it unprotesting—or, rather, he scarcely noticed it; for all his thoughts were now entirely taken up by one important subject—the time and manner of his escape.

Thanks to Dick's thoughtless liberality, he had now ample funds to carry him safely home. It was hardly likely that any more unexpected claims could be brought against him now, particularly as he had no intention of publishing his return to solvency. He might reasonably consider himself in a position to make his escape at the very first favourable opportunity.

When would that opportunity present itself? It must come soon. He could not wait long for it. Any hour might yet see him pounced upon and flogged heartily for some utterly unknown and unsuspected transgression; or the golden key which would unlock his prison bars might be lost in some unlucky moment; for his long series of reverses had made him loth to trust to Fortune, even when she seemed to look smilingly once more upon him.

Fortune's countenance is apt to be so alarmingly mobile with some unfortunates.

But in spite of the new facilities given him for escape, and his strong motives for taking advantage of them, he soon found to his utter dismay that he shrank from committing himself to so daring and dangerous a course, just as much as when he had tried to make a confidant of the Doctor.

For, after all, could he be sure of himself? Would his ill-luck suffer him to seize the one propitious moment, or would that fatal self-distrust and doubt that had paralysed him for the past week seize him again just at the crisis?

Suppose he did venture to take the first irrevocable step, could he rely on himself to go through the rest of his hazardous enterprise? Was he cool and wary enough? He dared not expect an uninterrupted run. Had he ruses and expedients at command on any sudden check?

If he could not answer all these doubts favourably, was it not sheer madness to take to flight at all?

He felt a dismal conviction that his success would have to depend, not on his own cunning, but on the forbearance or blindness of others. The slightest *contretemps* must infallibly upset him altogether.

The fact was, he had all his life been engaged in the less eventful and contentious branches of commerce. His will had seldom had to come in contact with others, and when it did so, he had found means, being of a prudent and cautious temperament, of avoiding disagreeable personal consequences by timely compromises or judicious employment of delegates. He had generally found his fellow-men ready to meet him reasonably as an equal or a superior.

But now he must be prepared to see in everyone he met a possible enemy, who would hand him over to the tyrant on the faintest suspicion. They were spies to be baffled or disarmed, pursuers to be eluded. The smallest slip in his account of himself would be enough to undo him.

No wonder that, as he thought over all this, his heart quailed within him.

They say—the paradox-mongers say—that it requires a far higher degree of moral courage for a soldier in action to leave the ranks under fire and seek a less distinguished position towards the rear, than would carry him on with the rest to charge a battery.

This may be true, though it might not prove a very valuable defence at a court-martial; but, at all events, Mr. Bultitude found, when it came to the point, that it was almost impossible for him to screw up his courage to run away.

It is not a pleasant state, this indecision whether to stay passively and risk the worst or avoid it by flight, and the worst of it is that, whatever course is eventually forced upon us, it finds us equally unprepared, and more liable from such indecision to bungle miserably in the sequel.

Paul might never have gained heart to venture, but for an unpleasant incident that took place during dinner and a discovery he made after it.

They happened to have a particularly unpopular pudding that day; a pallid preparation of suet, with an infrequent currant or two embalmed in it, and Paul was staring at his portion of this delicacy disconsolately enough, wondering how he should contrive to consume and, worse still, digest it, when his attention was caught by Jolland, who sat directly opposite him.

That young gentleman, who evidently shared the general prejudice against the currant pudding, was inviting Mr. Bultitude's attention to a little contrivance of his own for getting rid of it, which consisted in delicately shovelling the greater part of what was on his plate into a large envelope held below the table to receive it.

This struck Paul as a heaven-sent method of avoiding the difficulty, and he had just got the envelope which had held Barbara's letter out of his pocket, intending to follow Jolland's example, when the Doctor's voice made him start guiltily and replace the envelope in his pocket.

"Jolland," said the Doctor, "what have you got there?"

"An envelope, sir," explained Jolland, who had now got the remains of his pudding safely bestowed.

"What is in that envelope?" said the Doctor, who happened to have been watching him.

"In the envelope, sir? Pudding, sir," said Jolland, as if it were the most natural thing in the world to send bulky portions of pudding by post.

"And why did you place pudding in the envelope?" inquired the Doctor in his deepest tone.

Jolland felt a difficulty in explaining that he had done so because he wished to avoid eating it, and with a view to interring it later on in the playground: he preferred silence.

"Shall I tell you why you did it, sir?" thundered the Doctor. "You did it, because you were scheming to obtain a second portion—because you did not feel yourself able to eat both portions at your leisure here, and thought to put by a part to devour in secret at a future time. It's a most painful exhibition of pure piggishness. There shall be no pocketing at this table, sir. You will eat that pudding under my eye at once, and you will stay in and write out French verbs for two days. That will put an end to any more gorging in the garden for a time, at least."

Jolland seemed stupefied, though relieved, by the unexpected construction put upon his conduct, as he gulped down the intercepted fragments of pudding, while the rest diligently cleared their plates with as much show of appreciation as they could muster.

Mr. Bultitude shuddered at this one more narrow escape. If he had been detected—as he must have been in another instant—in smuggling pudding in an envelope he might have incautiously betrayed his real motives, and then, as the Doctor was morbidly sensitive concerning all complaints of the fare he provided, he would have got into worse trouble than the unfortunate Jolland, to say nothing of the humiliation of being detected in such an act.

It was a solemn warning to him of the dangers he was exposed to hourly, while he lingered within those walls; but his position was still more strongly brought home to him by the terrible discovery he made shortly afterwards.

He was alone in the schoolroom, for the others had all gone down into the playground, except Jolland, who was confined in one of the class-rooms below, when the thought came over him to test the truth of Dick's hint about a name cut on the Doctor's writing-table.

He stole up to it guiltily, and, lifting the slanting desk which stood there, examined the surface below. Dick had been perfectly correct. There it was, glaringly fresh and distinct, not large but very deeply cut and fearfully legible. "R. Bultitude." It might have been done that day. Dick had probably performed it out of bravado, or under the impression that he was not going to return after the holidays.

Paul dropped the desk over the fatal letters with a shudder. The slightest accidental shifting of it must disclose them—nothing but a miracle could have kept them concealed so long. When they did come to light, he knew from what he had seen of the Doctor, that the act would be considered as an outrage of the blackest and most desperate kind. He would most unquestionably get a flogging for it!

He fetched a large pewter ink-pot, and tried nervously to blacken the letters with the tip of a quill, to make them, if possible, rather less obtrusive than they were. All in vain; they only stood out with more startling vividness when picked out in black upon the brown-stained deal. He felt very like a conscience-stricken murderer trying to hide a corpse that *wouldn't* be buried. He gave it up at last, having only made a terrible mess with the ink.

That settled it. He must fly. The flogging must be avoided at all hazards. If an opportunity delayed its coming, why, he must do without the opportunity—he must make one. For good or ill, his mind was made up now for immediate flight.

All that afternoon, while he sat trying to keep his mind upon long sums in Bills of Parcels, which disgusted him as a business man, by the glaring improbability of their details, his eye wandered furtively down the long tables to where the Doctor sat at the head of the class. Every chance movement of the principal's elbow filled him with a sickening dread. A hundred times did those rudely carved letters seem about to start forth and denounce him.

It was a disquieting afternoon for Paul.

But the time dragged wearily on, and still the desk loyally kept its secret. The dusk drew on and the gas-burners were lit. The younger boys came up from the lower class-room and were sent out to play; the Doctor shortly afterwards dismissed his own class to follow them, and Paul and his companions had the room to themselves.

He sat there on the rough form with his slate before him, hearing half-unconsciously the shouts, laughter, and ring of feet coming up from the darkness outside, and the faint notes of a piano, which filtered through the double doors from one of the rooms, where a boy was practising Haydn's "Surprise," from Hamilton's exercise book, a surprise which he rendered as a mildly interjectional form of astonishment.

All the time Paul was racked with an intense burning desire to get up and run for it then, before it became too late; but cold fits of doubt and fear preserved him from such lunacy—he would wait, his chance might come before long.

His patience was rewarded; the Doctor came in, looking at his watch, and said, "I think these boys have had enough of it, Mr. Tinkler, eh? You can send them out now till tea-time."

Mr. Tinkler, who had been entangling himself frightfully in intricate calculations upon the blackboard, without making a single convert, was only too glad to take advantage of the suggestion, and Paul followed the rest into the playground with a sense of relief.

The usual "chevy" was going on there, with more spirit than usual, perhaps, because the darkness allowed of practical jokes and surprises, and offered great facilities for paying off old grudges with secrecy and despatch, and as the Doctor had come to the door of the greenhouse, and was looking on, the players exerted themselves still more, till the "prison" to which most of one side had been consigned by being run down and touched by their fleeter enemies was filled with a long line of captives holding hands and calling out to be released.

Paul, who had run out vaguely from his base, was promptly pursued and made prisoner by an unnecessarily vigorous thump in the back, after which he took his place at the bottom of the line of imprisoned ones.

But the enemy's spirit began to slacken; one after another of the players still left to the opposite side succeeded in outrunning pursuit and touching the foremost prisoner for the time being, so as to set him free by the rules of the game. The Doctor went in again, and the enemy relapsed as usual into total indifference, so that Paul, without exactly knowing how, soon found himself the only one left in gaol, unnoticed and apparently forgotten.

He could not see anything through the darkness, but he heard the voices of the boys disputing at the other side of the playground; he looked round; at his right was the indistinct form of a large laurel bush, behind that he knew was the playground gate. Could it be that his chance had come at last?

He slipped behind the laurel and waited, holding his breath; the dispute still went on; no one seemed to have noticed him, probably the darkness prevented all chance of that; he went on tip-toe to the gate—it was not locked.

He opened it very carefully a little way; it was forbearing enough not to creak, and the next moment he was outside, free to go where he would!

Escape, after all, was simple enough when he came to try it; he could hardly believe at first that he really was free at last; free with money enough in his pocket to take him home, with the friendly darkness to cover his retreat; free to go back and confront Dick on his own ground, and, by force, or fraud, get the Garudâ Stone into his own hands once more.

As yet he never doubted that it would be easy enough to convince his household, if necessary, of the truth of his story, and enlist them one and all on his side; all that he required, he thought, was caution; he must reach the house unobserved, and wait and watch, and the deuce would be in it if the stone were not safe in his pocket again before twelve hours had gone by.

All this time he was still within a hundred yards or so of the playground wall; he must decide upon some particular route, some definite method of ordering his flight; to stay where he was any longer would clearly be unwise, yet, where should he go first?

If he went to the station at once, how could he tell that he should be lucky enough to catch a train without having to wait long for it, and unless he did that, he would almost certainly be sought for first on the station platform, and might be caught before a train was due?

At last, with an astuteness he had not suspected himself of possessing, which was probably the result of the harrowing experiences he had lately undergone, he hit upon a plan of action. "I'll go to a shop," he thought, "and change this sovereign, and ask to look at a timetable—then, if I find I can catch a train at once, I'll run for it; if one is not due for some time, I can hang about near the station till it comes in."

With this intention he walked on towards the town till he came to a small terrace of shops, when he went into the first, which was a stationer's and toy-dealer's, with a stock in trade of cheap wooden toys and incomprehensible games, drawing slates, penny packets of stationery and cards of pen and pencil-holders, and a particularly stuffy atmosphere; the proprietor, a short man with a fat white face with a rich glaze all over it and a fringe of ragged brown whisker meeting under his chin, was sitting behind the counter posting up his ledger.

Paul looked round the shop in search of something to purchase, and at last said, more nervously than he expected to do, "I want a pencil-case, one which screws up and down." He thought a pencil-case would be an innocent, unsuspicious thing to ask for. The man set rows of cards containing pencil-cases of every imaginable shape on the counter before him, and when Mr. Bultitude had chosen and paid for one, the stationer asked if there would be anything else, and if he might send it for him. "You're one of Dr. Grimstone's young gentlemen up at Crichton House, aren't you, sir?" he added.

A guilty dread of discovery made Paul anxious to deny this at once. "No," he said; "oh no; no connection with the place. Ah, could you allow me to look at a time-table?"

"Certainly, sir; expectin' some one to-night or to-morrow p'raps. Let me see," he said, consulting a table which hung behind him. "There's a train from Pancras comes in in half an hour from now, 6.5 that is; there's another doo at 8.15, and one at 9.30. Then from Liverpool Street they run——"

"Thank you," said Mr. Bultitude, "but—but I want the up-trains."

"Ah," said the man, with a rather peculiar intonation, "I thought maybe your par or mar was comin' down. Ain't Dr. Grimstone got the times the trains go?"

"Yes," said Paul desperately, without very well knowing what he said, "yes, he has, but ah, not for this month; he—he sent me to inquire."

"Did he though?" said the stationer. "I thought you wasn't one of his young gentlemen?"

Mr. Bultitude saw what a fearful trap he had fallen into and stood speechless.

"Go along with you!" said the little stationer at last, with a not unkindly grin. "Lor bless you, I knew your face the minnit you come in. To go and tell me a brazen story like that! You're a young pickle, you are!"

Mr. Bultitude began to shuffle feebly towards the door. "Pickle, eh?" he protested in great discomposure. "No, no. Heaven knows I'm no pickle. It's of no consequence about those trains. Don't trouble. Good evening to you."

"Stop," said the man, "don't be in such a nurry now. You tell me what you want to know straightforward, and I don't mean to say as I won't help you so far as I can. Don't be afraid of my telling no tales. I've bin a schoolboy myself in my time, bless your 'art. I shouldn't wonder now if I couldn't make a pretty good guess without telling at what you're after. You've bin a catchin' of it hot, and you want to make a clean bolt of it. I ain't very far off, now, am I?"

"No," said Paul; for something in the man's manner inspired confidence. "I do want to make a bolt of it. I've been most abominably treated."

"Well, look here, I ain't got no right to interfere; and if you're caught, I look to you not to bring my name in. I don't want to get into trouble up at Crichton House and lose good customers, you see. But I like the looks of you, and you've always dealt 'ere pretty regular. I don't mind if I give you a lift. Just see here. You want to get off to London, don't you? What for is your business, not mine. Well, there's a train, express, stops at only one station on the way, in at 5.50. It's twenty minnits to six now. If you take that road just oppersite, it'll bring you out at the end of the Station Road; you can do it easy in ten minnits and have time to spare. So cut away, and good luck to you?"

"I'm vastly obliged to you," said Paul, and he meant it. It was a new experience to find anyone offering him assistance. He left the close little shop, crossed the road, and started off in the direction indicated to him at a brisk trot.

His steps rang out cheerfully on the path ironbound with frost. He was almost happy again under the exhilarating glow of unusual exercise and the excitement of escape and regained freedom.

He ran on, past a series of villa residences enclosed in varnished palings and adorned with that mediæval abundance of turrets, balconies, and cheap stained-glass, which is accepted nowadays as a guarantee of the tenant's culture, and a satisfactory substitute for effective drainage. After the villas came a church, and a few yards farther on the road turned with a sharp curve into the main thoroughfare leading to the station.

He was so near it that he could hear the shrill engine whistles, and the banging of trucks on the railway sidings echoed sharply from the neighbouring houses. He was saved, in sight of haven at last!

Full of delight at the thought, he put on a still greater pace, and turning the corner without looking, ran into a little party of three, which was coming in the opposite direction.

Fate's vein of irony was by no means worked out yet. As he was recovering from the collision, and preparing to offer or accept an apology, as the case might be, he discovered to his horror that he had fallen amongst no strangers.

The three were his old acquaintances, Coker, Coggs, and the virtuous Chawner—of whom he had fondly hoped to have seen the last for ever!

The moral and physical shock of such an encounter took all Mr. Bultitude's remaining breath away. He stood panting under the sickly rays of a street-lamp, the very incarnation of helpless, hopeless dismay.

"Hallo!" said Coker, "it's young Bultitude!"

"What do you mean by cannoning into a fellow like this?" said Coggs. "What are you up to out here, eh?"

"If it comes to that," said Paul, casting about for some explanation of his appearance, "what are you up to here?"

"Why," said Chawner, "if you want to know, Dick, we've been to fetch the *St. James' Gazette* for the Doctor. He said I might go if I liked, and I asked for Coker and Coggs to come too; because there was something I wanted to tell them, very important, and I have told them, haven't I, Corny?"

Coggs growled sulkily; Coker gave a tragic groan, and said: "I don't care when you tell, Chawner. Do it to-night if you like. Let's talk about something else. Bultitude hasn't told us yet how he came out here after us."

His last words suggested a pretext to Paul, of which he hastened to make use. "Oh," he said, "I? I came out here, after you, to say that Dr. Grimstone will not require the *St. James' Gazette*. He wants the *Globe* and, ah, the *Star* instead."

It did not sound a very probable combination; but Paul used the first names that occurred to him, and, as it happened, aroused no suspicions, for the boys read no newspapers.

"Well, we've got the other now," said Coker. "We shall have to go back and get the fellow at the bookstall to change it, I suppose. Come on, you fellows!"

This was at least a move in the right direction; for the three began at once to retrace their steps. But, unfortunately, all these explanations had taken time, and before they had gone many yards, Mr. Bultitude was horrified to hear the station-bell ring loudly, and immediately after a cloud of white steam rose above the station roof as the London train clanked cumbrously in, and was brought to with a prolonged screeching of brakes.

The others were walking very slowly. At the present pace it would be almost impossible to reach the train in time. He looked round at them anxiously. "H-hadn't we better run, don't you think?" he asked.

"Run!" said Coker scornfully. "What for? I'm not going to run. You can, if you like."

"Why, ah, really," said Paul briskly, very grateful for the permission; "do you know, I think I will!"

And run he did, with all his might, rushing headlong through the gates, threading his way between the omnibuses and under the Roman noses of the mild fly-horses in the enclosure, until at length he found himself inside the little booking-office.

He was not too late; the train was still at the platform, the engine getting up steam with a dull roar. But he dared not risk detection by travelling without a ticket. There was time for that, too. No one was at the pigeon-hole but one old lady.

But, unhappily, the old lady considered taking a ticket as a solemn rite to be performed with all due caution and deliberation. She had already catechised the clerk upon the number of stoppages during her proposed journey, and exacted earnest assurances from him that she would not be called upon to change anywhere in the course of it; and as Paul came up she was laying out the purchase-money for her ticket upon the ledge and counting it, which, the fare being high and the coins mostly halfpence, seemed likely to take some time.

"One moment, ma'am, if you please," cried Mr. Bultitude, panting and desperate. "I'm pressed for time."

"Now you've gone and put me out, little boy," said the old lady fussily. "I shall have to begin all over again. Young man, will you take and count the other end and see if it adds up right? There's a halfpenny wrong somewhere; I know there is."

"Now then," shouted the guard from the platform. "Any more going on?"

"I'm going on!" said Paul. "Wait for me. First single to St. Pancras, quick!"

"Drat the boy!" said the old lady angrily. "Do you think the world's to give way for you? Such impidence! Mind your manners, little boy, can't you? You've made me drop a threepenny bit with your scrouging!"

"First single, five shillings," said the clerk, jerking out the precious ticket.

"Right!" cried the guard at the same instant. "Stand back there, will you!"

Paul dashed towards the door of the booking-office which led to the platform; but just as he reached it a gate slammed in his face with a sharp click, through the bars of it he saw, with hot eyes, the tall, heavy carriages which had shelter and safety in them jolt heavily past, till even the red lamp on the last van was quenched in the darkness.

That miserable old woman had shattered his hopes at the very moment of their fulfilment. It was fate again!

As he stood, fiercely gripping the bars of the gate, he heard Coggs' hateful voice again.

"Hallo! so you haven't got the *Globe* and the other thing after all, then; they've shut you out?"

"Yes," said Mr. Bultitude in a hollow voice; "they've shut me out!"

16.
Hard Pressed

"Mark the poor wretch, to overshoot his troubles,

How he outruns the wind, and with what care

He cranks and crosses with a thousand doubles:

    The many musets through the which he goes

    Are like a labyrinth to amaze his foes."

As soon as the gate was opened, Paul went through mechanically with the others on to the platform, and waited at the bookstall while they changed the paper. He knew well enough that what had seemed at the time a stroke of supreme cunning would now only land him in fresh difficulties, if indeed it did not lead to the detection of his scheme. But he dared not interfere and prevent them from making the unlucky exchange. Something seemed to tie his tongue, and in sullen leaden apathy he resigned himself to whatever might be in store for him.

They passed out again by the booking-office. There was the old lady still at the pigeon-hole, trying to persuade the much-enduring clerk to restore a lucky sixpence she had given him by mistake, and was quite unable to describe. Mr. Bultitude would have given much just then to go up and shake her into hysterics, or curse her bitterly for the mischief she had done; but he refrained, either from an innate chivalry, or from a feeling that such an outburst would be ill-judged.

So, silent and miserable, with slow step and hanging head, he set out with his gaolers to render himself up once more at his house of bondage—a sort of involuntary Regulus, without the oath.

"Dickie, you were very anxious to run just now," observed Chawner, after they had gone some distance on their homeward way.

"We were late for tea—late for tea," explained Paul hastily.

"If you think the tea worth racing like that for, I don't," said Coggs viciously; "it's muck."

"You don't catch me racing, except for something worth having," said Coker.

One more flash of distinct inspiration came to Paul's aid in the very depths of his gloom. It was, in fact, a hazy recollection from English history of the ruse by which Edward I., when a prince, contrived to escape from his captors at Hereford Castle.

"Why—why," he said excitedly, "would you race if you had something worth racing for, hey? would you now?"

"Try us!" said Coker emphatically.

"What do you call 'something'?" inquired Chawner suspiciously.

"Well," said Mr. Bultitude; "what do you say to a shilling?"

"You haven't got a shilling," objected Coggs.

"Here's a shilling, see," said Paul, producing one. "Now then, I'll give this to any boy I see get into tea first!"

"Bultitude thinks he can run," said Coker, with an amiable unbelief in any disinterestedness. "He means to get in first and keep the shilling himself, I know."

"I'll back myself to run him any day," put in Coggs.

"So will I," added Chawner.

"Well, is it agreed?" Paul asked anxiously. "Will you try?"

"All right," said Chawner. "You must give us a start to the next lamp-post, though. You stay here, and when we're ready we'll say 'off'!"

They drew a line on the path with their feet to mark Paul's starting point, and went on to the next lamp. After a moment or two of anxious waiting he heard Coggs shout, all in one breath, "One-two-three-off!" and the sound of scampering feet followed immediately.

It was a most exciting and hotly contested race. Paul saw them for one brief moment in the lamplight. He saw Chawner scudding down the path like some great camel, and Coker squaring his arms and working them as if they were wings. Coggs seemed to be last.

He ran a little way himself just to encourage them, but, as the sound of their feet grew fainter and fainter, he felt that his last desperate ruse had taken effect, and with a chuckle at his own cleverness, turned round and ran his fastest in the opposite direction. He felt little or no interest in the result of the race.

Once more he entered the booking-office and, kneeling on a chair, consulted the time-board that hung on the wall over the sheaf of texts and the missionary box.

The next train was not until 7.25. A whole hour and twenty-five minutes to wait! What was he to do? Where was he to pass the weary time till then? If he lingered on the platform he would assuredly be recaptured. His absence could not remain long undiscovered and the station would be the first place they would search for him.

And yet he dared not wander away from the neighbourhood of the station. If he kept to the shops and lighted thoroughfares he might be recognised or traced. If, on the other hand, he went out farther into the country (which was utterly unknown to him), he had no watch, and it would be only too easy to lose his way, or miscalculate time and distance in the darkness.

To miss the next train would be absolutely fatal.

He walked out upon the platform, and on past the refreshment and waiting rooms, past the weighing machine, the stacked trucks and the lamp-room, meeting and seen by none—even the boy at the bookstall was busy with bread and butter and a mug of tea in a dark corner, and never noticed him.

He went on to the end of the platform where the planks sloped gently down to a wilderness of sheds, coaling stages and sidings; he could just make out the bulky forms of some tarpaulined cattle-vans and open coal-trucks standing on the lines of metals which gleamed in the scanty gaslights.

It struck him that one of these vans or trucks would serve his purpose admirably, if he could only get into it, and very cautiously he picked his way over the clogging ballast and rails, till he came to a low narrow strip of platform between two sidings.

He mounted it and went on till he came to the line of trucks and vans drawn up alongside; the vans seemed all locked, but at the end he found an empty coal-waggon in which he thought he could manage to conceal himself and escape pursuit till the longed-for 7.25 train should arrive to relieve him.

He stepped in and lay down in one corner of it, listening anxiously for any sound of search, but hearing nothing more than the dismal dirge of the telegraph wires overhead; he soon grew cold and stiff, for his enforced attitude was far from comfortable, and there was more coal-dust in his chosen retreat than he could have wished. Still it was secluded enough; it was not likely that it would occur to anyone to look for him there. Ten days ago Mr. Paul Bultitude would have found it hard to conceive himself lying down in a hard and grimy coal-truck to escape his son's schoolmaster, but since then he had gone through too much that was unprecedented and abnormal to see much incongruity in his situation—it was all too hideously real to be a nightmare.

But even here he was not allowed to remain undisturbed; after about half an hour, when he was beginning to feel almost secure, there came a sharp twanging of wires beneath, and two short strokes of a bell in the signal-box hard by.

He heard some one from the platform, probably the station-master, shout, "Look alive, there, Ing, Pickstones, some of you. There's those three trucks on the A siding to go to Slopsbury by the 6.30 luggage—she'll be in in another five minutes."

There were steps as if some persons were coming out of a cabin opposite—they came nearer and nearer: "These three, ain't it, Tommy?" said a gruff voice, close to Paul's ear.

"That's it, mate," said another, evidently Tommy's—"get 'em along up to the points there. Can't have the 6.30 standing about on this 'ere line all night, 'cos of the Limited. Now then, all together, shove! they've got the old 'orse on at the other end."

And to Paul's alarm he felt the truck in which he was begin to move ponderously on the greasy metals, and strike the next with its buffers with a jarring shock and a jangling of coupling chains.

He could not stand this; unless he revealed himself at once, or managed to get out of this delusive waggon, the six-whatever-it-was train would be up and carry him off to Slopsbury, a hundred miles or so farther from home; they would have time to warn Dick—he would be expected—ambushes laid for him, and his one chance would be gone for ever!

There was a whistle far away on the down line, and that humming vibration which announces an approaching train: not a moment to lose—he was afraid to attempt a leap from the moving waggons, and resolved to risk all and show himself.

With this intention he got upon his knees, and putting his head above the dirty bulwark, looked over and said softly, "Tommy, I say, Tommy!"

A porter, who had been laboriously employed below, looked up with a white and scared face, and staggered back several feet; Mr. Bultitude in a sudden panic ducked again.

"Bill!" Paul heard the porter say hoarsely, "I'll take my Bible oath I've never touched a drop this week, not to speak of—but I've got 'em again, Bill, I've got 'em again!"

"Got what agin?" growled Bill. "What's the matter now?"

"It's the jumps, Bill," gasped the other, "the 'orrors—they've got me and no mistake. As I'm a livin' man, as I was a shovin' of that there truck, I saw a imp—a gashly imp, Bill, stick its hugly 'ed over the side and say, 'Tommy,' it ses, jest like that—it ses, 'Tommy, I wants you!' I dursn't go near it, Bill. I'll get leave, and go 'ome and lay up—it glared at me so 'orrid, Bill, and grinned—ugh! I'll take the pledge after this 'ere, I will—I'll go to chapel Sundays reg'lar!"

"Let's see if there ain't something there first," said the practical Bill. "Easy with the 'oss up there. Now then," here he stepped on the box of the wheel and looked in. "Shin out of this, whatever y'are, we don't contrack to carry no imps on this line—Well, if ever I—Tommy, old man, it's all right, y'ain't got 'em this time—'ere's yer imp!"

And, reaching over, he hauled out the wretched Paul by the scruff of his neck in a state of utter collapse, and deposited him on the ground before him.

"That ain't your private kerridge, yer know, that ain't—there wasn't no bed made up there for you, that I know on. You ain't arter no good, now; you're a wagabone! that's about your size, I can see—what d'yer mean by it, eh?"

"Shet yer 'ed, Bill, will yer?" said Tommy, whose relief probably softened his temper, "this here's a young gent."

"Young gent, or no young gent," replied Bill sententiously, "he's no call to go 'idin' in our waggins and givin' 'ard-workin' men a turn. 'Old 'im tight, Tommy—here's the luggage down on us."

Tommy held him fast with a grip of iron, while the other porters coupled the trucks, and the luggage train lumbered away with its load.

After this the men slouched up and stood round their captive, staring at him curiously.

"Look here, my men," said Paul, "I've run away from school, I want to go on to town by the next train, and I took the liberty of hiding in the truck, because the schoolmaster will be up here very soon to look for me—you understand?"

"I understand," said Bill, "and a nice young party *you* are."

"I—I don't want to be caught," said Paul.

"Naterally," assented Tommy sympathetically.

"Well, can't you hide me somewhere where he won't see me? Come, you can do that?"

"What do you say, Bill?" asked Tommy.

"What'll the Guv'nor say?" said Bill dubiously.

"I've got a little money," urged Paul. "I'll make it worth your while."

"Why didn't you say that afore?" said Bill; "the Guv'nor needn't know."

"Here's half-a-sovereign between you," said Paul, holding it out.

"That's something like a imp," said Tommy warmly; "if all bogeys acted as 'andsome as this 'ere, I don't care how often they shows theirselves. We'll have a supper on this, mates, and drink young Delirium Trimminses' jolly good 'ealth. You come along o' me, young shaver, I'll stow you away right enough, and let you out when yer train comes in."

He led Paul on to the platform again and opened a sort of cupboard or closet. "That's where we keeps the brooms and lamp-rags, and them," he said; "it ain't what you may call tidy, but if I lock you in no one won't trouble you."

It was perfectly dark and the rags smelt unpleasantly, but Mr. Bultitude was very glad of this second ark of refuge, even though he did bruise his legs over the broom-handles; he was gladder still by-and-by, when he heard a rapid heavy footfall outside, and a voice he knew only too well, saying, "I want to see the station-master. Ha, there he is. Good evening, station-master, you know me—Dr. Grimstone, of Crichton House. I want you to assist me in a very unpleasant affair—the fact is, one of my pupils has had the folly and wickedness to run away."

"You don't say so!" said the station-master.

"It's only too true, I'm sorry to say; he seemed happy and contented enough, too; it's a black ungrateful business. But I must catch him, you know; he must be about here somewhere, I feel sure. You don't happen to have noticed a boy who looked as if he belonged to me? They can't tell me at the booking-office."

How glad Paul was now he had made no inquiries of the station-master!

"No," said the latter, "I can't say I have, sir, but some of my men may have come across him. I'll inquire—here, Ing, I want you; this gentleman here has lost one of his boys, have you seen him?"

"What sort of a young gentleman was he to look at?" Paul heard Tommy's voice ask.

"A bright intelligent-looking boy," said the Doctor, "medium height, about thirteen, with auburn hair."

"No, I ain't seen no intelligent boys with median 'eight," said Tommy slowly, "not leastways, to speak to positive. What might he 'ave on, now, besides his oburn 'air?"

"Black cloth jacket, with a wide collar," was the answer; "grey trousers, and a cloth cap with a leather peak."

"Oh," said Tommy, "then I see 'im."

"When—where?"

"'Bout arf an 'our since."

"Do you know where he is now?"

"Well," said Tommy, to Paul's intense horror, for he was listening, quaking, to every word of this conversation, which was held just outside his cupboard door.

"I dessay I could give a guess if I give my mind to it."

"Out with it, Ing, now, if you know; no tricks," said the station-master, who had apparently just turned to go away. "Excuse me, sir, but I've some matters in there to see after."

When he had gone, the Doctor said rather heatedly, "Come, you're keeping something from me, I *will* have it out of you. If I find you have deceived me, I'll write to the manager and get you sent about your business—you'd better tell me the truth."

"You see," said Tommy, very slowly, and reluctantly, "that young gent o' yourn *was* a gent."

"I tried my very best to render him so," said the Doctor stiffly, "here is the result—how did you discover he was one, pray?"

"'Cos he acted like a gent," said Tommy; "he took and give me a 'arf-suffering."

"Well, I'll give you another," said the Doctor, "if you can tell me where he is."

"Thankee, sir, don't you be afraid—you're a gent right enough, too, though you do 'appen to be a schoolmaster."

"Where is the unhappy boy?" interrupted the Doctor.

"Seems as if I was a roundin' on 'im, like, don't it a'most, sir?" said Tommy, with too evident symptoms of yielding in his voice. Paul shook so in his terror that he knocked down a broom or two with a clatter which froze his blood.

"Not at all," said the Doctor, "not at all, my good fellow; you're—ahem—advancing the cause of moral order."

"Oh, ah," said Tommy, obviously open to conviction. "Well, if I'm a doin' all that, I can't go fur wrong, can I? And arter all, we mayn't like schools or schoolmasters, not over above, but we can't get on without 'em, I s'pose. But, look ye here, sir—if I goes and tells you where you can get hold of this here boy, you won't go and wallop him now, will ye?"

"I can make no bargains," said the Doctor; "I shall act on my own discretion."

"That's it," said Tommy, unaccountably relieved, "spoke like a merciful Christian gen'leman; if you don't go actin' on nothing more nor your discretion, you can't hurt him much, I take it. Well then, since you've spoke out fair, I don't mind putting you on his track like."

If the door of the cupboard had not been locked, Paul would undoubtedly have burst out and yielded himself up, to escape the humiliation of being sold like this by a mercenary and treacherous porter. As it was, he had to wait till the inevitable words should be spoken.

"Well, you see," went on Tommy, very slowly, as if struggling with the remnants of a conscience, "it was like this here—he comes up to me, and says—your young gen'leman, I mean—says he, 'Porter, I wants to 'ide, I've run away.' And I says to him, says I, 'It's no use your 'anging about 'ere,' I says, "cause, if you do, your guv'nor (meanin' no offence to you, sir) 'll be comin' up and ketchin' of you on the 'op.' 'Right you are, porter,' says he to me, 'what do you advise?' he says. 'Well,' I says, 'I don't know as I'm right in givin' you no advice at all, havin' run away from them as has the care on you,' I says; 'but if *I* was a young gen'leman as didn't want to be ketched, I should just walk on to Dufferton; it ain't on'y three mile or so, and you'll 'ave time for to do it before the up-train comes along there.' 'Thankee, porter,' he says, 'I'll do that,' and away he bolts, and for anything I know, he's 'arf way there by this time."

"A fly!" shouted the Doctor excitedly, when Tommy had come to the end of his veracious account. "I'll catch the young rascal now—who has a good horse? Davis, I'll take you. Five shillings if you reach Dufferton before the up-train. Take the——"

The rest was lost in the banging of the fly door and the rumble of wheels; the terrible man had been got safely off on a wrong scent, and Paul fell back amongst the lumber in his closet, faint with the suspense and relief.

Presently he heard Tommy's chuckling whisper through the keyhole: "Are you all right in there, sir? he's safe enough now—orf on a pretty dance. You didn't think I was goin' to tell on ye, did ye now? I ain't quite sech a cur as that comes to, particular when a young gent saves me from the 'orrors, and gives me a 'arf-suffering. I'll see you through, you make yourself easy about that."

Half an hour went slowly by for Mr. Bultitude in his darkness and solitude. The platform gradually filled, as he could tell by the tread of feet, the voices, and the scent of cigars, and at last, welcome sound, he heard the station bell ringing for the up-train.

It ran in the next minute, shaking the cupboard in which Paul crouched, till the brushes rattled. There was the usual blind hurry and confusion outside as it stopped. Paul waited impatiently inside. The time passed, and still no one came to let him out. He began to grow alarmed. Could Tommy have forgotten him? Had he been sent away by some evil chance at the critical moment? Two or three times his excited fancy heard the fatal whistle sound for departure. Would he be left behind after all?

But the next instant the door was noiselessly unlocked. "Couldn't do it afore," said honest Tommy. "Our guv'nor would have seen me. Now's your time. Here's a empty first-class coach I've kept for ye. In with you now."

He hoisted Paul up the high footboard to an empty compartment, and shut the door, leaving him to sink down on the luxurious cushions in speechless and measureless content. But Tommy had hardly done so before he reappeared and looked in. "I say," he suggested, "if I was you, I'd get under the seat before you gets to Dufferton, otherways your guv'nor'll be spottin' you. I'll lock you in."

"I'll get under now; some one might see me here," said Paul; and, too anxious for safety to thank his preserver, he crawled under the low, blue-cushioned seat, which left just room enough for him to lie there in a very cramped and uncomfortable position. Still he need not stay there after the train had once started, except for five minutes or so at Dufferton.

Unfortunately he had not been long under the seat before he heard two loud imperious voices just outside the carriage door.

"Porter! guard! Hi, somebody! open this door, will you; it's locked."

"This way, sir," he heard Tommy's voice say outside. "Plenty of room higher up."

"I don't want to go higher up. I'll go here. Just open it at once, I tell you."

The door was opened reluctantly, and two middle-aged men came in. "Always take the middle carriage of a train," said the first. "Safest in any accident, y'know. Never heard of a middle carriage of a train getting smashed up, to speak of."

The other sat heavily down just over Paul, with a comfortable grunt, and the train started, Paul feeling naturally annoyed by this intrusion, as it compelled him to remain in seclusion for the whole of the journey. "Still," he thought, "it is lucky that I had time to get under here before they came in; it would have seemed odd if I had done it afterwards." And he resigned himself to listen to the conversation which followed.

"What was it we were talking about just now?" began the first. "Let me see. Ah! I remember. Yes; it was a very painful thing—very, indeed, I assure you."

There is a certain peculiar and uncomfortable suspicion that attacks most of us at times, which cannot fairly be set down wholly to self-consciousness or an exaggerated idea of our own importance. I mean the suspicion that a partly-heard conversation must have ourselves for its subject. More often than not, of course, it proves utterly unfounded, but once in a way, like most presentiments, it finds itself unpleasantly fulfilled.

Mr. Bultitude, though he failed to recognise either of the voices, was somehow persuaded that the conversation had something to do with himself, and listened with eager attention.

"Yes," the speaker continued; "he was never, according to what I hear, a man of any extraordinary capacity, but he was always spoken of as a man of standing in the City, doing a safe business, not a risky one, and so on, you know. So, of course, his manner, when I called, shocked me all the more."

"Ah!" said the other. "Was he violent or insulting, then?"

"No, no! I can only describe his conduct as eccentric—what one might call reprehensibly eccentric and extravagant. I didn't call exactly in the way of business, but about a poor young fellow in my house, who is, I fear, rather far gone in consumption, and, knowing he was a Life Governor, y'know, I thought he might give me a letter for the hospital. Well, when I got up to Mincing Lane——"

Paul started. It was as he had feared, then; they *were* speaking of him!

"When I got there, I sent in my card with a message that, if he was engaged or anything, I would take the liberty of calling at his private house, and so on. But they said he would see me. The clerk who showed me in said: 'You'll find him a good deal changed, if you knew him, sir. We're very uneasy about him here,' which prepared me for something out of the common. Well, I went into a sort of inner room, and there he was, in his shirt-sleeves, busy over some abomination he was cooking at the stove, with the office-boy helping him! I never was so taken aback in my life. I said something about calling another time, but Bultitude——"

Paul groaned. The blow had fallen. Well, it was better to be prepared and know the worst.

"Bultitude says, just like a great awkward schoolboy, y'know, 'What's your name? How d'ye do? Have some hardbake, it's just done?' Fancy finding a man in his position cooking toffee in the middle of the day, and offering it to a perfect stranger!"

"Softening of the brain—must be," said the other.

"I fear so. Well, he asked what I wanted, and I told him, and he actually said he never did any business now, except sign his name where his clerks told him. He'd worked hard all his life, he said, and he was tired of it. Business was, I understood him to say, 'all rot!'"

"Then he wouldn't promise me votes or give me a letter or anything, without consulting his head clerk; he seemed to know nothing whatever about it himself, and when that was over, he asked me a quantity of frivolous questions which appeared to have a sort of catch in them, as far as I could gather, and he was exceedingly angry when I wouldn't humour him."

"What kind of questions?"

"Well, really I hardly know. I believe he wanted to know whether I would rather be a bigger fool than I looked or look a bigger fool than I was, and he pressed me quite earnestly to repeat some foolishness after him, about 'being a gold key,' when he said 'he was a gold lock,' I was very glad to get away from him, it was so distressing."

"They tell me he has begun to speculate, too, lately," said the other. "You see his name about in some very queer things. It's a pitiful affair altogether."

Paul writhed under his seat with shame. How could he, even if he succeeded in ousting Dick and getting back his old self, how could he ever hold up his head again after this?

Why, Dick must be mad. Even a schoolboy would have had more caution when so much depended on it. But none would suspect the real cause of the change. These horrible tales were no doubt being circulated everywhere!

The conversation fell back into a less personal channel again after this; they talked of "risks," of some one who had only been "writing" a year and was doing seven thousand a week, of losses they had been "on," and of the uselessness of "writing five hundred on everything," and while at this point the train slackened and stopped—they had reached Dufferton.

There was an opening of doors all along the train, and sounds of some inquiry and answer at each. The voices became audible at length, and, as he had expected, Paul found that the Doctor, not having discovered him on the platform, was making a systematic search of the train, evidently believing that he had managed to slip in somewhere unobserved.

It was a horrible moment when the door of his compartment was flung open and a stream of ice-cold air rushed under the blue cloth which, fortunately for Paul, hung down almost to the floor.

Some one held a lantern up outside, and by its rays Paul saw from behind the hanging the upper half of Dr. Grimstone appear, very pale and polite, at the doorway. He remained there for some moments without speaking, carefully examining every corner of the compartment.

The two men on the seats drew their wraps about them and shivered, until at length one said rather testily—"Get in, sir; kindly get in if you're coming on, please. This draught is most unpleasant!"

"I do not propose to travel by this train, sir," said the Doctor; "but, as a person entrusted with the care of youth, permit me to inquire whether you have seen (or, it may be assisted to conceal) a small boy of intelligent appearance——"

"Why should we conceal small boys of intelligent appearance about us, pray?" demanded the man who had described his visit to Mincing Lane. "And may we ask you to shut that door, and make any communications you wish to make through the window, or else come in and sit down?"

"That's not an answer to my question, sir," retorted the Doctor. "I notice you carefully decline to say whether you have seen a boy. I consider your manner suspicious, sir; and I shall insist on searching this carriage through and through till I find that boy!"

Mr. Bultitude rolled himself up close against the partition at these awful words.

"Guard, guard!" shouted the first gentleman. "Come here. Here's a violent person who will search this carriage for something he has lost. I won't be inconvenienced in this way without any reason whatever! He says we're hiding a boy in here!"

"Guard!" said the Doctor, quite as angrily, "I insist upon looking under these seats before you start the train. I've looked through every other carriage and he must be in here. Gentlemen, let me pass, I'll get him if I have to travel in this compartment to town with you!"

"For peace and quietness sake, gentlemen," said the guard, "let him look round, just to ease his mind. Lend me your stick a minute, sir, please. I'll turn him out if he's anywhere about this here compartment!"

And with this he pulled Dr. Grimstone down from the footboard and mounted it himself; after which he began to rummage about under the seats with the Doctor's heavy stick.

Every lunge found out some tender part in Mr. Bultitude's person and caused him exquisite torture; but he clenched his teeth hard to prevent a sound, while he thought each fresh dig must betray his whereabouts.

"There," said the guard at last; "there really ain't no one there, sir, you see. I've felt everywhere and—— Hello, I certainly did feel something just then, gentlemen!" he added, in an undertone, after a lunge which took all the breath out of Paul's body. All was lost now!

"You touch that again with that confounded stick if you dare!" said one of the passengers. "That's a parcel of mine. I won't have you poking holes through it in that way. Don't tell that lunatic behind you, he'll be wanting it opened to see if his boy's inside! Now perhaps you'll let us alone!"

"Well, sir," said the guard at last to the Doctor, as he withdrew, "he ain't in there. There's nothing under any of the seats. Your boy'll be comin' on by the next train, most likely—the 8.40. We're all behind. Right!"

"Good night, sir," said the first passenger as he leant out of the window, to the baffled schoolmaster on the platform. "You've put us to all this inconvenience for nothing, and in the most offensive way too. I hope you won't find your boy till you're in a better temper, for his sake."

"If I had you out on this platform, sir," shouted the angry Doctor, "I'd horsewhip you for that insult. I believe the boy's there and you know it. I——"

But the train swept off and, to Paul's joy and thankfulness, soon left the Doctor, gesticulating and threatening, miles behind it.

"What a violent fellow for a schoolmaster, eh?" said one of Paul's companions, when they were fairly off again. "I wasn't going to have him turning the cushions inside out here; we shouldn't have settled down again before we got in!"

"No; and if the guard hasn't, as it is, injured that Indian shawl in my parcel, I shall be—— Why, bless my soul, that parcel's not under the seat after all! It's up in the rack. I remember putting it there now."

"The guard must have fancied he felt something; and yet—— Look here, Goldicutt; just feel under here with your feet. It certainly does seem as if something soft was—eh?"

Mr. Goldicutt accordingly explored Paul's ribs with his boot for some moments, which was very painful.

"Upon my word," he said at last, "it really does seem very like it. It's not hard enough for a bag or a hat-box. It yields distinctly when you kick it. Can you fetch it out with your umbrella, do you think? Shall we tell the guard at the next——? Lord, it's coming out of its own accord. It's a dog! No, my stars— it's the boy, after all!"

For Paul, alarmed at the suggestion about the guard, once more felt inclined to risk the worst and reveal himself. Begrimed with coal, smeared with whitewash, and covered with dust and flue, he crawled slowly out and gazed imploringly up at his fellow-passengers.

After the first shock of surprise they lay back in their seats and laughed till they cried.

"Why, you young rascal!" they said, when they recovered breath, "you don't mean to say you've been under there the whole time?"

"I have indeed," said Paul. "I—I didn't like to come out before."

"And are you the boy all this fuss was about? Yes? And we kept the schoolmaster off without knowing it! Why, this is splendid, capital! You're something like a boy, you little dog, you! This is the best joke I've heard for many a day!"

"I hope," said Paul, "I haven't inconvenienced you. I could not help it, really."

"Inconvenienced us? Gad, your schoolmaster came very near inconveniencing us and you too. But there, he won't trouble any of us now. To think of our swearing by all our gods there was no boy in here, and vowing he shouldn't come in, while you were lying down there under the seat all the time! Why, it's lovely! The boy's got pluck and manners too. Shake hands, young gentleman, you owe us no apologies. I haven't had such a laugh for many a day!"

"Then you—you won't give me up?" faltered poor Paul.

"Well," said the one who was called Goldicutt, and who was a jovial old gentleman with a pink face and white whiskers, "we're not exactly going to take the trouble of getting out at the next station, and bringing you back to Dufferton, just to oblige that hot-tempered master of yours, you know; he hasn't been so particularly civil as to deserve that."

"But if he were to telegraph and get some one to stop me at St. Pancras?" said Paul nervously.

"Ah, he might do that, to be sure—sharp boy this—well, as we've gone so far, I suppose we must go through with the business now and smuggle the young scamp past the detectives, eh, Travers?"

The younger man addressed assented readily enough, for the Doctor had been so unfortunate as to prejudice them both from the first by his unjustifiable suspicions, and it is to be feared they had no scruples in helping to outwit him.

Then they noticed the pitiable state Mr. Bultitude was in, and he had to give them a fair account of his escape and subsequent adventures, at which even their sympathy could not restrain delighted shouts of laughter—though Paul himself saw little enough in it all to laugh at; they asked his name, which he thought more prudent, for various reasons, to give as "Jones," and other details, which I am afraid he invented as he went on, and altogether they reached Kentish Town in a state of high satisfaction with themselves and their protégé.

At Kentish Town there was one more danger to be encountered, for with the ticket collector there appeared one of the station inspectors. "Beg pardon, gentlemen," said the latter, peering curiously in, "but does that young gent in the corner happen to belong to either of you?"

The white-whiskered gentleman seemed a little flustered at this downright inquiry, but the other was more equal to the occasion. "Do you hear that, Johnny, my boy," he said, to Paul (whom they had managed during the journey to brush and scrape into something approaching respectability), "they want to know if you belong to me. I suppose you'll allow a son to belong to his father to a certain extent, eh?" he asked the inspector.

The man apologised for what he conceived to be a mistake. "We've orders to look out for a young gent about the size of yours, sir," he explained; "no offence meant, I'm sure," and he went away satisfied.

A very few minutes more and the train rolled in to the terminus, under the same wide arch beneath which Paul had stood, helpless and bewildered, a week ago.

"Now my advice to you, young man," said Mr. Goldicutt, as he put Paul into a cab, and pressed half-a-sovereign into his unwilling hand, "is to go straight home to Papa and tell him all about it. I daresay he won't be very hard on you—here's my card, refer him to me if you like. Good-night, my boy, good-night, and good luck to you. Gad, the best joke I've had for years!"

And the cab rolled away, leaving them standing chuckling on the platform, and, as Paul found himself plunging once more into the welcome roar and rattle of London streets, he forgot the difficulties and dangers that might yet lie before him in the thought that at last he was beyond the frontier, and, for the first time since he had slipped through the playground gate, he breathed freely.

17.
A Perfidious Ally

"But homeward—home—what home? had he a home?

His home—he walk'd;

Then down the long street having slowly stolen,

His heart foreshadowing all calamity,

His eyes upon the stones, he reached his home."

Paul had been careful, whilst in the hearing of his friends, to give the cabman a fictitious address, but as soon as he reached the Euston Road, he stopped the man and ordered him to put him down at the church near the south end of Westbourne Terrace, for he dared not drive up openly to his own door.

At last he found himself standing safely on the pavement, looking down the long line of yellow lamps of his own terrace, only a few hundred yards from home.

But though his purpose was now within easy reach, his spirits were far from high; his anxiety had returned with tenfold power; he felt no eagerness or exultation; on the contrary, the task he had set himself had never before seemed so hopeless, so insurmountable.

He stood for some time by the railing of the church, which was lighted up for evening service, listening blankly to the solemn drone of the organ within, unable to summon up resolution to move from the spot and present himself to his unsuspecting family.

It was a cold night, with a howling wind, and high in the blue black sky fleecy clouds were coursing swiftly along; he obliged himself to set out at last, and walked down the flags towards his house, shivering as much from nervousness as cold.

There was a dance somewhere in the terrace that evening, a large one; as far as he could see there were close ranks of carriages with blazing lamps, and he even fancied he could hear the shouts of the link-boys and the whistles summoning cabs.

As he came nearer, he had a hideous suspicion, which soon became a certainty, that the entertainment was at his own house; worse still, it was of a kind and on a scale calculated to shock and horrify any prudent householder and father of a family.

The balcony above the portico was positively hung with gaudy Chinese lanterns, and there were even some strange sticks and shapes up in one corner that looked suspiciously like fireworks. Fireworks in Westbourne Terrace! What would the neighbours think or do?

Between the wall which separates the main road from the terrace and the street front there were no less than four piano-organs, playing, it is to be feared, by express invitation; and there was the usual crowd of idlers and loungers standing about by the awning stretched over the portico, listening to the music and loud laughter which came from the brilliantly lighted upper rooms.

Paul remembered then, too late, that Barbara in that memorable letter of hers had mentioned a grand children's party as being in contemplation. Dick had held his tongue about it that morning; and he himself had not thought it was to be so soon.

For an instant he felt almost inclined to turn away and give the whole thing up in sick despair—even to return to Market Rodwell and brave the Doctor's anger; for how could he hope to explain matters to his family and servants, or get the Garudâ Stone safely into his hands again before all these guests, in the whirl and tumult of an evening party?

And yet he dared not, after all, go back to Crichton House—that was too terrible an alternative, and he obviously could not roam the world to any extent, a runaway schoolboy to all appearance, and with less than a sovereign in his pocket!

After a short struggle, he felt he must make his way in, watch and wait, and leave the rest to chance. It was his evil fate, after all, that had led him on to make his escape on this night of all others, and had allowed him to come through so much, only to be met with these unforeseen complications just when he might have imagined the worst was over.

He forced his way through the staring crowd, and went down the steps into the area; for he naturally shrank from braving the front door, with its crowd of footmen and hired waiters.

He found the door in the basement open, which was fortunate, and slipped quietly through the pantry, intending to reach the hall by the kitchen stairs. But here another check met him. The glass door which led to the stairs happened to be shut, and he heard voices in the kitchen, which convinced him that if he wished to escape notice he must wait quietly in the darkness until the door was opened for him, whenever that might be.

The door from the pantry to the kitchen was partly open, however, and Mr. Bultitude could not avoid hearing everything that passed there, although every fresh word added to his uneasiness, until at last he would have given worlds to escape from his involuntary position of eavesdropper.

There were only two persons just then in the kitchen: his cook, who, still in her working dress, was refreshing herself after her labours over the supper with a journal of some sort, and the housemaid, who, in neat gala costume, was engaged in fastening a pin more securely in her white cap.

"They haven't give me a answer yet, Eliza," said the cook, looking up from her paper.

"Lor, cook!" said Eliza, "you couldn't hardly expect it, seeing you only wrote on Friday."

"No more I did, Eliza. You see it on'y began to come into my mind sudden like this last week. I'm sure I no more dreamt———. But they've answered a lady who's bin in much the same situation as me aperiently. You just 'ark to this a minute." And she proceeded to read from her paper: "'*Lady Bird.*— You ask us (1) what are the signs by which you may recognise the first dawnings of your lover's affection. On so delicate a matter we are naturally averse from advising you; your own heart must be your best guide. But perhaps we may mention a few of the most usual and infallible symptoms'— What sort of a thing is a symptim, Eliza?"

"A symptim, cook," explained Eliza, "is somethink wrong with the inside. Her at my last place in Cadogan Square had them uncommon bad. She was what they call æsthetical, pore young thing. Them infallible ones are always the worst."

"It don't seem to make sense though, Eliza," objected cook doubtfully. "Hear how it goes on: 'Infallible symptoms. If you have truly inspired him with a genuine and lasting passion' (don't he write beautiful?) 'passion, he will continually haunt those places in which you are most likely to be found' (I couldn't tell you the times master's bin down in my kitching this last week); 'he will appear awkward and constrained in your presence' (anything more awkward than master *I* never set eyes on. He's knocked down one of the best porcelain vegetables this very afternoon!); 'he will beg for any little favours, some trifle, it may be, made by your own hand' (master's always a-asking if I've got any of those doughnuts to give away); 'and, if granted, he will treasure them in secret with pride and rapture' (I don't think master kep' any of them doughnuts though, Eliza. I saw him swaller five; but you couldn't treasure a doughnut, not to mention——— I'll make him a pincushion when I've time, and see what he does with it). 'If you detect all these indications of liking in the person you suspect of paying his addresses to you, you may safely reckon upon bringing him to your feet in a very short space of time. (2) Yes, fuller's earth will make them exquisitely white.'"

"There, Eliza!" said cook, with some pride, when she had finished; "if it had been meant for me it couldn't have been clearer. Ain't it written nice? And on'y to think of my bringing master to my feet! It seems almost too much for a cook to expect!"

"I wouldn't say so, cook; I wouldn't. Have some proper pride. Don't let him think he's only to ask and have! Why, in the *London Journal* last week there was a dook as married a governess; and I should 'ope as a cook ranked above a governess. Nor yet master ain't a dook; he's only in the City! But are you sure he's not only a-trifling with your affections, cook? He's bin very affable and pleasant with all of us lately."

"It ain't for me to speak too positive, Eliza," said cook almost bashfully, "nor to lay bare the feelings of a bosom, beyond what's right and proper. You're young yet, Eliza, and don't understand these things—leastways, it's to be hoped not" (Eliza having apparently tossed her head); "but do you remember that afternoon last week as master stayed at home a-playin' games with the children? I was a-goin' upstairs to fetch my thimble, and there, on the bedroom landin', was master all alone, with one of Master Dick's toy-guns in his 'and, and a old slouch 'at on his head.

"'Have you got a pass, cook?' he says, and my 'art came right up into my mouth, he looked that severe and lofty at me. I thought he was put out about something."

"I said I didn't know as it was required, but I could get one, I says, not knowing what he was alludin' to all the same."

"But he says, quite soft and tender-like," (here Paul shivered with shame), "'No, you needn't do that, cook, there ain't any occasion for it; only,' he says, 'if you haven't got no pass, you'll have to give me a kiss, you know, cook!' I thought I should have sunk through the stairs, I was that overcome. I saw through his rouge with half an eye."

"Why, he said the same to me," said Eliza, "only I had a pass, as luck had it, which Miss Barbara give me. I'd ha' boxed his ears if he'd tried it, too, master or no master!"

"You talk light, Eliza," said the cook sentimentally, "but you weren't there to see. It wasn't only the words, it was the way he said it, and the 'ug he gave me at the time. It was as good as a proposal. And, I tell you, whatever you may say—and mark my words—I 'ave 'opes!"

"Then, if I was you, cook," said Eliza, "I'd try if I could get him to speak out plain in writing; then, whatever came of it, there'd be as good as five hundred pounds in your pockets."

"Love-letters!" cried the cook, "why, Lord love you, Eliza—— Why, William, how you made me jump! I thought you was up seein' to the supper-table."

"The pastrycook's man is looking after all that, Jane," said Boaler's voice. "I've been up outside the droring-room all this time, lookin' at the games goin' on in there. It's as good as a play to see the way as master is a unbendin' of himself, and such a out and out stiff-un as he used to be, too! But it ain't what I like to see in a respectable house. I'm glad I give warning. It doesn't do for a man in my position to compromise his character by such goings on. I never see anything like it in any families I lived with before. Just come up and see for yourself. You needn't mind about cleanin' of yourself—they won't see you."

So the cook allowed herself to be persuaded by Boaler, and the two went up to the hall, and, to Mr. Bultitude's intense relief, forgot to close the glazed door which cut him off from the staircase.

As he followed them upstairs at a cautious interval, and thought over what he had just so unwillingly overheard, he felt as one who had just been subjected to a moral showerbath. "That dreadful woman!" he groaned. "Who would have dreamed that she would get such horrible ideas into her head? I shall never be able to look either of those women in the face again: they will both have to go—and she made such excellent soup, too. I do hope that miserable Dick has not been fool enough to write to her—but no, that's too absurd."

But more than ever he began to wish that he had stayed in the playground.

When he reached the hall he stood there for some moments in anxious deliberation over his best course of proceeding. His main idea was to lie in wait somewhere for Dick, and try the result of an appeal to his better feelings to acknowledge his outcast parent and abdicate gracefully.

If that failed, and there was every reason to expect that it would fail, he must threaten to denounce him before the whole party. It would cause a considerable scandal no doubt, and be extremely repugnant to his own feelings, but still he must do it, or frighten Dick by threatening to do it, and at all hazards he must contrive during the interview to snatch or purloin the magic stone; without that he was practically helpless.

He looked round him: the study was piled up with small boys' hats and coats, and in one corner was a kind of refined bar, where till lately a trim housemaid had been dispensing coffee and weak lemonade; she might return at any moment, he would not be safe there.

Nor would the dining-room be more secluded, for in it there was an elaborate supper being laid out by the waiters which, as far as he could see through the crack in the door, consisted chiefly of lobsters, trifle, and pink champagne. He felt a grim joy at the sight, more than he would suffer for this night's festivities.

As he stole about, with a dismal sense of the unfitness of his sneaking about his own house in this guilty fashion, he became gradually aware of the scent of a fine cigar, one of his own special Cabañas. He wondered who had the impudence to trespass on his cigar-chest; it could hardly be one of the children.

He traced the scent to a billiard room which he had built out at the side of the house, which was a corner one, and going down to the door opened it sharply and walked in.

Comfortably imbedded in the depths of a long well-padded lounging chair, with a spirit case and two or three bottles of soda water at his elbow, sat a man who was lazily glancing through the *Field* with his feet resting on the mantelpiece, one on each side of the blazing fire. He was a man of about the middle size, with a face rather bronzed and reddened by climate, a nose slightly aquiline and higher in colour, quick black eyes with an uneasy glance in them, bushy black whiskers, more like the antiquated "Dundreary" type than modern fashion permits, and a wide flexible mouth.

Paul knew him at once, though he had not seen him for some years; it was Paradine, his disreputable brother-in-law—the "Uncle Marmaduke" who, by importing the mysterious Garudâ Stone, had brought all these woes upon him; he noticed at once that his appearance was unusually prosperous, and that the braided smoking coat he wore over his evening clothes was new and handsome. "No wonder," he thought bitterly, "the fellow has been living on me for a week!" He stood by the cue-rack looking at him for some time, and then he said with a cold ironic dignity that (if he had known it) came oddly from his boyish lips: "I hope you are making yourself quite comfortable?"

Marmaduke put down his cigar and stared: "Uncommonly attentive and polite of you to inquire," he said at last, with a dubious smile, which showed a row of very white teeth, "whoever you are. If it will relieve your mind at all to know, young man, I'm happy to say I am tolerably comfortable, thanks."

"I—I concluded as much," said Paul, nearly choked with rage.

"You've been very nicely brought up," said Uncle Marmaduke, "I can see that at a glance. So you've come in here, like me, eh? because the children bore you, and you want a quiet gossip over the world in general? Sit down then, take a cigar, if you don't think it will make you very unwell. I shouldn't recommend it myself, you know, before supper—but you're a man of the world and know what's good for you. Come along, enjoy yourself till you find yourself getting queer—then drop it."

Mr. Bultitude had always detested the man—there was an underbred swagger and familiarity in his manner that made him indescribably offensive; just now he seemed doubly detestable, and yet Paul by a strong effort succeeded in controlling his temper.

He could not afford to make enemies just then, and objectionable as the man was, his astuteness made him a valuable ally; he determined, without considering the risk of making such a confident, to tell him all and ask his advice and help.

"Don't you know me, Paradine?"

"I don't think I have the privilege—you're one of Miss Barbara's numerous young friends, I suppose? and yet, now I look at you, you don't seem to be exactly got up for an evening party; there's something in your voice, too, I ought to know."

"You ought," said Paul, with a gulp. "My name is Paul Bultitude!"

"To be sure!" cried Marmaduke. "By Jove, then, you're my young nephew, don't you know; I'm your long-lost uncle, my boy, I am indeed (I'll excuse you from coming to my arms, however; I never was good at family embraces). But, I say, you little rascal, you've never been asked to these festivities, you ought to be miles away, fast asleep in your bed at school. What in the name of wonder are you doing here?"

"I've—left school," said Paul.

"So I perceive. Sulky because they left you out of all this, eh? Thought you'd turn up in the middle of the banquet, like the spectre bridegroom—'the worms they crawled in, and the worms they crawled out,' eh? Well, I like your pluck, but, ahem—I'm afraid you'll find they've rather an unpleasant way of laying your kind of apparitions."

"Never mind about that," said Paul hurriedly; "I have something I must tell you—I've no time to lose. I'm a desperate man!"

"You are," Paradine assented with a loud laugh, "oh, you are indeed! 'a desperate man.' Capital! a stern chase, eh? the schoolmaster close behind with the birch! It's quite exciting, you know, but, seriously, I'm very much afraid you'll catch it!"

"If," began Mr. Bultitude in great embarrassment, "if I was to tell you that I was not myself at all—but somebody else, a—in fact, an entirely different person from what I seem to you to be—I suppose you would laugh?"

"I beg your pardon," said his brother-in-law politely, "I don't think I quite catch the idea."

"When I assure you now, solemnly, as I stand here before you, that I am not the miserable boy whose form I am condemned to—to wear, you'll say it is incredible?"

"Not at all—by no means, I quite believe you. Only (really it's a mere detail), but I should rather like to know, if you're not that particular boy, what other boy you may happen to be. You'll forgive my curiosity."

"I'm not a boy at all—I'm your own unhappy brother-in-law, Paul! You don't believe me, I see."

"Oh, pardon me, it's perfectly clear! you're not your own son, but your own father—it's a little confusing at first, but no doubt common enough. I'm glad you mentioned it, though."

"Go on," said Paul bitterly, "make light of it—you fancy you are being very clever, but you will find out the truth in time!"

"Not without external assistance, I'm afraid," said Paradine calmly. "A more awful little liar for your age I never saw!"

"I'm tired of this," said Paul. "Only listen to reason and common sense!"

"Only give me a chance."

"I tell you," protested Paul earnestly, "it's the sober awful truth—I'm not a boy, it's years since I was a boy—I'm a middle-aged man, thrust into this, this humiliating form."

"Don't say that," murmured the other; "it's an excellent fit—very becoming, I assure you."

"Do you want to drive me mad with your clumsy jeers?" cried Paul. "Look at me. Do I speak, do I behave, like an ordinary schoolboy?"

"I really hope not—for the sake of the rising generation," said Uncle Marmaduke, chuckling at his own powers of repartee.

"You are very jaunty to-day—you look as if you were well off," said Paul slowly. "I remember a time when a certain bill was presented to me, drawn by you, and appearing to be accepted (long before I ever saw it) by me. I consented to meet it for my poor Maria's sake, and because to disown my signature would have ruined you for life. Do you remember how you went down on your knees in my private room and swore you would reform and be a credit to your family yet? You weren't quite so well off, or so jaunty then, unless I am very much mistaken."

These words had an extraordinary effect upon Uncle Marmaduke; he turned ashy white, and his quick eyes shifted restlessly as he half rose from his chair and threw away his unfinished cigar.

"You young hound!" he said, breathing hard and speaking under his breath. "How did you get hold of that—that lying story? Your father must have let it out! Why do you bring up bygones like this? You—you're a confounded, disagreeable little prig! Who told you to play an ill-natured trick of this sort on an uncle, who may have been wild and reckless in his youth—was in fact—but who never, never misused his relation towards you as—as an uncle?"

"How did I get hold of the story?" said Paul, observing the impression he had made. "Do you think if I were really a boy of thirteen I should know as much about you as I do? Do you want to know more? Ask, if you dare! Shall I tell you how it was you left your army coach without going up for examination? Will you have the story of your career in my old friend Parkinson's counting-house, or the real reason of your trip to New York, or what it was that made your father add that codicil, cutting you off with a set of engravings of the 'Rake's Progress,' and a guinea to pay for framing them? I can tell you all about it, if you care to hear."

"No!" shrieked Paradine, "I won't listen. When you grow up, ask your father to buy you a cheap Society journal. You're cut out for an editor of one. It doesn't interest me."

"Do you believe my story or not?" asked Paul.

"I don't know. Who could believe it?" said the other sullenly. "How can you possibly account for it?"

"Do you remember giving Maria a little sandal-wood box with a small stone in it?" said Paul.

"I have some recollection of giving her something of that kind. A curiosity, wasn't it?"

"I wish I had never seen it. That infernal stone, Paradine, has done all this to me. Did no one tell you it was supposed to have any magic power?"

"Why, now I think of it, that old black rascal, Bindabun Doss, did try to humbug me with some such story; said it was believed to be a talisman, but the secret was lost. I thought it was just his stingy way of trying to make the rubbish out as something priceless, as it ought to have been, considering all I did for the old ruffian."

"You told Maria it was a talisman. Bindabun what's-his-name was right. It is a talisman of the deadliest sort. I'll soon convince you, if you will only hear me out."

And then, in white-hot wrath and indignation, Mr. Bultitude began to tell the story I have already attempted to sketch here, dwelling bitterly on Dick's heartless selfishness and cruelty, and piteously on his own incredible sufferings, while Uncle Marmaduke, lolling back in his armchair with an attempt (which was soon abandoned) to retain a smile of amused scepticism on his face, heard him out in complete silence and with all due gravity.

Indeed, Paul's manner left him no room for further unbelief. His tale, wild and improbable as it was, was too consistent and elaborate for any schoolboy to have invented, and, besides, the imposture would have been so entirely purposeless.

When his brother-in-law had come to the end of his sad history, Paradine was silent for some time. It was some relief to know that the darkest secrets of his life had not been ferreted out by a phenomenally sharp nephew; but the change in the situation was not without its drawbacks—it remained to be seen how it might affect himself. He already saw his reign in Westbourne Terrace threatened with a speedy determination unless he played his cards well.

"Well," he said at last, with a swift, keen glance at Paul, who sat anxiously waiting for his next words; "suppose I were to say that I think there may be something in this story of yours, what then? What is it you want me to do for you?"

"Why," said Paul, "with all you owe to me, now you know the horrible injustice I have had to bear, you surely don't mean to say that you won't help me to right myself?"

"And if I did help you, what then?"

"Why, I should be able to recover all I have lost, of course," said Mr. Bultitude. He thought his brother-in-law had grown very dull.

"Ah, but I mean, what's to become of *me*?"

"You?" repeated Paul (he had not thought of that). "Well, hum, from what I know and what you know that I know about your past life, you can't expect me to encourage you to remain here?"

"No," said Uncle Marmaduke. "Of course not; very right and proper."

"But," said Paul, willing to make all reasonable concessions, "anything I can do to advance your prospects—such as paying your passage out to New York, you know, and so on—I should be very ready to do."

"Thank you!" said the other.

"And even, if necessary, provide you with a small fund to start afresh upon—honestly," said Paul; "you will not find me difficult to deal with."

"It's a dazzling proposition," remarked Paradine drily. "You have such an alluring way of putting things. But the fact, is, you'll hardly believe it, but I'm remarkably well off here. I am indeed. Your son, you know, though not you (except as a mere matter of form), really makes, as they say of the marmalade in the advertisements, an admirable substitute. I doubt, I do assure you, whether you yourself would have received me with quite the same warmth and hospitality I have met with from him."

"So do I," said Paul; "very much."

"Just so; for, without your admirable business capacity and extraordinary firmness of character, you know, he has, if you'll excuse my saying so, a more open guileless nature, a more entire and touching faith in his fellow-man and brother-in-law, than were ever yours."

"To say that to me," said Paul hotly, "is nothing less than sheer impudence."

"My dear Paul (it does seem deuced odd to be talking to a little shrimp like you as a grown-up brother-in-law. I shall get used to it presently, I daresay). I flatter myself I am a man of the world. We're dealing with one another now, as the lawyers have it, at arm's length. Just put yourself in my place (you're so remarkably good at putting yourself in other people's places, you know). Look at the thing from my point of view. Accidentally dropping in at your offices to negotiate (if I could) a small temporary loan from anyone I chanced to meet on the premises, I find myself, to my surprise, welcomed with effusion into what I then imagined to be your arms. More than that, I was invited here for an indefinite time, all my little eccentricities unmentioned, overlooked. I was deeply touched (it struck me, I confess, at one time that you must be touched too), but I made the best use of my opportunities. I made hay while the sun shone."

"Do you mean to make me lose my temper?" interrupted Paul. "It will not take much more."

"I have no objection. I find men as a rule easier to deal with when they have once lost their temper, their heads so often go too. But to return: a man with nerve and his fair share of brains, like myself, only wants a capitalist (he need not be a millionaire) at his back to conquer the world. It's not by any means my first campaign, and I've had my reverses, but I see victory in my grasp, sir, in my grasp at last!"

Paul groaned.

"Now you—it's not your fault, I know, a mere defect of constitution; but you, as a speculator, were, if I may venture to put it so, not worth your salt; no boldness, no dash, all caution. But your promising son is a regular whale on speculation, and I may tell you that we stand in together in some little ventures that would very probably make your hair stand on end—*you* wouldn't have touched them. And yet there's money in every one of them."

"*My* money!" said Paul savagely; "and it won't come out again."

"You don't know much about these things, you see," said Marmaduke; "I tell you I have my eye on some fine openings for capital."

"Your pockets always were very fine openings for capital," retorted Paul.

"Ha, ha, deuced sharp that! But, to come to the point, you were always a sensible practical kind of a fellow, and you must see, that, for me to back you up and upset this young rascal who has stepped into your slippers, might be morally meritorious enough, but, treating it from a purely pecuniary point of view, it's not business."

"I see," said Mr. Bultitude heavily; "then you side against me?"

"Did I ever say I would side against you? Let us hear first what you propose to do."

Paul, upon this, explained that, as he believed the Stone still retained its power of granting one wish to any other person who happened to get hold of it, his idea was to get possession of it somehow from Dick, who probably would have it about him somewhere, and then pass it on to some one whom he could trust not to misuse it so basely.

"A good idea that, Paul, my boy," said Paradine, smiling; "but you don't imagine our young friend would be quite such an idiot as not to see your game! Why, he would pitch the Stone in the gutter or stamp it to powder, rather than let you get hold of it."

"He's quite capable of it," said Paul; "in fact, he threatened to do worse than that. I doubt if I shall ever be able to manage it myself; but what am I to do? I must try, and I've no time to lose about it either."

"I tell you this," said Marmaduke, "if you let him see you here, it's all up with you. What you want is some friend to manage this for you, some one he won't suspect. Now, suppose I were willing to risk it for you?"

"You!" cried Paul, with involuntary distrust.

"Why not?" said Marmaduke, with a touch of feeling. "Ah, I see, you can't trust me. You've got an idea into your head that I'm a thorough-paced rascal, without a trace of human feeling about me. I daresay I deserve it, I daresay I do; but it's not generous, my boy, for all that. I hope to show you your mistake yet, if you give me the chance. You allow yourself to be prejudiced by the past, that's where you make your mistake. I only put before you clearly and plainly what it was I was giving up in helping you. A fellow may have a hard cynical kind of way of putting things, and yet, take my word for it, Paul, have a heart as tender as a spring chicken underneath. I believe I'm something like that myself. I tell you I'm sorry for you. I don't like to see a family man of your position in such a regular deuce of a hole. I feel bound to give you a lift out of it, and let my prospects take their own chance. I leave the gratitude to you. When I've done, kick me down the doorsteps if you like. I shall go out into the world with the glow of self-approval (and rapid motion) warming my system. Take my advice, don't attempt to tackle Master Dick yourself. Leave him to me."

"If I could only make up my mind to trust you!" muttered Paul.

"The old distrust!" cried Marmaduke; "you can't forget. You won't believe a poor devil like me can have any gratitude, any disinterestedness left in him. Never mind, I'll go. I'll leave it to you. I'll send Dick in here, and we shall see whether he's such a fool as you think him."

"No," said Paul, "no; I feel you're right; that would never do."

"It would be for my advantage, I think," said the other, "but you had better take me while I am in a magnanimous mood, the opportunity may never occur again. Come, am I to help you or not? Yes or no?"

"I must accept," said Paul reluctantly; "I can't find Boaler now, and it might take hours to make him see what I wanted. I'll trust to your honour. What shall I do?"

"Do? Get away from this, he'll be coming in here very soon to see me. Run away and play with the children or hide in the china closet—anything but stay here."

"I—I must be here while you are managing him," objected Paul.

"Nonsense!" said Paradine angrily. "I tell you it will spoil all, unless you—who's that? it's his step—too late now—dash it all! Behind that screen, quick—don't move for your life till I tell you you may come out!"

Mr. Bultitude had no choice; there was just time to set up an old folding screen which stood in a corner of the room and slip behind it before the door opened.

It might not be the highest wisdom to trust everything to his new ally in this manner; but what else could he do, except stand by in forced inactivity while the momentous duel was being fought out? Just then, at all events, he saw no other course.

18.
Run to Earth

"The is noon in this hous schuld bynde me this night."

—*The Coke's Tale of Gamelyn.*

Dick burst open the door of the billiard-room rather suddenly, and then stood holding on to the handle and smiling down upon his relative in a happy and affectionate but rather weak manner.

"So here you are!" he said. "Been lookin' for you everywhere. What's good of shutting 'self in here? Come up and play gamesh. No? Come in and have shupper. I've had shupper."

"So I perceive," observed Uncle Marmaduke; and the fact was certainly obvious enough.

"Tell y'what I did," giggled the wretched Dick. "You know I never did get what I call regular good blow out—always some one to shay 'had quite 'nough' 'fore I'd begun. So I thought this time I would have a tuck-in till—till I felt tired, and I—he-he-he—I got down 'fore anybody elsh and helped myshelf. Had first go-in. No one to help to thingsh. No girlsh to bother. It was prime! When they've all gone up again you and me'll go in and have shome more, eh?"

"You're a model host," said his uncle.

"It's a good shupper," Dick went on. "I ought to know. I've had some of everything. It'sh almost too good for kids. But it'sh a good thing I went in first. After I'd been in a little time I saw a sponge-cake on the table, and when I tried it, what d'ye think I found? It was as full inside of brandy-an'-sherry as it could be. All it could do to shtand! I saw d'rectly it washn't in condition come to table, and I said, 'Take it away! take it away! It'sh drunk; it'sh a dishgraceful sight for children!' But they wouldn't take it away; sho I had to take it away. But you can't take away a whole tipshy-cake!"

"I am quite sure you did your best," murmured Paradine.

"Been having such gamesh upstairs!" said Dick, with another giggle. "That lil' Dolly Merridew's jolly girl. Not sho nice as Dulcie, though. Here, you, let'sh go up and let off fireworksh on balcony, eh? Letsh have jolly lark!"

"No, no," said his uncle. "You and I are too old for that sort of thing. You should leave the larks to the young fellows."

"How do you know I'm too old for sorterthing?" said Dick, with an offended air.

"Well, you're not a young man any longer, you know. You ought to behave like the steady old buffer you look."

"Why?" demanded Dick; "why should I behave like shteady ole buffer, when I don't feel shteady ole buffer? What do you want shpoil fun for? Tell you I shall do jus' zackly wharriplease. And, if you shay any more, I'll punch y' head!"

"No, no," said his uncle, slightly alarmed at this intimation. "Come, you're not going to quarrel with me, I'm sure!"

"All ri'," said Dick. "No; I won' quarrel. Don' wanter quarrel anybody."

"That's right," said Paradine. "I knew you were a noble fellow!"

"Sho I am," said Dick, shaking hands with effusion. "Sho are you. Nearly ash noble 'sh me. There, you're jolly good fellow. I say, I've goo' mind tell you something. Make you laugh. But I won't; not now."

"Oh, you can tell me," said Marmaduke. "No secrets between friends, you know."

"Shan't tell you now," said Dick. "Keep shecret little longer."

"Do you know, my friend, that there's something very odd about you I've noticed lately? Something that makes me almost fancy sometimes you're not what you pretend to be."

Dick sat down heavily on one of the leather benches placed against the wall.

"Eh, what d'you shay?" he gasped. "Shay tharragain."

"You look to me," said Marmaduke slowly, "like some one excellently made up for the part of heavy father, without a notion how to play it. Dick, you young dog, you see I know you! You can't take me in with all this. You'd better tell me all about it."

Dick seemed almost sobered by this shock.

"You've found me out," he repeated dully. "Then it's all up. If you've found me out, everybody elsh can find me out!"

"No, no; it's not so bad as that, my boy. I've better eyes than most people, and then I had the privilege of knowing your excellent father rather well once upon a time. You haven't studied his little peculiarities closely enough; but you'll improve. By the way, where *is* your excellent father all this time?"

"He's all right," said Dick, beginning to chuckle. "He-he. He's at school, he is!"

"At school. You mean to say you've put him to school at his time of life! He's rather old for that sort of thing, isn't he? They don't take him on the ordinary terms, do they?"

"Ah," said Dick, "that'sh where it is. He isn't old, you see, now, to look at."

"Not old to look at! Then how on earth—— I should like to know how you managed all that. What have you been doing to the poor gentleman?"

"That'sh my affair," said Dick. "An' if I don' tell you you won' find that out anyway!"

"There's only one way you could have done it," said Paradine, pretending to hesitate. "It must have been done by some meddling with magic. Now what—— Let me see—yes—— Surely the Stone I brought your poor mother from India was given to me as a talisman of some sort? You can't have been sharp enough to get hold of that!"

"How did you know?" cried Dick sharply. "Who told you?"

"I am right, then? Well, you are a clever fellow. I should like to know how you did it, now?"

"Did it with the Shtone," said Dick, evidently discomposed by such unexpected penetration, but unable to prevent a little natural complacency. "All my own idea. No one helped me. It—it washn't sho bad for me, wash it?"

"Bad! it was capital!" cried Marmaduke enthusiastically. "It was a stroke of genius! And so my Indian Stone has done all this for you. Sounds like an Arabian Night, by Jove! By-the-by, you don't happen to have it about you, do you? I should rather like to look at it again. It's a real curiosity after this."

Paul trembled with anxiety. Would Dick be induced to part with it? If so, he was saved! But Dick looked at his uncle's outstretched hand, and wagged his head with tipsy cunning.

"I dareshay you would," he said, "but I'm not sho green as all that. Don't let that Stone out of my hands for anyone."

"Why, I only wanted to look at it for a minute or two," said Marmaduke; "I wouldn't hurt it or lose it."

"You won' get chance," said Dick.

"Oh, very well," said Paradine carelessly, "just as you please, it doesn't matter; though when we come to talk things over a little, you may find it better to trust me more than that."

"Wha' do you mean?" said Dick uneasily.

"Well, I'll try to explain as well as I can, my boy (drink a little of this soda water first, it's an excellent thing after supper); there, you're better now, aren't you? Now, I've found you out, as you see; but only because I knew something of the powers of this Stone of yours, and guessed the rest. It doesn't at all follow that other people, who know nothing at all, will be as sharp; if you're more careful about your behaviour in future—unless, unless, young fellow——" and here he paused meaningly.

"Unless what?" asked Dick suspiciously.

"Unless I chose to tell them what I've found out."

"What would you tell them?" said Dick.

"What? Why, what I know of this talisman; tell them to use their eyes; they wouldn't be very long before they found out that something was wrong. And when one or two of your father's friends once get hold of the idea, your game will be very soon over—you know that as well as I do."

"But," stammered Dick, "you wouldn't go and do beastly mean thing like that? I've not been bad fellow to you."

"The meanness, my dear boy, depends entirely upon the view you take of it. Now, the question with me, as a man of honour (and I may tell you an over-nice sense of honour has been a drawback I've had to struggle against all my life), the question with me is this: Is it not my plain duty to step in and put a stop to this topsy-turvy state of things, to show you up as the barefaced young impostor you are, and restore my unhappy brother-in-law to his proper position?"

"Very well expressed," thought Paul, who had been getting uncomfortable; "he has a heart, as he said, after all!"

"How does that seem to strike you?" added Paradine.

"It shtrikes me as awful rot," said Dick, with refreshing candour.

"It's the language of conscience, but I don't expect you to see it in the same light. I don't mind confessing to you, either, that I'm a poor devil to whom money and a safe and respectable position (all of which I have here) are great considerations. But whenever I see the finger of duty and honour and family affection all beckoning me along a particular road, I make a point of obeying their monitions—occasionally. I don't mean to say that I never have bolted down a back way, instead, when it was made worth my while, or that I never will."

"I wonder what he's driving at now," thought Paul.

"I don't know about duty and honour, and all that," said Dick; "my head aches, it's the noise they're making upstairs. Are you goin' to tell?"

"The fact is, my dear boy, that when one has had a keen sense of honour in constant use for several years, it's like most other articles, apt to become a little the worse for wear. Mine is not what it used to be, Dicky (that's your name, isn't it?). Our powers fail as we grow old."

"I don' know what you're talking about!" said Dick helplessly. "Do tell me what you mean to do."

"Well then, your head's clear enough to understand this much, I hope," said Paradine a little impatiently, "that, if I did my duty and exposed you, you wouldn't be able to keep up the farce for a single hour, in spite of all your personal advantages—you know that, don't you?"

"I shpose I know that," said Dick feebly.

"You know too, that if I could be induced—mind, I don't say I can—to hold my tongue and stay on here and look after you and keep you from betraying yourself by any more of these schoolboy follies, there's not much fear that anyone else will ever find out the secret——"

"Which are you going to do, then?" said Dick.

"Suppose I say that I like you, that you have shown me more kindness in a single week than ever your respectable father has since I first made his acquaintance? Suppose I say that I am willing to let the sense of honour and duty, and all the rest of it, go overboard together; that we two together are a match for Papa, wherever he may be and whatever he chooses to say and do?"

There was a veiled defiance in his voice that seemed meant for more than Dick, and alarmed Mr. Bultitude; however, he tried to calm his uneasiness and persuade himself that it was part of the plot.

"Will you say that?" cried Dick excitedly.

"On one condition, which I'll tell you by-and-by. Yes, I'll stand by you, my boy, I'll coach you till I make you a man of business every bit as good as your father, and a much better man of the world. I'll show you how to realise a colossal fortune if you only take my advice. And we'll pack Papa off to some place abroad where he'll have no holidays and give no trouble!"

"No," said Dick firmly; "I won't have that. After all, he's my governor."

"Do what you like with him then, he can't do much harm. I tell you, I'll do all this, on one condition—it's a very simple one——"

"What is it?" asked Dick.

"This. You have, somewhere or other, the Stone that has done all this for you—you may have it about you at this very moment—ah!" (as Dick made a sudden movement towards his white waistcoat) "I thought so! Well, I want that Stone. You were afraid to leave it in my hands for a minute or two just now; you must trust me with it altogether."

Paul was relieved; of course this was merely an artifice to recover the Garudâ Stone, and Marmaduke was not playing him false after all—he waited breathlessly for Dick's answer.

"No," said Dick, "I can't do that; I want it too."

"Why, man, what use is it to you? it only gives you one wish, you can't use it again."

Dick mumbled something about his being ill, and Barbara wishing him well again.

"I suppose I can do that as well as Barbara," said his uncle. "Come, don't be obstinate, give me the Stone; it's very important that it should be in safe hands."

"No," said Dick obstinately; he was fumbling all the time irresolutely in his pockets; "I mean to keep it myself."

"Very well then, I have done with you. To-morrow morning I shall step up to Mincing Lane, and then to your father's solicitor. I think his offices are in Bedford Row, but I can easily find out at your father's place. After that, young man, you'll have a very short time to amuse yourself in, so make the best of it."

"No, don't leave me, let me alone for a minute," pleaded Dick, still fumbling.

At this a sudden suspicion of his brother-in-law's motives for wishing to get the Stone into his own hands overcame all Paul's prudence. If he was so clever in deceiving Dick, might he not be cheating *him*, too, just as completely? He could wait no longer, but burst from behind the screen and rushed in between the pair.

"Go back!" screamed Paradine. "You infernal old idiot, you've ruined everything!"

"I won't go back," said Paul, "I don't believe in you. I'll hide no longer. Dick, I forbid you to trust that man."

Dick had risen in horror at the sudden apparition, and staggered back against the wall, where he stood staring stupidly at his unfortunate father with fixed and vacant eyes.

"Badly as you've treated me, I'd rather trust you than that shifty plausible fellow there. Just look at me, Dick, and then say if you can let this cruelty go on. If you knew all I've suffered since I have been among those infernal boys, you would pity me, you would indeed.... If you send me back there again, it will kill me.... You know as well as I do that it is worse for me than ever it could be for you.... You can't really justify yourself because of a thoughtless wish of mine, spoken without the least intention of being taken at my word. Dick, I may not have shown as much affection for you as I might have done, but I don't think I deserve all this. Be generous with me now, and I swear you will never regret it."

Dick's lips moved; there really was something like pity and repentance in his face, muddled and dazed as his general expression was by his recent over-indulgence, but he said nothing.

"Give papa the Stone by all means," sneered Paradine. "If you do, he will find some one to wish the pair of you back again, and then, back you go to school again, the laughing-stock of everybody, you silly young cub!"

"Don't listen to him, Dick," urged Paul. "Give it to me, for Heaven's sake; if you let him have it, he'll use it to ruin us all."

But Dick turned his white face to the rival claimants and said, getting the words out with difficulty: "Papa, I'm shorry. It is a shame. If I had the Shtone, I really would give it you, upon my word-an'-honour I would. But—but, now I can't ever give it up to you. It'sh gone. Losht!"

"Lost!" cried Marmaduke. "When, where? When do you last recollect seeing it? you must know!"

"In the morning," said Dick, twirling his chain, where part of the cheap gilt fastening still hung.

"No; afternoon. I don't know," he added helplessly.

Paul sank down on a chair with a heartbroken groan; a moment ago he had felt himself very near his goal, he had regained something of his old influence over Dick, he had actually managed to touch his heart—and now it was all in vain!

Paradine's jaw fell; he, too, had had his dreams of doing wonderful things with the talisman after he had cajoled Dick to part with it. Whether the restoration of his brother-in-law formed any part of his programme, it is better, perhaps, not to inquire. His dreams were scattered now; the Stone might be anywhere, buried in London mud, lying on railway ballast, or ground to powder by cartwheels. There was little chance, indeed, that even the most liberal rewards would lead to discovery. He swore long and comprehensively.

As for Mr. Bultitude, he sat motionless in his chair, staring in dull, speechless reproach at the conscience-stricken Dick, who stood in the corner blinking and whimpering with an abject penitence, odd and painful to see in one of his portly form. The children had now apparently finished supper, for there were sounds above as of dancing, and "Sir Roger de Coverley," with its rollicking, never-wearying repetition, was distinctly audible above the din and laughter. Once before, a week ago that very day, had that heartless piano mocked him with its untimely gaiety.

But things were not at their worst even yet, for, while they sat like this, there was a sharp, short peal at the house-bell, followed by loud and rather angry knocking, for carriages being no longer expected, the servants and waiters had now closed the front-door, and left the passage for the supper-room.

"The visitors' bell!" cried Paul, roused from his apathy; and he rushed to the window which commanded a side-view of the portico; it might be only a servant calling for one of the children, but he feared the worst, and could not rest till he knew it.

It was a rash thing to do, for as he drew the blind, he saw a large person in a heavy Inverness cloak standing on the steps, and (which was worse) the person both saw and recognised *him*!

With fascinated horror, Mr. Bultitude saw the Doctor's small grey eyes fixed angrily on him, and knew that he was hunted down at last.

He turned to the other two with a sort of ghastly composure: "It's all over now," he said. "I've just seen Dr. Grimstone standing on my doorstep; he has come after me."

Uncle Marmaduke gave a malicious little laugh: "I'm sorry for you, my friend," he said, "but I really can't help it."

"You can," said Paul; "you can tell him what you know. You can save me."

"Very poor economy that," said Marmaduke airily. "I prefer spending to saving, always did. I have my own interests to consider, my dear Paul."

"Dick," said poor Mr. Bultitude, disgusted at this exhibition of selfishness, "you said you were sorry just now. Will you tell him the truth?"

But Dick was quite unnerved, he cowered away, almost crying; "I daren't, I daren't," he stammered; "I—I can't go back to the fellows like this. I'm afraid to tell him. I—I want to hide somewhere."

And certainly he was in no condition to convince an angry schoolmaster of anything whatever, except that he was in a state very unbecoming to the head of a family.

It was all over; Paul saw that too well, he dashed frantically from the fatal billiard-room, and in the hall met Boaler preparing to admit the visitor.

"Don't open the door!" he screamed. "Keep him out, you mustn't let him in. It's Dr. Grimstone."

Boaler, surprised as he naturally was at his young master's unaccountable appearance and evident panic, nevertheless never moved a muscle of his face; he was one of those perfectly bred servants, who, if they chanced to open the door to a ghoul or a skeleton, would merely inquire, "What name, if you please?"

"I must go and ask your Par, then, Master Dick; there's time to 'ook it upstairs while I'm gone. I won't say nothing," he added compassionately.

Paul lost no time in following this suggestion, but rushed upstairs, two or three steps at the time, stumbling at every flight, with a hideous nightmare feeling that some invisible thing behind was trying to trip up his heels.

He rushed blindly past the conservatory, which was lit up by Chinese lanterns and crowded with little "Kate Greenaway" maidens crowned with fantastic headdresses out of the crackers, and comparing presents with boy-lovers; he upset perspiring waiters with glasses and trays, and scattered the children sitting on the stairs, as he bounded on in his reckless flight, leaving crashes of glass behind him.

He had no clear idea of what he meant to do; he thought of barricading himself in his bedroom and hiding in the wardrobe; he had desperate notions of getting on to the housetop by means of a step-ladder and the sky-light above the nursery landing; on one point he was resolved—he would not be retaken *alive*!

Never before in this commonplace London world of ours was an unfortunate householder hunted up his own staircase in this distressing manner; even his terror did not blind him to the extreme ignominy and injustice of his position.

And below he heard the bell ringing more and more impatiently, as the Doctor still remained on the wrong side of the door. In another minute he must be admitted—and then!

Who will not sympathise with Mr. Bultitude as he approaches the crisis of his misfortunes? I protest, for my own part, that as I am compelled to describe him springing from step to step in wild terror, like a highly respectable chamois before some Alpine marksman, my own heart bleeds for him, and I hasten to end my distressing tale, and make the rest of it as little painful as I may with honesty.

19.
The Reckoning

MONTR. The father is victorious.

BELF. Let us haste

To gratulate his conquest.

1ST CAPT. We to mourn

The fortune of the son.

MASSINGER. *The Unnatural Combat.*

Poor Mr. Bultitude, springing wildly upstairs in a last desperate effort to avoid capture, had now almost reached his goal. Just above him was the nursery landing, with its little wooden gate, and near it, leaning against the wall, was a pair of kitchen steps, with which he had hopes of reaching the roof, or the cistern loft, or some other safe and inaccessible place. Better a night spent on the slates amongst the chimney-pots than a bed in that terrible No. 6 Dormitory!

But here, too, fate was against him. He was not more than half-a-dozen steps from the top, when, to his unspeakable horror, he saw a small form in a white frock and cardinal-red sash come running out of the nursery, and begin to descend slowly and cautiously, clinging to the banisters with one chubby little hand.

It was his youngest son, Roly, and as soon as he saw this, he lost hope once and for all; he could not escape being recognised, the child would probably refuse to leave him, and even if he did contrive to get away from him, it would be hopeless to make Roly understand that he was not to betray his hiding-place.

So he stopped on the stairs, aghast at this new misfortune, and feeling himself at the end of all his resources. Roly knew him at once, and began to dance delightedly up and down on the stair in his little bronze shoes. "Buzzer Dicky," he cried, "dear buzzer Dicky, tum 'ome to party!"

"It's not brother Dicky," said Paul miserably; "it's all a mistake."

"Oh, but it is though," said Roly; "and you don't know what Roly's found."

"No, no," said Paul, trying to pass (which, as Roly persisted in leaping joyously from side to side of the narrow stair, was difficult); "you shall show me another time. I'm in a hurry, my boy, I've got an appointment."

"Roly's got something better than that," observed the child.

Mr. Bultitude, in spite of his terror, was too much afraid of hurting him by brushing roughly past to attempt such a thing, so he tried diplomacy. "Well, what has Roly found—a cracker?"

"No, no, better than a cwacker—you guess."

"I can't guess," said Paul; "never mind, I don't want to know."

"Well then," said Roly, "there." And he slowly unclosed a fat little fist, and in it Paul saw, with a revulsion of feeling that turned him dizzy and faint, the priceless talisman itself, the identical Garudâ Stone, with part of the frail gilt ring still attached to it.

The fastening had probably given way during Master Dick's uproarious revels in the drawing-room, and Roly must have picked it up on the carpet shortly afterwards.

"Isn't it a pitty sing?" said Roly, insisting that his treasure should be duly admired.

"A very pretty thing," said his father, hoarse and panting; "but it's mine, Roly, it's mine!"

And he tried to snatch it, but Roly closed his fist over it and pouted, "It isn't yours," he said, "it's Roly's. Roly found it."

Paul's fears rose again; would he be wrecked in port after all? His ear, unnaturally strained, caught the sound of the front door being opened, he heard the Doctor's deep voice booming faintly below, then the noise of persons ascending.

"Roly shall have it, then," he said perfidiously, "if he will say after me what I tell him. Say, 'I wish Papa and Brother Dick back as they were before,' Roly."

"Ith it a game?" asked Roly, his face clearing and evidently delighted with his eccentric brother Dick, who had run all the way home from school to play games with him on the staircase.

"No—yes!" cried Paul, "it's a very funny game; only do what I tell you. Now say, 'I wish Papa and Brother Dick back again as they were before.' I'll give you a sugar-plum if you say it nicely."

"What sort of sugar-plum?" demanded Roly, who inherited business instincts.

"Any sort you like best!" almost shrieked Paul; "oh, do get on!"

"Lots of sugar-plums, then. 'I with'—I forget what you told me—oh, 'I with Papa and——' there'th thomebody tummin' upsthairs!" he broke off suddenly; "it'h nurth tummin' to put me to bed. I don't want to go to bed yet."

"And you shan't go to bed!" cried Paul, for he too thought he heard some one. "Never mind nurse, finish the—the game."

—'Papa and Buzzy Dicky back again as—as they were before,' repeated Roly at last. "What a funny—ow, ow, it'h Papa! it'h Papa! and he told me it wath Dicky. I'm afwaid! Whereth Dicky gone to? I want Bab, take me to Bab!"

For the Stone had done its work once more, and this time with happier results; with a supreme relief and joy, which no one who has read this book can fail to understand, Mr. Bultitude felt that he actually was his old self again.

Just when all hope seemed cut off and relief was most unlikely, the magic spell that had caused him such intolerable misery for one hideous week was reversed by the hand of his innocent child.

He caught Roly up in his arms and kissed him as he had never been kissed in his whole life before, at least by his father, and comforting him as well as he could, for the poor child had naturally received rather a severe shock, he stepped airily down the staircase, which he had mounted with such different emotions five minutes before.

On his way he could not resist going into his dressing-room and assuring himself by a prolonged examination before the cheval-glass that the Stone had not played him some last piece of jugglery; but he found everything quite correct; he was the same formal, precise and portly person, wearing the same morning dress even as on that other Monday evening, and he went on with greater confidence.

He took care, however, to stop at the first window, when he managed, after some coaxing, to persuade Roly to give up the Garudâ Stone. As soon as he had it in his hands again, he opened the window wide and flung the dangerous talisman far out into the darkness. Not till then did he feel perfectly secure.

He passed the groups of little guests gathered about the conservatory, and lower down he met Boaler, the nurse, and one or two servants and waiters, rushing up in a state of great anxiety and flurry; even Boaler's usual composure seemed shaken. "Please, sir," he asked, "the schoolmaster gentleman, Master Dick—he've run upstairs, haven't you seen him?"

Paul had almost forgotten Dick in his new happiness; there would be a heavy score to settle with him; he had the upper hand once more, and yet, somehow, he did not feel as much righteous wrath and desire for revenge as he expected to do.

"Don't be alarmed," he said, waving them back with more benignity than he thought he had in him. "Master Dick is safe enough. I know all about it. Where is Dr. Grimstone? In the library, eh? Very well, I will see him there."

And leaving Roly with the nurse, he went down to the library; not, if the truth must be told, without a slight degree of nervousness, unreasonable and unaccountable enough now, but quite beyond his power to control.

He entered the room, and there, surrounded by piles of ticketed hats and coats, under the pale light of one gas-burner, he saw the terrible man before whom he had trembled for the last seven horrible days.

A feeling of self-defence made Paul assume rather more than his old stiffness as he shook hands. "I am very glad to see you, Dr. Grimstone," he said, "but your coming at this time forces me to ask if there is any unusual reason for, for my having the—a—pleasure of seeing you here?"

"I am exceedingly distressed to have to say that there is," said the Doctor solemnly, "or I should not have troubled you at this hour. Try to compose yourself, my dear sir, to bear this blow."

"I will," said Paul, "I will try."

"The fact is then, and I know how sad a story it must be for a parent's ear, but the fact is, that your unhappy boy has had the inconceivable rashness to quit my roof." And the Doctor paused to watch the effect of his announcement.

"God bless my soul!" cried Paul. "You don't say so!"

"I do indeed; he has, in short, run away. But don't be alarmed, my dear Mr. Bultitude, I think I can assure you he is quite safe at the present moment" ("Thank Heaven, he is!" thought Paul, thinking of his own marvellous escape). "I should certainly have recaptured him before he could have left the railway station, where he seems to have gone at once, only, acting on information (which I strongly suspect now was intentionally misleading), I drove on to the station on the up-line, thinking to find him there. He was not there, sir, I believe he never went there at all; but, guessing how matters were, I searched the train, carriage by carriage, compartment by compartment, when it came up."

"I am very sorry you should have had so much trouble," said Paul, with a vivid recollection of the exploring stick; "and so you found him?"

"No, sir," said the Doctor passionately, "I did not find him, but he was there; he must have been there! but the shameless connivance of two excessively ill-bred persons, who positively refused to allow me access to their compartment, caused him to slip through my fingers."

Mr. Bultitude observed, rather ungratefully, that, if this was so, it was a most improper thing for them to do.

"It was, indeed, but it is of no consequence fortunately. I was forced to wait for the next train, but that was not a very slow one, and so I was able to come on here before a very late hour and acquaint you with what had taken place."

"Thank you very much," said Paul.

"It's a painful thing to occur in a school," observed the Doctor after a pause.

"Most unfortunate," agreed Paul, coughing.

"So apt to lead persons who are not acquainted with the facts to imagine that the boy was unhappy under my care," continued the Doctor.

"In this case, I assure you, I have no doubts," protested Paul with politeness and (seldom a possible combination) perfect truth.

"Very kind of you to say so; really, it's a great mystery to me. I certainly, as I felt it my duty to inform you at the time, came very near inflicting corporal punishment upon him this morning—very near. But then he was pardoned on your intercession; and, besides, the boy would never have run away for fear of a flogging."

"Oh, no, perfectly absurd!" agreed Paul again.

"Such a merry, high-spirited lad, too," said the Doctor, sincerely enough; "popular with his schoolfellows; a favourite (in spite of his faults) with his teachers."

"No, was he though?" said Paul with more surprise, for he had not been fortunate enough to reap much vicarious benefit from his son's popularity, as he could not help remembering.

"All this, added to the comforts (or, may I say, the luxuries?) he enjoyed under my supervision, does make it seem very strange and ungrateful in the boy to take this sudden and ill-considered step."

"Very, indeed; but do you know, Dr. Grimstone, I can't help thinking—and pray do not misunderstand me if I speak plainly—that, perhaps, he had reasons for being unhappy you can have no idea of?"

"He would have found me ready to hear any complaints and prompt to redress them, sir," said the Doctor. "But, now I think of it, he certainly did appear to have something on his mind which he wished to tell me; but his manner was so strange and he so persistently refused to come to the point, that I was forced to discourage him at last."

"You did discourage him, indeed!" said Paul inwardly, thinking of those attempted confidences with a shudder. "Perhaps some of his schoolfellows may have—eh?" he said aloud.

"My dear sir," exclaimed the Doctor, "quite out of the question!"

"Do you think so?" said Paul, not being able to resist the suggestion. "And yet, do you know, some of them did not appear to me to look very—very good-natured, now."

"A more manly, pleasant, and gentlemanly set of youths never breathed!" said the Doctor, taking up the cudgels for his boys, and, to do him justice, probably with full measure of belief in his statement. "Curious now that they should have struck you so differently!"

"They certainly did strike me very differently," said Paul. "But I may be mistaken."

"You are, my dear sir. And, pardon me, but you had no opportunity of testing your opinion."

"Oh, pardon me," retorted Paul grimly, "I had indeed!"

"A cursory visit," said the Doctor, "a formal inspection—you cannot fairly judge boys by that. They will naturally be reserved and constrained in the presence of an elder. But you should observe them without their knowledge—you want to know them, my dear Mr. Bultitude, you want to go among them!"

It was the very last thing Paul did want—he knew them quite well enough, but it was of no use to say so, and he merely assented politely.

"And now," said the Doctor, "with regard to your misguided boy. I have to tell you that he is here, in this very house. I tracked him here, and, ten minutes ago, saw him with my own eyes at one of your windows.

"Here!" cried Paul, with a well-executed start; "you astonish me!"

"It has occurred to me within the last minute," said the Doctor, "that there may be a very simple explanation of his flight. I observe you are giving a—a juvenile entertainment on a large scale."

"I suppose I am," Paul admitted. "And so you think——?"

"I think that your son, who doubtless knew of your intention, was hurt at being excluded from the festivities and, in a fit of mad wilful folly, resolved to be present at them in spite of you."

"My dear Doctor," cried Paul, who saw the conveniences of this theory, "that must be it, of course—that explains it all!"

"So grave an act of insubordination," said the Doctor, "an act of double disobedience—to your authority and mine—deserves the fullest punishment. You agree with me, I trust?"

The memory of his wrongs overcame Mr. Bultitude for the moment: "Nothing can be too bad for the little scoundrel!" he said, between his teeth.

"He shall have it, sir, I swear to you; he shall be made to repent this as long as he lives. This insult to me (and of course to you also) shall be amply atoned for. If you will have the goodness to deliver him over to my hands, I will carry him back at once to Market Rodwell, and to-morrow, sir, to-morrow, I will endeavour to awaken his conscience in a way he will remember!"

The Doctor was more angry than an impartial lover of justice might perhaps approve of, but then it must be remembered that he had seen himself completely outwitted and his authority set at nought in a very humiliating fashion.

However, his excessive wrath cooled Paul's own resentment instead of inflaming it; it made him reflect that, after all, it was he who had the best right to be angry.

"Well," he said, rather coldly, "we must find him first, and then consider what shall be done to him. If you will allow me I will ring and——"

But before he could lay his hand upon the bell the library door opened, and Uncle Marmaduke made his appearance, dragging with him the unwilling Dick: the unfortunate boy was effectually sobered now, pale and trembling and besmirched with coal-dust—in fact, in very much the same plight as his ill-used father had been in only three hours ago.

There was a brazen smile of triumph on Mr. Paradine's face as he met Paul's eyes with a knowing wink, which the latter did not at all understand.

Such audacity astonished him, for he could hardly believe that Paradine, after his perfidious conduct in the billiard-room, could have the clumsy impudence to try to propitiate him now.

"Here he is, my boy," shouted Paradine; "here's the scamp who has given us all this trouble! He came into the billiard-room just now and told me who he was, but I would have nothing to do with him of course. Not my business, as I told him at the time. Then—(I think I have the pleasure of seeing Dr. Grimstone? just so) well, then you, sir, arrived—and he made himself scarce. But when I saw him in the act of making a bolt up the area, where he had been taking shelter apparently in the coal-cellar, I thought it was time to interfere, and so I collared him. I have much pleasure in handing him over now to the proper authorities."

And, letting Dick go, he advanced towards his brother-in-law, still with the same odd expression of having a secret understanding with him, which made Paul's blood boil.

"Stand where you are, sir," said Paul to his son. "No, Dr. Grimstone, allow me—leave him to me for the present, please."

"That's much better," whispered Paradine approvingly; "capital. Keep it up, my boy; keep it up! Papa's as quiet as a lamb now. Go on."

Then Paul understood; his worthy brother-in-law had not been present at the last transformation and was under a slight misapprehension: he evidently imagined that he had by this last stroke made himself and Dick masters of the situation—it was time to undeceive him.

"Have the goodness to leave my house at once, will you!" he said sternly.

"You young fool!" said Marmaduke, under his breath, "after all I have done for you, too! Is this your gratitude? You know you can't get on without me. Take care what you're about!"

"If you can't see that the tables are turned at last," said Paul slowly, "you're a duller knave than I take you to be."

Marmaduke started back with an oath: "It's a trick," he said savagely; "you want to get rid of me."

"I certainly intend to," said Paul. "Are you satisfied? Do you want proofs—shall I give them—I did just now in the billiard-room?"

Paradine went to Dick and shook him angrily: "You young idiot!" he said, in a furious aside, "why didn't you tell me? What did you let me make a fool of myself like this for, eh?"

"I did tell you," muttered Dick, "only you wouldn't listen. It just serves you right!"

Marmaduke soon collected himself after this unexpected shock; he tried to shake Paul's hands with an airy geniality. "Only my little joke," he said, laughing; "ha, ha, I thought I should take you in!... Why, I knew it directly....

I've been working for you all the time—but it wouldn't have done to let you see my line."

"No," said Paul; "it was not a very straight one, as usual."

"Well," said Marmaduke, "I shouldn't have stopped Master Dick there if I hadn't been on your side, should I now? I knew you'd come out of it all right, but I had a difficult game to play, don't you know? I don't wonder that you didn't follow me just at first."

"You've lost your game," said Paul; "it's no use to say any more. So now, perhaps, you'll go?"

"Go, eh?" said Paradine, without showing much surprise at the failure of so very forlorn a hope, "oh, very well, just as you please, of course. Let your poor wife's only brother go from your doors without a penny in the world!—but I warn you that a trifle or so laid out in stopping my mouth would not be thrown away. Some editors would be glad enough of a sensation from real life just now, and I could tell some very odd tales about this little affair!"

"Tell them, if a character for sanity is of no further use to you," said Paul. "Tell them to anyone you can get to believe you—tell the crossing-sweeper and the policemen, tell your grandmother, tell the horse-marines—it will amuse them. Only, you shall tell them on the other side of my front door. Shall I call anyone to show you out?"

Paradine saw his game was really played out, and swaggered insolently to the door: "Not on my account, I beg," he said. "Good-bye, Paul, my boy, no more dissolving views. Good-bye, my young friend Richard, it was good fun while it lasted, eh? like the Servian crown—always a pleasant reminiscence! Good evening to you, Doctor. By the way, for educational purposes let me recommend a 'Penang lawyer'—buy one as you go back for the boys—just to show them you haven't forgotten them!"

And, having little luggage to impede him, the front door closed upon him shortly afterwards—this time for ever.

When he had gone, Dick looked imploringly at his father and then at the Doctor, who, until Paradine's parting words had lashed him into fury again, had been examining the engravings on the walls with a studied delicacy during the recent painful scene, and was now leaning against the chimney-piece with his arms folded and a sepulchral gloom on his brow.

"Richard," said Mr. Bultitude, in answer to the look, "you have not done much to deserve consideration at my hands."

"Or at mine!" added the Doctor ominously.

"No," said Dick, "I know I haven't. I've been a brute. I deserve a jolly good licking."

"You do," said his father, but in spite of his indignation, the broken-down look of the boy, and the memory of his own sensations when waiting to be caned that morning, moved him to pity. And then Dick had shown some compunction in the billiard-room: he was not entirely lost to feeling.

"Well," he said at last, "you've acted very wrongly. Because I thought it best that you should not—ahem, leave your studies for this party, you chose to disobey me and alarm your master by defying my orders and coming home by stealth—that was your object, I presume?"

"Y—yes," said Dick, looking rather puzzled, but seeing that he was expected to agree; "that was it."

"You know as well as I do what good cause I have to be angry; but, if I consent to overlook your conduct this time, if I ask Dr. Grimstone to overlook it too" (the Doctor made an inarticulate protest, while Dick stared, incredulous), "will you undertake to behave better for the future—will you?"

Dick's voice broke at this, and his eyes swam—he was effectually conquered. "Oh, I will!" he cried, "I will, really. I never meant to go so far when I began."

"Then, Dr. Grimstone," said Paul, "you will do me a great favour if you will take no further notice of this. You see the boy is sorry, and I am sure he will apologise to you amply for the grave slight he has done you. And by the way—I should have mentioned it before—but he will have to leave your care at the end of the term for a public school—I intend to send him to Harrow, so he will require some additional preparation, perhaps: I may leave that in your hands?"

Dr. Grimstone looked deeply offended, but he only said, "I will see to that myself, my dear sir. I am sorry you did not tell me this earlier. But, may I suggest that a large public school has its pitfalls for a boy of your son's disposition? And I trust this leniency may not have evil consequences, but I doubt it—I greatly doubt it."

As for Dick, he ran to his father, and hung gratefully on to his arm with a remorseful hug, a thing he had never dared to do, or thought of attempting, in his life till then.

"Dad," he said in a choked voice, "you're a brick! I don't deserve any of it, but I'll never forget this as long as I live."

Mr. Bultitude too, felt something spring up in his heart which drew him towards the boy in an altogether novel manner, but no one will say that either was the worse for it.

"Well," he said mildly, "prove to me that I have made no mistake. Go back to Crichton House now, work and play well, and try to keep out of mischief for the rest of the term. I trust to you," he added, in a lower tone, "while you remain at Market Rodwell, to keep my—my connection with it a secret; you owe that at least to me. You may probably have—ahem, some inconveniences to put up with—inconveniences you are not prepared for. You must bear them as your punishment."

And soon afterwards a cab was called, and Dr. Grimstone prepared to return to Market Rodwell, with the deserter, by the last train.

As Paul shook hands through the cab window with his prodigal son, he repeated his warning. "Mind," he said, "*you* have been at school all this past week; you have run away to attend this party, you understand? Good-bye, my boy, and here's something to put in your pocket, and another for Jolland; but he need not know it comes from me." And when Dick opened his hand afterwards, he found two half-sovereigns in it.

So the cab rolled away, and Paul went up to the drawing-room, where, although he certainly allowed the fireworks on the balcony and in the garden to languish forgotten on their sticks, he led all the other revels up to an advanced hour with jovial *abandon* quite worthy of Dick, and none of his little guests ever suspected the change of host.

When it was all over, and the sleepy children had driven off, Paul sat down in an easy chair by the bright fire which sparkled frostily in his bedroom, to think gratefully over all the events of the day—events which were beginning already to take an unreal and fantastic shape.

Bitterly as he had suffered, and in spite of the just anger and thirst for revenge with which he had returned, I am glad to say he did not regret the spirit of mildness that had stayed his hand when his hour of triumph came.

His experiences, unpleasant as they had been, had had their advantages: they had drawn him and his family closer together.

In his daughter Barbara, as she wished him good-night (knowing nothing, of course, of the escape), he had suddenly become aware of a girlish freshness and grace he had never looked for or cared to see before. Roly after this, too, had a claim upon him he could never wish to forget, and even with the graceless Dick there was a warmer and more natural feeling on both sides—a strange result, no doubt, of such unfilial behaviour, but so it was.

Mr. Bultitude would never after this consider his family as a set of troublesome and thankless incumbrances; thanks to Dick's offices during the interregnum, they would henceforth throw off their reserve and constraint in their father's presence, and in so doing, open his eyes to qualities of which he had hitherto been in contented ignorance.

It would be pleasanter perhaps to take leave of Mr. Bultitude thus, as he sits by his bedroom fire in the first flush of supreme and unalloyed content.

But I feel almost bound to point out a fact which few will find any difficulty in accepting, namely, that, although the wrong had been retrieved without scandal or exposure, for which Paul could not be too thankful, there were many consequences which could not but survive it.

Neither father nor son found himself exactly in the same position as before their exchange of characters.

It took Mr. Bultitude considerable time and trouble to repair all the damage his son's boyish excesses had wrought both at Westbourne Terrace and in the City. He found the discipline of his clerks' room and counting-house sorely relaxed, and his office-boy in particular attempted a tone towards him of such atrocious familiarity that he was indignantly dismissed, much to his astonishment, the very first day. And probably Paul will never quite clear himself of the cloud that hangs over a man of business who, in the course of however well regulated a career, is known to have been at least once "a little odd."

And his home, too, was distinctly demoralised: his cook was an artist, unrivalled at soups and entrées; but he had to get rid of her notwithstanding.

It was only too evident that she looked upon herself as the prospective mistress of his household, and he did not feel called upon as a parent to fulfil any expectations which Dick's youthful cupboard love had unintentionally excited.

For some time, as fresh proof of Dick's extravagances came home to him, Paul found it cost him no little effort to restrain a tendency to his former bitterness and resentment, but he valued the new understanding between himself and his son too highly to risk losing it again by any open reproach, and so with each succeeding discovery the victory over his feelings became easier.

As for Dick, he found the inconveniences at which his father had hinted anything but imaginary, as will perhaps be easily understood.

It was an unpleasant shock to discover that in one short week his father had contrived somehow to procure him a lasting unpopularity. He was obviously looked upon by all, masters and boys, as a confirmed coward and sneak. And although some of his companions could not fairly reproach him on the latter score, the imputation was particularly galling to Dick, who had always treated such practices with sturdy contempt.

He was sorely tempted at times to right himself by declaring the real state of the case; but he remembered his promise and his father's unexpected clemency and his gratitude always kept him silent.

He never quite understood how it was that the whole school seemed to have an impression that they could kick and assault him generally with perfect impunity; but a few very unsuccessful experiments convinced them that this was a popular error on their part.

Although, however, in everything else he did gradually succeed in recovering all the ground his father had lost him, yet there was one respect in which, I am sorry to say, he found all his efforts to retrieve himself hopeless.

His little sweetheart, with the grey eyes and soft brown hair, cruelly refused to have anything more to do with him. For Dulcie's pride had been wounded by what she considered his shameless perfidy on that memorable Saturday by the parallel bars; the last lingering traces of affection had vanished before Paul's ingratitude on the following Monday, and she never forgave him.

She did not even give him an opportunity of explaining himself, never by word or sign up to the last day of the term showing that she was even aware of his return. What was worse, in her resentment she transferred her favour to Tipping, who became her humble slave for a too brief period; after which he was found wanting in polish, and was ignominiously thrown over for the shy new boy Kiffin, whose head Dick found a certain melancholy pleasure in punching in consequence.

This was Dick's punishment, and a very real and heavy one he found it. He is at Harrow now, where he is doing fairly well; but I think there are moments even yet when Dulcie's charming little face, her pretty confidences, and her chilling disdain, are remembered with something as nearly resembling a heartache as a healthy unsentimental boy can allow himself.

Perhaps, if some day he goes back once more to Crichton House "to see the fellows," this time with the mysterious glamour of a great public school about him, he may yet obtain forgiveness, for she is getting horribly tired of Kiffin, who, to tell the truth, is something of a milksop.

As for the Garudâ Stone, I really cannot say what has become of it. Perhaps it was dashed to pieces on the cobble-stones of the stables behind the terrace, and a good thing too. Perhaps it was not, and is still in existence, with all its dangerous powers as ready for use as ever it was; and in that case the best I can wish my readers is, that they may be mercifully preserved from finding it anywhere, or if they are unfortunate enough to come upon it, that they may at least be more careful with it than Mr. Paul Bultitude, by whose melancholy example I trust they will take timely warning.

And with these very sincere wishes I beg to bid them a reluctant farewell.

Milton Keynes UK
Ingram Content Group UK Ltd.
UKHW020829231024
450026UK00004B/475